SweaterBabe.com's

Fabulous
& Flirty Crochet

QUARRY

SweaterBabe.com's

Fabulous
& Flirty Crochet

Gorgeous Sweater
and Accessory Patterns
from Los Angeles' Top
Crochet Designer

Katherine Lee

GLOUCESTER MASSACHUSETTS

QUARRY BOOKS

First published in the United States of America by
Quarry Books, a member of
Quayside Publishing Group
33 Commercial Street
Gloucester, Massachusetts 01930-5089
Telephone: (978) 282-9590
Fax: (978) 283-2742
www.rockpub.com

Library of Congress Cataloging-in-Publication Data
Lee, Katherine (Katherine W. C.)
    Sweaterbabe.com's fabulous and flirty crochet : gorgeous sweater and accessory patterns from Los Angeles' top crochet designer / Katherine Lee.
        p.   cm.
    ISBN 1-59253-216-0 (pbk.)
    1. Crocheting—Patterns. 2. Sweaters. I. Title.
TT825.L38829 2006
746.43'40432—dc22   2005025324
                                                                              CIP

ISBN-13: 978-1-59253-216-2
ISBN-10: 1-59253-216-0

10 9 8 7 6 5 4 3

Cover Design: Rockport Publishers
Book Design: Rockport Publishers
Production: *tabula rasa* graphic design
Photography: Allan Penn Photography
Technical Editor: Jean Lampe
Stitching Illustrations: Judy Love

Printed in China

Contents

Introduction

WELCOME! I am thrilled to introduce this new, exclusive collection of twenty fabulous and flirty crochet sweater and accessory patterns inspired by the fresh and sexy Hollywood lifestyle. These enticing projects are sure to persuade you to pick up your crochet hook and create something extraordinary!

In this collection, you will find a range of patterns for beginners to advanced crocheters—from cardigans, sweaters, and sleek tank tops for all seasons to gorgeous scarves, handbags, wraps, and more. Some are crocheted quickly and make perfect gifts, while others are a little more involved but are well worth the effort. You'll see a wonderful variety of stitch patterns that make each project unique and exciting to crochet.

Rather than the trendy, fancy yarns that only last a few seasons, I chose the more classically beautiful yarns that lend themselves to the intricate look of crochet stitches used in these patterns. Because of this, these yarns are easily substituted—so feel free to dive into your yarn stash or to splurge on a luxurious blend you've been eyeing.

My love of crochet began when I learned the craft at just eight years old. The only interesting crochet books I ever found were in Japanese bookstores. The elaborate lace patterns and stitch variety in these books showed a level of creativity that I'd never seen in crochet books published in the United States, which typically contained variations on the granny square and uninspired double crochet stitches. Even as a little girl, I always wondered

"You'll see a wonderful variety of stitch patterns that make each project unique and exciting to crochet."

why there were no great American crochet pattern books. I imagined that perhaps one day I would design my *own* collection. . . .

Once I turned crocheting and knitting into my career, I began publishing my designs in magazines and books. While the demand for knitting has taken off more quickly, renewed demand for crochet has indeed begun to follow right along. I receive many emails through my website, SweaterBabe.com, from crocheters desperately searching for fresh and fashionable patterns like mine. These pleas inspired me to create my own crochet pattern collection.

Numerous influences have inspired this collection: I have always been drawn to shaped, sophisticated silhouettes, enhanced by great detailing. Living in Los Angeles amidst the glitter and glitz of the

entertainment industry, I am surrounded by the latest fashions worn by the glamorous Hollywood celebrities and the young and stylish hipsters of the city.

Crochet is ideal for creating intricate-looking lace fabrics. Even simple combinations of crochet stitches can create beautiful woven textures. Crochet is more fluid than knitting (which has a more gridlike structure) and lends itself to creating sexier shapes and curves.

I've taken advantage of these wonderful characteristics of crochet in this new collection. I've also added many special shaping and finishing details to create original designs that I hope you will love as much as I do.

Enjoy crocheting your next masterpiece!

Katherine Lee
Founder and Designer
SweaterBabe.com
LOS ANGELES, CALIFORNIA

PURSE

7 1/2" (19 cm)

12" (30.5 cm)

4" (10 cm)

LEFT
FRONT

20" (51 cm)

5 1/4" (14.5 cm)

9 1/4" (23.5 cm)

Basics

While crochet can look intimidating to those who have never learned it, it is actually a very old craft based entirely on the concept of using a hook to pull loops through loops. A chain is first created using this technique. Then, rows of new loops are built on top of the rows of previous loops, creating a crochet fabric that merely began as a ball of yarn and a hook.

Crochet is similar to knitting in many ways, but it lends itself more easily to creating more varied shapes and textures and is often considered faster than knitting. Learning to knit involves the challenge of holding and balancing two needles, one in each hand, while simultaneously holding the yarn in position. Learning to crochet is a bit simpler: it mainly involves just one hand (usually the right hand), which holds the hook (just like a pencil or a steak knife) and maneuvers it to create the stitches. The other hand holds the crochet work as it is completed and guides the yarn so it can flow easily and be accessible for the hook.

Whether you learn, or refresh your memory of, crochet from a book, a friend, or a relative, begin with the basic stitches while you get used to handling the yarn and the hook. Before you know it, these basic stitches will become automatic for you and you will be ready to try out new stitch variations and techniques that open up a world of wonderful stitch patterns and effects uniquely created with crochet.

The patterns in this collection present a range of stitch variations and techniques worked into beautiful shapes and silhouettes that I hope will inspire you to pick up your hook and start crocheting.

Crochet Hooks

Crochet hooks are made in a variety of materials. Steel, aluminum, and plastic are most commonly used, though you can also find hooks made of wood, bamboo, silver, or gold. The size of the crochet hook is based on the thickness of the hook, measured by the diameter of the shank. Some hooks have a flattened area (called the *grip* or *thumb rest*) next to the shank, where you rest your thumb, while the index or forefinger rests on the shank, which permits balance and leverage. Some hooks even have rubbery covers to make it more comfortable for your hands when you crochet often or for long periods of time.

Which type of hook you choose is mostly a matter of personal preference. Try crocheting with the various types to see what works best for you, is most comfortable for your grip and hand size, and allows your crocheting to go smoothly.

Plastic and aluminum hooks are most widely available and are great for their lightness, smooth construction, and cost. Bamboo and other wood hooks can be preferred for their warm and natural feel, but often the tips of the hooks are not as pointy, which may make them harder to work with if you need to insert your hook frequently into tighter stitches versus open spaces.

Below is a crochet hook size conversion chart to help you match the U.S. sizing with the metric sizes found in other countries. Sizes are based on the diameter of the hook and are usually embossed or printed on the crochet hook itself; however, it is a good idea to keep and store your hooks in their original packaging to keep them organized and to help track which sizes you own. Sometimes sizes may also vary among crochet hook manufacturers. When in doubt,

Crochet Hook Size Conversions	
U.S.	**METRIC**
B/1	2.00mm
C/2	2.50mm
D/3	3.00mm
E/4	3.50mm
F/5	4.00mm
G/6	4.50mm
H/8	5.00mm
I/9	5.50mm
J/10	6.00mm
K/10.5	7.00mm
L/11	8.00mm
M/13	9.00mm
N/15	10.00mm
P/16	11.50mm

it is best to follow the metric sizes. As with knitting, crochet can be very addictive and soon enough you'll own a multitude of hook sizes and styles.

Yarn and Yarn Substitution

To create the same results as in the samples in this book, use the exact yarn specified in each pattern. The Yarn Resources section, on page 142, can help you locate a specific yarn if your local yarn shop doesn't carry it. Also, try searching for the yarn on the Web, where you'll find many online yarn shops that sell these yarns.

Most of the yarns used in this book are fairly classic yarns that can be easily substituted. Standardized yarn weight information is provided in each pattern, along with fiber content and yardage information. In addition, page 141 includes a photo of the yarns.

Whether you are substituting yarn to use up your stash, changing fibers because you prefer cotton over wool, or for any other reason, be sure your new yarn choice matches the given gauge so you can be assured that your finished measurements will be correct. While this is less important for the scarves, shawls, and purses in this book, it is very important for the sweaters, tops,

and cardigans. Sometimes you will need to change your hook size up or down from what is listed in the materials section of the pattern to meet the gauge. Don't be concerned if you need to change your hook size, as it is your gauge that matters, not what hook size gets you the required gauge.

Each pattern lists the standard yarn weight used. Find a substitute that falls into the same yarn weight. The suggested needle/hook size and gauge on the yarn ball band should be similar to what you see in the yarn standards chart on the next page.

The chart on the following page, developed by The Yarn Council of America, offers an overview of yarns, gauge ranges, and recommended needle and hook sizes. For more information, visit their website: www.yarnstandards.com.

Remember to always buy enough substitute yarn based on the total yardage required by the pattern, not by the total weight. Total yardages are listed in the materials section of each pattern. To determine the number of balls of yarn that you'll need to purchase, just divide the total yardage required by the number of yards per ball listed on your new yarn's ball band. The result is the number of balls you will need.

Other Tools for Crochet

Crochet can be a very portable hobby. Besides your hook and yarn, all you generally need are a pair of scissors, a yarn tapestry needle for weaving in loose ends and sewing pieces together, a tape measure, and sewing pins if you need to sew larger pieces together or pin your pieces flat for blocking. It is also a great idea to always have a calculator handy and to keep pen and paper by your side to keep track of which row or round you are on. Post-it notes can come in really handy for tracking your progress as well.

Pattern Instructions

All of the crochet patterns in this book are written using the standard abbreviations and style common to most published patterns. Please refer to pages 16–17 for all abbreviations and symbols used in this book. Any special stitches or techniques used in a pattern are noted and explained at the beginning of that pattern. In addition, all of the stitches and techniques used are listed at the top of the instructions to help you quickly determine which patterns fit your skill level.

Pattern stitch instructions are listed separately so you can use the stitches in creating your own projects. Also, they are explained using both written instructions and diagrams. Whether you choose to follow the written

Standard Yarn Weight System
Categories of Yarn, Gauge Ranges, and Recommended Needle and Hook Sizes

Yarn weight symbol and category	**1** SUPER FINE	**2** FINE	**3** LIGHT	**4** MEDIUM	**5** BULKY	**6** SUPER BULKY
Types of yarns in category	sock, fingering, baby	sport, baby	DK, light worsted	worsted, afghan, aran	chunky, craft, rug	bulky, roving
Knit gauge range* in stockinette stitch to 4 inches	27-32 sts	23-26 sts	21-24 sts	16-20 sts	12-15 sts	6-11 sts
Recommended needle in metric size range	2.25-3.25 mm	3.25-3.75 mm	3.75-4.5 mm	4.5-5.5 mm	5.5-8 mm	8 mm and larger
Recommended needle in U.S. size range	1 to 3	3 to 5	5 to 7	7 to 9	9 to 11	11 and larger
Crochet gauge* ranges in single crochet to 4 inches	21-32 sts	16-20 sts	12-17 sts	11-14 sts	8-11 sts	5-9 sts
Recommended hook in metric size range	2.25-3.5 mm	3.5-4.5 mm	4.5-5.5 mm	5.5-6.5 mm	6.5-9 mm	9 mm and larger
Recommended hook U.S. size range	B-1 to E-4	E-4 to 7	7 to I-9	I-9 to K-10 ½	K-10 ½ to M-13	M-13 and larger

*GUIDELINES ONLY: The above reflects the most commonly used gauges and needle or hook sizes for specific yarn categories.

instructions or the diagram, it is a good idea to refer to both to double check your interpretation of a complicated pattern stitch. Symbols used in the diagrams are listed in the symbols section on page 17.

The pattern stitch diagrams are visual representations of the crochet pattern as it is actually worked. Remember that you are seeing the "right side" of the work in the diagrams, so if the first row (and therefore all of the odd numbered rows) of a pattern stitch is read from right to left, the next row (and all subsequent even rows) should be read from left to right. Row numbers are included to indicate from which end to begin reading the diagram. For motifs that are worked in the round, you are only seeing the "right side" in the diagrams since the work will never be turned.

In the diagrams, each basic stitch is represented by a symbol that resembles the stitch. Where the stitch is drawn shows exactly where the stitch should be placed. In some cases, for example, in wavy pattern stitches, the scale of a stitch may look longer or shorter than similar stitches. This is done only in order to keep the diagram positioning correct and does not indicate that you should try to make that stitch longer or shorter by altering your technique in any way.

Pattern stitch instructions begin with the number of chains required for the base or starting chain. For example, if it says "Ch a multiple of 8, plus 2 extra," the pattern stitch can be worked over any multiple of the number 8, plus 2, that is, 18 chains, 26 chains, 34 chains, etc.

Brackets are used to indicate a set of instructions that will be repeated multiple times in a row. Simply work the instructions in the brackets the number of times stated immediately after the close bracket. Parentheses, in contrast, are used to indicate a set of instructions that need to be worked all into one stitch or space.

Different sizes are represented in each pattern using parentheses. Before beginning any pattern with multiple sizes, determine which size is best based on the finished measurements given at the beginning of the instructions as well as on the schematic provided at the end of each pattern. Once you determine which size you are following, it is a good idea to go through the pattern and circle or highlight the numbers that apply specifically to your size. For example, most patterns will

have size Small instructions, with sizes Medium and Large following in the parentheses. If that pattern specifies to chain 30 (35, 40), the 30 is for the size Small, the 35 is for the size Medium, and the 40 applies to size Large. If there is only one number, then it applies to all three sizes. Sometimes, you will see a header such as "for size Medium only," which will block off a set of instructions just for size Medium. Then, the instructions will say "for all sizes" to indicate that the next section applies to all of the sizes.

Measuring Gauge

To ensure that your finished measurements are the same as in the instructions, your crochet gauge must match what is stated in the instructions. This is especially important for the apparel items in this book and if you are substituting a different yarn than was originally used in the sample. Before beginning a pattern, make a swatch by working the pattern stitch indicated in the gauge section of the instructions for a few inches, using the crochet hook size listed in the materials section. This crochet hook size is only the suggested size— whatever hook size obtains the correct gauge is the right size to use. Making a swatch that is at least 4" x 4" (10 x 10 cm) is best. Lay the swatch flat on a table and use a ruler or measuring tape to measure your gauge. You may need to block your swatch first if it does not lie flat and you plan to block the finished

piece as well. If you find that you have fewer stitches than the listed gauge for the measurement given, your stitches are larger than required, and you will want to redo your swatch using a hook size smaller than what you used for the last swatch. If you find that you have more stitches than the listed gauge for the measurement given, your stitches are smaller than required, and you will want to redo your swatch using a larger hook size. Once you match the gauge as closely as possible, you'll have the correct crochet hook size to use for the project. It's important to also check your gauge often as you crochet. The weight of the item, the weather, or how relaxed you are can all play a part in altering the gauge as you work.

Sewing Pieces Together

Finished crochet pieces can be sewn together to create garments as you would sew fabric or finished knit pieces. Holding the right sides together, use a yarn tapestry needle threaded with a strand of the same yarn, and seam using a back stitch. Be sure to allow a small seam allowance. Especially with the bulkier yarns, the seam allowance should be no more than one stitch in order to keep the seams from getting too bulky. If you are using a particularly nubby yarn, you can always use a basic cotton or wool in the same color for sewing your pieces together.

Blocking

Sometimes, finished crocheted pieces and seams can be smoothed or flattened out by blocking. Blocking can often help flatten edges and edgings to allow their detail to show. The method of blocking—wet or steam—should be based on the yarn content and care instructions listed on the yarn ball bands. When in doubt, test the blocking method on a swatch before touching your finished crochet pieces.

Wet blocking is done by pinning the piece down to its finished measurements on a flat surface using rust-proof pins. The piece can then be sprayed lightly with water and allowed to fully dry, naturally and out of the sun. Alternately, damp towels can be laid on top of the piece. Wait until the towels and the crochet piece are completely dry before removing the pins.

A pinned piece can be steam blocked instead by running a steam iron (set at a temperature according to the fabric content) one to two inches above the surface of the piece. Do not press the iron down on the fabric, or the stitches will get flattened and the natural texture will be lost. Allow to dry naturally and completely as well.

Be especially careful when blocking luxury fibers, such as silk, which can easily be ruined by overzealous blocking! Check the yarn label and test your blocking method gently on a swatch first.

Care of Finished Crocheted Projects

Check the yarn ball bands for laundering instructions. Some garments can be washed gently by hand in a mild detergent. Never wring the water out. Just gently squeeze and roll in a towel to press the water out. Lay the item out flat to dry (out of the sun), pinning to measurements (as you would when blocking) if needed to reshape.

Stitch Glossary

For illustrations demonstrating the basic techniques and stitches used in crochet, and in the patterns in this book, refer to the Stitch Glossary that starts on page 134.

Levels of Difficulty

Each project in this book is rated by level of difficulty based on the following definitions. In addition, each project lists the Stitches and Techniques that are used in that project to help you determine what skill level is needed to successfully create that project.

Beginner

Projects using basic crochet stitches, repeating stitch patterns, simple color changes, and minimal shaping and finishing.

Intermediate

Projects using crochet stitch combinations and variations to create more involved stitch patterns and shaping.

Advanced

Projects using crochet stitch combinations and variations to create intricate stitch patterns, more detailed shaping, and refined finishing.

Errata

While every effort has been made to be accurate and complete with each pattern, mistakes and typos do occasionally happen. We are sorry for any inconvenience. Please visit SweaterBabe.com for the latest updates on any corrections.

Please keep in mind that we strive to reproduce the color of the crocheted pieces found in this book as accurately as possible. However, due to ink variations that can occur during the printing process, there may be some slight color difference between the suggested yarn color and the photo of the actual project.

Abbreviations

The following are the standardized abbreviations used throughout the instructions in this book:

approx	approximately
beg	beginning
bet	between
ch(s)	chain(s)
cl	cluster
cm	centimeter(s)
cont	continue(ing)
dec	decrease
1dc/rf	1 double crochet around the front of the stem of the double crochet in the previous row
1dc/rb	1 double crochet around the back of the stem of the double crochet in the previous row
dc	double crochet
Dc2Cl	2-double crochet cluster stitch
Dc2tog	2-double crochets worked together
Dc3Cl or Dc3tog	3-double crochet cluster stitch
Dc4Cl	4-double crochet cluster stitch
Dc5Cl	5-double crochet cluster stitch
dtr	double treble
DTr2Cl	2-double treble cluster stitch
DTr3Cl	3-double treble cluster stitch
g	gram(s)
hdc	half double crochet
Hdc4tog	4-half double crochet puff stitch
Hdc5tog	5-half double crochet puff stitch
hk	hook
inc	increase

lp(s)	loop(s)
m	meter(s)
mm	millimeter(s)
oz	ounce(s)
patt	pattern
PuffCl	puff stitch cluster
rem	remain(ing)
rep	repeat
rnd	round
RS	right side of work
sc	single crochet
sk	skip
sl st	slip stitch
sp(s)	space(s)
st(s)	stitch(es)
t-ch	turning chain (beginning chain)
tog	together
tr	treble
TrCl	2-treble cluster
WS	wrong side of work
yd	yard(s)
yo	yarn over
[ ]	repeat instructions in brackets the number of times indicated right after the close bracket
( )	work instructions in parentheses in the same stitch or space indicated right after the close parenthesis
*	repeat the instructions following the single asterisk as instructed

International Crochet Symbols

Here is a key to the crochet symbols used in the pattern stitch diagrams:

○ chain (ch)

● slip st (sl st)

+ single crochet (sc)

T half double crochet (hdc)

Ŧ double crochet (dc)

Ŧ treble (tr)

Ŧ double treble (dtr)

V 2 dc worked in a single st

W 3 dc worked in a single st

W 4 dc worked in a single st

W 5 dc worked in a single st

W 6 dc worked in a single st

Ö Dc2tog cluster worked in a single st

⊕ Dc3tog cluster worked in a single st

Ⓤ Puff or cluster stitch worked in a single st. The horizontal bars and extra vertical lines are added depending on the actual stitches involved (hdc, dc, tr, etc.)

Ⓜ Puff or cluster stitch worked in a space or several sts

Ⱥ 2 dc cluster worked in a space or several sts

Ⱥ 3 dc cluster worked in a space or several sts

Ⱥ 2 tr cluster worked in a space or several sts

Ⱥ 3 tr cluster worked in a space or several sts

Ƭ 1 dc/rf (or FPdc)—work 1 dc around the back of the stem (post) of the dc in the previous row, which will cause the dc to lie in the back of the work.

Ƭ 1 dc/rb (or BPdc)—work 1 dc around the back of the stem (post) of the dc in the previous row, which will cause the dc to lie in the back of the work.

Ƭ Bullion stitch—Yarn over as many times as indicated in the instructions; insert the hook into stitch or space as specified; yarn over once more; draw through a loop; yarn over again and draw through all loops; chain 1 to complete the bullion stitch.

⊗ 3-stitch picot closed with a slip st. A picot can be made using any number of chains; follow instructions as specified.

◯ Joining a chain into a ring with a slip stitch.

1 Fabulous & Flirty projects

INTERMEDIATE

Bold Lace Cardigan **35**

Ruffled-Strap Tank **36**

Textured Shaped
Purse **37**

INTERMEDIATE

Flirty Skirt **38**

Ruffled Scarf **39**

ADVANCED

Spaghetti-Strap
Top **20**

Shawl-Collared Wrap
Cardigan **24**

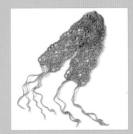

Macramé Belt **31**

Spaghetti-Strap Top

This close-fitting, spaghetti-strap top has all the detailing of a fine silk camisole. The yarn is a luxe blend of mohair and silk. It is crocheted in a simple shell stitch with lacy crocheted flowers accenting the top. Double straps, with ties only on the right shoulder, complete the look.

Instructions begin on page 42

Sumptuous Striped Scarf

Add a little color and luxury to your life with this sumptuous scarf, which is crocheted in a simple stitch that creates pretty heart-shaped scallops. Pick your favorite colors and make your own color combination. This is a great project for using up your yarn stash as well. And if you're feeling particularly ambitious, use the wavy striped pattern stitch to make a gorgeous striped afghan.

Instructions begin on page 48

Moroccan Slippers

Crochet yourself a pair of fanciful slippers inspired by stylish Moroccan footwear. The pattern is mostly single and double crochet, with a few puff stitches to create the openwork inset. These slippers are crocheted using a large size J/10 (6 mm) hook so they make a great weekend or evening project and a nice alternative gift item to the usual scarf. Great for using up your yarn stash as well.

Instructions begin on page 50

Evening Scarf

Scarves make the ultimate evening accessories. This one is crocheted in an easy lace pattern using a spectacular mohair yarn with glittery silver accents. Its skinnier shape and generous length are perfect for wearing loosely draped around your neck or casually thrown over one shoulder. Long, skinny fringe adds to the sexy feel. An easy project that makes a perfect gift.

Instructions begin on page 54

Shawl-Collared Wrap Cardigan

Cardigans are ideal for wearing year-round. This one is an easy favorite with its very wearable and romantic shape. The cozy shawl collar is beautifully shaped. The unique open pattern contrasts well with the solid collar and split cuffs, which are worked in a simple single crochet stitch. A feminine, fitted shape and set-in sleeves make this an easy choice for both casual and dress-up events. This cardigan is worked in a wonderfully soft angora and wool blend yarn.

Instructions begin on page 56

Textured Cloche Hat

Hats are great for instant gratification. This one can be crocheted in a flash using a big size L/11 (8 mm) hook. Its two-tone design is done with a very simple, yet complicated looking textured stitch, giving a new look to a classic hat shape. This hat is so quick to make, you'll be tempted to make several as gifts.

Instructions begin on page 66

Tortoise-Handled Purse

Here's a fun crocheted purse to brighten any outfit. The purse is crocheted in a simple textured stitch using a bold cotton and viscose blend yarn. Fuzzy wool stripes in a coordinating shade add a slightly sporty appeal. A big crocheted flower and beautiful tortoise shell–look handles are the finishing touches for this elegant and fun purse.

Instructions begin on page 68

Elegant Rectangular Stole

Treat yourself to a luxurious wrap in a decadent yarn blend. This rectangular stole is created with octagonal motifs joined together as you work the last round of each motif. The smaller motifs are crocheted and joined into the stole to fill in the holes between rows of the larger motifs. The result is a breathtaking stole that is perfect for breezy evenings and special occasions.

Instructions begin on page 71

Lush Cowl-Neck Sweater

Here is a sophisticated, yet cozy top you'll reach for again and again. The generous and flattering cowl neckline accents the open lace stitch. Solid, "ribbed" cuffs and a high waistband give the sweater lots of shape and strong style. This sweater is made with a soft, cloud-like mohair blend yarn.

Instructions begin on page 74

Chunky Flower Hat

Wonderful shades of red are used to crochet this charming flower trim hat. Simple cluster stitches at the top center create a pretty floral effect. The bulky yarn gives it great texture. A flirty little flower adds the finishing touch.

Instructions begin on page 78

Chunky Striped Car Coat

Beautiful shades of red work together to create this bold, striking car coat. The shaped silhouette and contrasting solid-color cuffs and collar add unique touches to this versatile piece. Mostly worked in double crochet, it is a relatively fast project. A self-belt completes the look.

Instructions begin on page 80

Macramé Belt

It's like wearing a piece of artwork around your hips. This lacy crocheted belt is a great accessory for a simple tunic, long t-shirt, or denim skirt. A special stitch, called the bullion stitch, gives it the unique macramé appearance, and is set against a web of chain-5 arches. While the bullion stitch is a little tricky at first, the effect is well worth the effort.

Instructions begin on page 86

Flutter-Sleeve Top

Fluttery sleeves on this delicate top add a truly feminine touch. The body is crocheted in a simple stitch, accented with a band of single crochet just below the bust. An open lace stitch is used in the upper bodice and contrasts beautifully with the solid stitch below. A shapely v-neck and a pretty crochet flower complete the look.

Instructions begin on page 88

Slim-Fitting Cardigan

Here's a lovely cardigan with lots of romantic touches. The slim shape is worked in an all-over wavy pattern stitch. The pretty collar, cuffs, and button bands are worked in a wide, distinctive lace border. Pearl buttons add a glamorous and vintage finishing touch.

Instructions begin on page 96

Romantic Summer Shawl

Add a little bohemian touch to your wardrobe with this lacy, romantic triangular shawl. It's crocheted in a soft cotton blend tape yarn in an open lace pattern with a large K/10 (7 mm) hook. The resulting fabric has wonderful drape and texture. A long-fringe finish adds to its flirty appeal. This shawl would also be stunning in a lightweight alpaca yarn. You'll never reach for that pashmina again.

Instructions begin on page 104

Bold Lace Cardigan

Make a bold statement with this chunky shaped jacket. Distinctively ribbed collar, cuffs, and front edges complement the textured stitch. Three-quarter-length sleeves and a shorter length complete the shapely look.

Instructions begin on page 107

Ruffled-Strap Tank

This ruffled-strap tank is sexy and sweet at the same time. The tank is crocheted in an all-over lace stitch, which has a beautifully intricate look. The shaped neckline and slim straps with ruffled trim make for a very flattering top. The drawstring tie accentuating the color change adds a nice finishing touch. Perfect with jeans for a casual, yet sexy look or with a cream-colored suit for an elegant, sophisticated look.

Instructions begin on page 114

Textured Shaped Purse

Here is a purse that shows crocheted stitch definition at its best. It is crocheted in a wonderfully classic wool yarn in a simple double crochet stitch that creates a great texture. The textured fabric contrasts nicely with a smooth antique-look wood handle. The shaped bottom adds to the vintage effect. Choose a unique vintage fabric to line the purse for maximum appeal.

Instructions begin on page 123

Flirty Skirt

A flirty skirt is a perfect way to update your wardrobe—with great color and flair to boot! The skirt is crocheted in a cotton yarn blended with Tencel for fabulous drape and softness. The bright color combination is earthy and youthful, yet the A-line shape makes it very elegant and sophisticated. A self-sash at the waist adds a fun accent and allows you to decide if you prefer your skirts to hit at the waist or ride a little lower on your hips. The skirt also has three buttons at the side.

Instructions begin on page 126

Ruffled Scarf

This ruffled-end scarf is an easy project to crochet. The yarn, a unique blend of mohair and sparkle, adds lots of interest to the scarf. Using a bulky size J/10 (6 mm) hook, this project can be made in a weekend. The scarf is a little wider than most, allowing it to double as a pretty evening shoulder wrap.

Instructions begin on page 132

section **2**

Fabulous & Flirty

project instructions

BEGINNER

Sumptuous Striped
Scarf **48**

Evening Scarf **54**

Textured Cloche
Hat **66**

Chunky Flower
Hat **78**

INTERMEDIATE

Moroccan Slippers **50**

Tortoise-Handled
Purse **68**

Elegant Rectangular
Stole **71**

Lush Cowl-Neck
Sweater **74**

INTERMEDIATE

Chunky Striped
Car Coat **80**

Flutter-Sleeve Top **88**

Slim-Fitting
Cardigan **96**

Romantic Summer
Shawl **104**

Spaghetti-Strap Top

To Fit Bust Size

32–34 (35–36, 37–39, 40–42)"
[81.5–86.5 (89–91.5, 94–99, 101.5–106.5) cm]

Finished Bust Size

32 (35, 37 ½, 40 ½)" [81.5 (89, 95, 103) cm]
Size 32"–34" shown.
Note: Instructions are given for smallest size, with larger sizes in parentheses. Where there is only one instruction, it applies to all sizes.

Materials

A fine-weight mohair blend yarn:
Color A total yardage required: 458 (458, 458, 687) yd [420 (420, 420, 630) m]; Color B total yardage required: 229 yd (210 m).

Shown:

Rowan Kid Silk Haze (70% Super Kid Mohair, 30% Silk; approx 229 yd [210 m] per ⅞ oz [25 g] ball):
Color A: #583 Blushes, 2 (2, 2, 3) balls;
Color B: #606 Candy Girl, 1 ball.

Sizes G/6 (4.5 mm) and F/5 (4 mm) crochet hook or size to obtain gauge.

Notions

Long sewing pins with colored heads; yarn tapestry needle.

SHELL PATTERN STITCH

Repeat rows 2 and 3 for shell pattern stitch.

Gauge

Seven 5-dc shells = 10" (25.5 cm) and 8 rows = 3" (7.5 cm) in shell pattern st using size G/6 (4.5 mm) crochet hook. Take time to check gauge.

Stitches and Techniques Used

(See pages 134–140)

Slip st, single crochet, double crochet, treble, multiple stitches into 1 stitch, cluster st.

Pattern Stitches

Shell Pattern Stitch

Ch a multiple of 6 plus 2 extra.
Row 1: Work 1 sc in 2nd ch from hk, *sk 2 ch, 5 dc in next ch, sk 2 ch, 1 sc in next ch; rep from * to end, turn.
Row 2: Ch 3 (counts as 1 dc), 2 dc in 1st sc, *sk 2 dc, 1 sc in next dc, sk 2 dc, 5 dc in next sc; rep from * ending last rep with 3 dc in last sc, turn.
Row 3: Ch 1, 1 sc in 1st dc, *sk 2 dc, 5 dc in next dc, sk 2 dc, 1 sc in next dc; rep from * ending last rep with 1 sc in top of t-ch, turn.
Rep rows 2 and 3 for shell pattern st.

Notes:
Treble Cluster (TrCl)—
Yo 2 times, insert hk in st or sp, yo, draw lp through work, yo, draw through 2 lps, yo, draw through 2 lps, yo 2 times, insert hk in same st or sp, yo, draw lp through work, yo, draw through 2 lps, yo, draw through 2 lps, yo, draw through rem 3 lps on hk.

Back

With A and size G/6 (4.5 mm) hk, ch 68 (74, 80, 86).

FLORAL EDGING

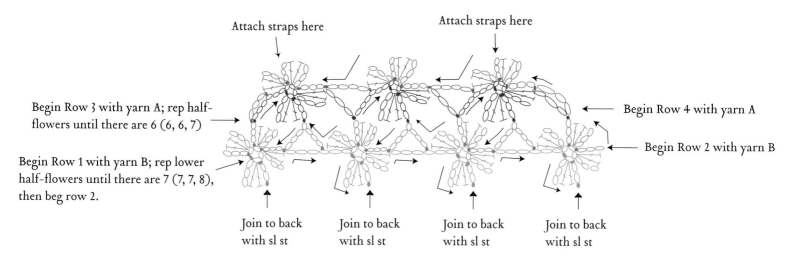

Attach straps here

Attach straps here

Begin Row 3 with yarn A; rep half-flowers until there are 6 (6, 6, 7)

Begin Row 1 with yarn B; rep lower half-flowers until there are 7 (7, 7, 8), then beg row 2.

Begin Row 4 with yarn A

Begin Row 2 with yarn B

Join to back with sl st

Join to back with sl st

Join to back with sl st

Join to back with sl st

Work in shell pattern st for 5 (5, 7, 7) rows: 11 (12, 13, 14) 5-dc shells.

Shape waist as follows:

Row 6 (6, 8, 8): Ch 3, 1 dc in 1st sc, *sk 2 dc, 1 sc in next dc, sk 2 dc, 5 dc in next sc; rep from * ending last rep with 2 dc in last sc, turn.

Row 7 (7, 9, 9): Ch 1, sk 2 dc, 4 dc in next sc, sk 2 dc, 1 sc in next dc, *sk 2 dc, 5 dc in next sc, sk 2 dc, 1 sc in next dc; rep from * ending last rep with 4 dc in last sc, sl st in top of t-ch, turn.

Row 8 (8, 10, 10): Ch 1, sk 1 dc, 1 sc in next dc, *sk 2 dc, 5 dc in next sc, sk 2 dc, 1 sc in next dc; rep from * to end, sk last dc and t-ch, turn: 10 (11, 12, 13) 5-dc shells remain.

Note: The dec are completed at this point; beg with the next row the patt shifts. Work as follows:

Row 9 (9, 11, 11): Rep row 2 of shell pattern st.

Row 10 (10, 12, 12): Rep row 3 of shell pattern st.

Rows 11 (11, 13, 13) to 18 (20, 22, 22): Rep rows 2 and 3 of shell pattern st 4 (5, 5, 5) more times.

Begin chest shaping as follows:

Row 19 (21, 23, 23): Ch 3, 3 dc in 1st sc, *sk 2 dc, 1 sc in next dc, sk 2 dc, 5 dc in next sc; rep from * ending last rep with 4 dc in last sc, turn.

Row 20 (22, 24, 24): Ch 3, 1 dc in 1st sc, 1 sc in next dc, *sk 2 dc, 5 dc in next sc, sk 2 dc, 1 sc in next dc; rep from * to t-ch, 2 dc in top of t-ch, turn.

Row 21 (23, 25, 25): Ch 1, sk 2 dc, 5 dc in next sc, *sk 2 dc, 1 sc in next dc, sk 2 dc, 5 dc in next sc; rep from * ending last rep with sk 2 dc, 4 dc in last sc, sl st in top of t-ch, turn.

Row 22 (24, 26, 26): Ch 3, 2 dc in 1st sc, 1 sc in next dc, sk 2 dc, 5 dc in next sc, *sk

2 dc, 1 sc in next dc, sk 2 dc, 5 dc in next sc; rep from * ending last rep with 3 dc in t-ch, turn.

Row 23 (25, 27, 27): Rep row 3 of shell pattern st: 11 (12, 13, 14) 5-dc shells.

Row 24 (26, 28, 28): Rep row 2 of shell pattern st.

Rows 25 (27, 29, 29) to 28 (30, 32, 34): Rep rows 3 and 2 of shell pattern st 2 (2, 2, 3) more times. Fasten off.

Front

Work same as for BACK through row 28 (30, 32, 34), but do not fasten off. Shape armholes as follows:

Row 29 (31, 33, 35): Sl st in 1st 6 sts, ch 1, 1 sc in next dc, *sk 2 dc, 5 dc in next sc, sk 2 dc, 1 sc in next dc; rep from * to last 6 sts, sk next 2 dc, sk next sc, sk last 2 dc, and sk t-ch, turn: 9 (10, 11, 12) 5-dc shells remain.

Row 30 (32, 34, 36): Sl st in 1st 3 sts, ch 1, 1 sc in next dc, *sk next 2 dc, 5 dc in next sc, sk 2 dc, 1 sc in next dc; rep from * to last 4 sts, sk next 2 dc, sk last sc, and sk t-ch, turn: 8 (9, 10, 11) 5-dc shells remain.

Row 31 (33, 35, 37): Sk 1st sc, sl st in next 2 dc, ch 1, 1 sc in next dc, *sk 2 dc, 5 dc in next sc, sk 2 dc, 1 sc in next dc; rep from * to last 4 sts, sk next 2 dc, sk last sc, and sk t-ch, turn: 7 (8, 9, 10) 5-dc shells remain.

For Sizes X-Small and Small Only

Fasten off.

For Sizes Medium and Large Only

Row — (—, 36, 38): Rep row 2 of shell pattern st.
Fasten off.

Floral Edging for Back Piece

Notes:

1. Each flower has 4 petals. The bottom 2 petals are worked on one row. The top 2 petals are worked on the next row.

2. As row 1 is worked, each flower is attached to the back piece with a sl st as the 1st petal is being worked.

3. Rows 1 and 3 are worked with the fabric (in this case the back piece) turned upside down. For rows 2 and 4, turn fabric right side up (as is usually done for crochet) to work the row.

First, use sewing pins to mark sts where flower trim will be attached to the last row of back piece.

For size X-SMALL, with WS of last row facing you, start counting from the right, as if you were working the next row: sk 1st 12 sts, mark next st, [sk 6 sts, mark next st] 6 times—7 marker pins.

For size SMALL, with WS of last row facing you, start counting from the right, as if you were working the next row: sk 1st 12 sts, mark next st, [sk 7 sts, mark next st] 6 times—7 marker pins.

For size MEDIUM, with WS of last row facing you, start counting from the right, as if you were working the next row: sk 1st 12 sts, mark next st, [sk 8 sts, mark next st] 6 times—7 marker pins.

For size LARGE, with WS of last row facing you, start counting from the right, as if you were working the next row: sk 1st 12 sts, mark next st, [sk 8 sts, mark next st, sk 7 sts, mark next st] 3 times, sk 8 sts, mark next st—8 marker pins.

Make the Flowers

Beg with the 1st flower at the top left (back left shoulder) of the BACK piece. Lay the BACK piece on a table in front of you, with RS facing you and upside down, that is, with top edge closer to you and bottom hem away from you. With B and size F/5 (4 mm) hk, ch 4.

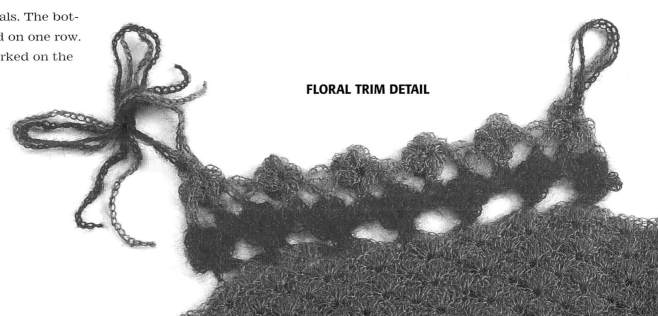

FLORAL TRIM DETAIL

Row 1: Sl st in 4th ch from hk to form a ring for flower #1, ch 3, 2 dc in ring, join to BACK piece with a sl st in the st with 1st marker pin on the BACK piece, ch 2, sl st in ring, (ch 3, 2 dc) in ring (bottom 2 petals of flower #1 completed); *ch 10, sl st in 4th ch from hk to form a ring for next flower, twist around (counter-clockwise) to work next sts in ring, ch 3, 2 dc in ring, join to BACK piece with a sl st at next marker pin, ch 2, sl st in ring, (ch 3, 2 dc) in ring (bottom 2 petals of next flower completed); rep from * 5 (5, 5, 6) more times: 7 (7, 7, 8) half-flowers.

Row 2: Turn BACK piece right-side up to complete top 2 petals of flowers. Ch 3, sl st in ring of flower #7 (7, 7, 8), ch 3, (2 dc, ch 3, sl st, ch 3, 2 dc) in same ring, sl st in 3rd ch of next ch-6 arch [flower #7 (7, 7, 8) completed], ch 7, *sl st in top of next dc of next flower, ch 3 (sl st, ch 3, 2 dc, ch 3, sl st, ch 3, 2 dc) in ring of same flower, sl st in 3rd ch of next ch-6 arch [next flower completed], ch 7; rep from * 5 (5, 5, 6) more times, ending last rep with ch 3, sl st in same ring [instead of sl st in 3rd ch of ch-6 arch] to complete last flower (flower #1). Fasten off B.
Turn BACK piece upside down again. Join A with size F/5 (4 mm) hk to top corner of flower #1 (top corner of petal opposite petal that is attached to BACK piece).

Row 3: *Ch 10, sl st in 4th ch from hk to form a ring, ch 3, 2 dc in ring, sl st in 4th ch of next ch-7 arch, ch 3, sl st in same ring, ch 3, 2 dc in same ring, ch 3, sl st in top of ch-3 of center petal of next flower from row 2; rep from * to end, turn piece right-side up: 6 (6, 6, 7) half-flowers.

Row 4: Ch 3, sl st in top of next dc of flower #6 (6, 6, 7), ch 3, sl st in ring, (ch 3, 2 dc, ch 3, sl st, ch 3, 2 dc) in same ring, sl st in 3rd ch of next ch-6 arch, ch 4, *sl st in top of next dc of next flower, ch 3 (sl st, ch 3, 2 dc, ch 3, sl st, ch 3, 2 dc) in ring of same flower, sl st in 3rd ch of next ch-6 arch, ch 4; rep from * ending last rep with ch 3, sl st in 1st ch at beg of row 3. Fasten off.

Floral Edging for Front Piece

Use sewing pins to mark sts where flower trim will be attached to the last row of FRONT piece.

For size X-SMALL, with WS of last row facing you, start counting from the right, as if you were working the next row: mark the 1st sc, [sk 6 sts, mark next st] 6 times—7 marker pins.

For size SMALL, with WS of last row facing you, start counting from the right, as if you were working the next row: mark the 1st sc, [sk 7 sts, mark next st] 6 times—7 marker pins.

For size MEDIUM, with WS of last row facing you, start counting from the right, as if you were working the next row: mark the 1st sc, [sk 8 sts, mark next st] 6 times—7 marker pins.

For size LARGE, with WS of last row facing you, start counting from the right, as if you were working the next row: mark the 1st st, [sk 8 sts, mark next st, sk 7 sts, mark next st] 3 times, sk 8 sts, mark next st—8 marker pins. Work 7 (7, 7, 8)-flower edging as for Back piece, following marker pins.

Left Double Strap

With 2 strands of A and size G/6 (4.5 mm) hk, ch 27. Fasten off.
With 2 strands of B and size G/6 (4.5 mm) hk, ch 27. Fasten off.
Sew ends of straps to top corners of flowers on BACK and FRONT for left shoulder strap.

Right Double Tie Straps

With 2 strands of A and size G/6 (4.5 mm) hk, ch 70. Fasten off. Rep to make 1 more strap in A.
With 2 strands of B and size G/6 (4.5 mm) hk, ch 70. Fasten off. Rep to make 1 more strap in B.
Sew one strap of each color to back corner flower and one strap of each color to front corner flower for right shoulder tie straps. Knot unsewn strap ends tightly and clip yarn close to knots.

Finishing

Sew side seams.

Bottom Edging

Attach B at bottom right corner (at the seam) of FRONT piece with RS facing and size G/6 (4.5 mm) hk.

Rnd 1: Ch 5, 1 TrCl in same sp used to attach, 1 sc in base of next 5-dc shell from row 1 of FRONT piece, *(1 TrCl, ch 1, 1 TrCl, ch 1, 1 TrCl) in base of next 5-dc shell from row 2 of FRONT piece, 1 sc in base of next 5-dc shell from row 1 of FRONT piece; rep from * to side seam; (1 TrCl, ch 1, 1 TrCl, ch 1, 1 TrCl) at side seam, 1 sc in base of next 5-dc shell from row 1 of BACK piece, **(1 TrCl, ch 1, 1 TrCl, ch 1, 1 TrCl) in base of next 5-dc shell from row 2 of FRONT piece, 1 sc in base of next 5-dc shell from row 1 of FRONT piece; rep from ** to 1st side seam, (1 TrCl, ch 1, 1 tr) in same sp as beg ch-5, join with a sl st in 4th ch of beg ch-5. Fasten off.

Weave in all loose ends. Very gently steam press flowers only to help flatten.

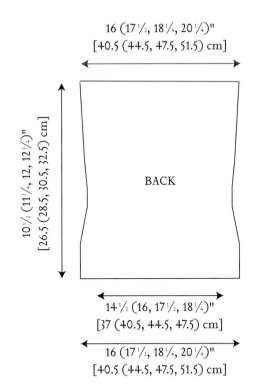

16 (17½, 18¾, 20¼)"
[40.5 (44.5, 47.5, 51.5) cm]

10½ (11¼, 12, 12¾)"
[26.5 (28.5, 30.5, 32.5) cm]

BACK

14½ (16, 17½, 18¾)"
[37 (40.5, 44.5, 47.5) cm]

16 (17½, 18¾, 20¼)"
[40.5 (44.5, 47.5, 51.5) cm]

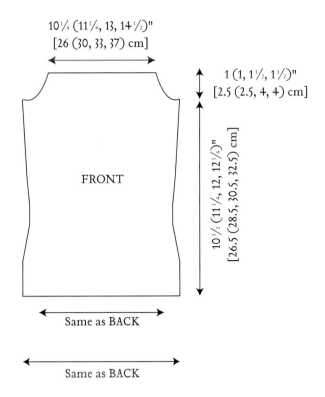

10¼ (11¼, 13, 14½)"
[26 (30, 33, 37) cm]

1 (1, 1½, 1½)"
[2.5 (2.5, 4, 4) cm]

FRONT

10½ (11¼, 12, 12¾)"
[26.5 (28.5, 30.5, 32.5) cm]

Same as BACK

Same as BACK

(Measurements do not include floral trim or edging)

Sumptuous Striped Scarf

Finished Size

Width: 8" (20.5 cm)

Length: 78" (198 cm) long, excluding fringe

Materials

A light-weight microfiber or cotton blend yarn: Colors A, B, and C, total yardage required: 336 yd (308 m) each.

Shown:

Lion Brand Micro Spun (100% Microfiber Acrylic; approx 168 yd [154 m] per 2 ½ oz [70 g] ball):

Color A: #143 Lavender, 2 balls.

Color B: #146 Fuchsia, 2 balls.

Color C: #98 French Vanilla, 2 balls.

Note: The scarf featured here used 1 ball each of B and C. However, because there was very little yarn left over in these 2 colors, I recommend readers purchase 2 balls each of B and C.

Size I/9 (5.5 mm) crochet hook or size to obtain gauge.

Notions

Yarn tapestry needle

Gauge

5 (2 dc, ch 3, 1 sc, ch 3, 2 dc) groups (from even-numbered rows) = 13"

WAVY STRIPE PATTERN STITCH

Repeat rows 2 through 5 for wavy stripe pattern stitch.

(33 cm) and 10 rows = 4" (10 cm) in wavy stripe pattern st using size I/9 (5.5 mm) crochet hook. Take time to check gauge.

Stitches and Techniques Used

(See pages 134–140)

Single crochet, double crochet, working into an arch, fringe.

Pattern Stitches

Wavy Stripe Pattern Stitch

Ch a multiple of 9 plus 6 extra.

Row 1: Sk 6 ch, 1 sc in next ch, sk 2 ch, 5 dc in next ch, *sk 2 ch, 1 sc in next ch, ch 3, sk 2 ch, 1 sc in next ch, sk 2 ch, 5 dc in next ch; rep from * ending with sk 2 ch, 1 sc in next sc, ch 1, sk 1 ch, 1 dc in next ch, turn.

Row 2: Ch 1, 1 sc in 1st dc, sk next ch-1 sp, sk next sc, *1 dc in each of next 2 dc, ch 3, 1 sc in next dc, ch 3, 1 dc in each of next 2 dc, 1 sc in next ch-3 sp; rep from * ending last rep with 1 sc in top of t-ch, turn.

Row 3: Ch 3, 2 dc in 1st sc, *sk next 2 dc, 1 sc in next ch-3 sp, ch 3, 1 sc in next ch-3 sp, 5 dc in next sc; rep from * ending last rep with 3 dc in last sc, turn.

Row 4: Ch 1, 1 sc in 1st dc, *ch 3, 1 dc in each of next 2 dc, 1 sc in next ch-3 sp, 1 dc in each of next 2 dc, ch 3, 1 sc in next dc; rep from * ending with 1 sc in top of t-ch, turn.

Row 5: Ch 4, 1 sc in 1st ch-3 sp, *5 dc in next sc, 1 sc in next ch-3 sp, ch 3, 1 sc in next ch-3 sp; rep from * ending last rep with ch 1, 1 dc in last sc, turn.

Rep rows 2 through 5 for pattern st.

Note: When joining the new color or cutting off the old color, always leave at least a 7" (18 cm) tail of yarn. These tails can be incorporated into the fringe when finishing the scarf.

With A, loosely ch 276.

Rows 1 and 2: Work rows 1 and 2 of Wavy Stripe pattern st. Change to B.

Rows 3 and 4: Work rows 3 and 4 of Wavy Stripe pattern st. Change to C.

Rows 5 and 6: Work rows 5 and 2 of Wavy Stripe pattern st. Change to A.

Rows 7 and 8: Work rows 3 and 4 of Wavy Stripe pattern st. Change to C.

Rows 9 and 10: Work rows 5 and 2 of Wavy Stripe pattern st. Change to B.

Rows 11 and 12: Work rows 3 and 4 of Wavy Stripe pattern st. Change to A.

Rows 13 and 14: Work rows 5 and 2 of Wavy Stripe pattern st. Change to C.

Rows 15 and 16: Work rows 3 and 4 of Wavy Stripe pattern st. Change to A.

Rows 17 and 18: Work rows 5 and 2 of Wavy Stripe pattern st. Change to B.

Rows 19 and 20: Work rows 3 and 4 of Wavy Stripe pattern st.
Fasten off.

Finishing

Cut 12" (30.5 cm) lengths of yarn for fringe. Use 2 strands of the same color for each fringe. Attach 2 fringes to each end of the corresponding color stripe. Incorporate 7" (18 cm) yarn tails from color changes into fringes, and trim excess to match fringe length.

Weave in all loose ends. Lightly steam.

Moroccan Slippers

To Fit Ladies Shoe Sizes
4-6 ½ (7-8 ½, 8 ½+) U.S. shoe size
Finished Sole Length
9 (10, 11)" [23 (25.5, 28) cm]
Sizes: Small, Medium, and Large.
Size Small shown.
Note: Instructions are given for smallest size, with larger sizes in parentheses. Where there is only one instruction, it applies to all sizes.

Materials

A medium-weight wool blend yarn:
Colors A and B: 127 yd [116 m] each.

Shown:

Classic Elite Montera (50% Llama, 50% Wool; 127 yd [116 m] per 3 ½ oz [100 g] ball):
Color A: #3888 Magenta, 1 ball;
Color B: #3885 Bolsita Orange, 1 ball.
This amount will make more than 1 pair of the smallest size if you switch the colors for the second pair. Or, make an extra pair of soles and attach on top of the existing soles for additional strength and warmth.

Size J/10 (6 mm) crochet hook or size to obtain gauge.

Notions

Yarn tapestry needle

Gauge

8 sc = 3" (7.5 cm) and 4 rows = 1" (2.5 cm) in basic sc st using size J/10 (6 mm) crochet hook. Take time to check gauge.

Stitches and Techniques Used

(See pages 134–140)
Slip st, single crochet, half double crochet, double crochet, treble, multiple stitches into 1 stitch, cluster st, puff st, working into an arch, working in back loop only, working in the round, joining in the round.

Notes:
1. To work a "dec 1" [insert hk in next st, yo, pull lp through] 2 times, yo, pull through 3 lps on hk.
2. To work a "dec 2" [insert hk in next st, yo, pull lp through] 3 times, yo, pull through 4 lps on hk.
3. To work a "Puff st" [yo, insert hk in st, yo, pull lp through] 3 times, yo, pull through all lps on hk, ch 1 tightly to close puff st.

4. To work a "Puff St Cluster" (PuffCl) *[yo, insert hk in 1st st, yo, pull lp through] 3 times*; rep from * to * in 2nd st; rep from * to * in 3rd st; yo, pull through all lps on hk, ch 1 tightly to close PuffCl.

Sole

With A, ch 16 (19, 22).

For Size Small Only

Rnd 1: Work 2 sc in 2nd ch from hk, 1 sc in each of next 13 ch, 2 sc in next ch, rotate work counter-clockwise and cont working on opposite side of base ch to complete the rnd, 2 sc in same ch as last 2 sc, 1 sc in each of next 13 ch, 2 sc in opposite side of 1st 2 sc, join with a sl st to 1st sc: 34 sc.

For Size Medium Only

Rnd 1: Work 2 sc in 2nd ch from hk, 1 hdc in each of next 16 ch, 2 sc in next ch, turn work counter-clockwise and cont working on opposite side of base ch to complete the rnd, 2 sc in same ch as last 2 sc, 1 hdc in each of next 16 ch, 2 sc in opposite side of 1st 2 sc, join with a sl st to 1st sc: 40 sts.

For Size Large Only

Rnd 1: Work 2 sc in 2nd ch from hk, 1 dc in each of next 19 ch, 2 sc in next ch, turn work counter-clockwise and cont working on opposite side of base ch to complete the rnd, 2 sc in same ch as last 2 sc, 1 dc in each of next 19 ch, 2 sc in opposite side of 1st 2 sc, join with a sl st to 1st sc: 46 sts.

For All Sizes

Rnd 2: Ch 3, 2 dc in same st as sl st, 1 dc in each of next 15 (18, 21) sts, 3 dc in each of next 2 sts, 1 dc in each of next 15 (18, 21) sts, 3 dc in next st, join with a sl st to top of ch-3: 42 (48, 54) dc (counting ch-3 as 1 dc).

Rnd 3: Ch 1, 2 sc in same ch as sl st, 2 sc in each of next 2 dc, 1 sc in each of next 15 (18, 21) dc, 2 sc in each of next 6 dc, 1 sc in each of next 15 (18, 21) dc, 2 sc in each of next 3 dc, join with a sl st to 1st sc: 54 (60, 66) sc.

Rnd 4: Ch 1, 1 sc in same sc as sl st, 1 sc in next sc, 1 hdc in each of next 4 sc, 1 dc in each of next 19 (22, 25) sc, 2 dc in next sc, 2 tr in each of next 2 sc, 2 dc in next sc, 1 dc in each of next 19 (22, 25) sc, 1 hdc in each of next 4 sc, 1 sc in each of next 2 sc, join with a sl st to 1st sc with B: 58 (64, 70) sts.

Slipper Sides and Top

Rnd 5: With B, ch 1, working in Back Loop only of each st, 1 sc in same sc as sl st and in each st around, join with a sl st to 1st sc with A: 58 (64, 70) sc.

For Size Small Only

Rnd 6: With A, ch 1, 1 sc in same sc as sl st and in each of next 27 sc, dec 1 over next 2 sc (dec 1 completed for toe shaping), 1 sc in each of next 28 sc, join with a sl st to 1st sc: 57 sts.

For Size Medium Only

Rnd 6: With A, ch 2, sk 1st sc, 1 hdc in each of next 30 sc, yo, insert hk in next sc, yo, insert hk in next sc, yo, pull through 5 lps on hk, (dec 1 completed for toe shaping), 1 hdc in each of next 31 sc, join with a sl st to top of ch-2: 63 sts (counting ch-2 as 1 st).

For Size Large Only

Rnd 6: With A, ch 3, sk 1st sc, 1 dc in each of next 33 sc, work 1 dc in next sc

SLIPPER SOLE MEASUREMENTS

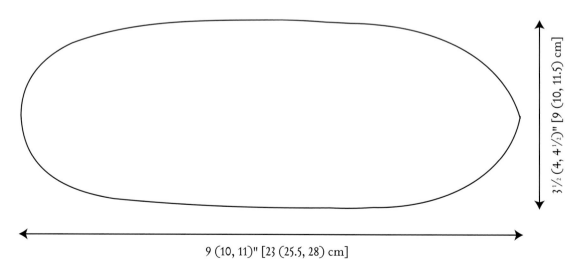

3 ½ (4, 4 ½)" [9 (10, 11.5) cm]

9 (10, 11)" [23 (25.5, 28) cm]

until 2 lps remain on hk, work 2nd dc in next sc until 3 lps remain on hk, yo, pull through 3 lps on hk, (dec 1 completed for toe shaping), 1 dc in each of next 34 sc, join with a sl st to top of ch-3: 69 sts (counting ch-3 as 1 st).

For All Sizes

Rnd 7: Ch 1, 1 sc in same place as sl st and in each of next 16 (19, 22) sts, sk next 2 sts, (1 Puff st, ch 2, 1 Puff st) in next st, sk next 2 sts, 1 sc in next st, sk next 2 sts, work 1st part of PuffCl in next st, sk next 2 sts, work 2nd part of PuffCl in next st, sk next 2 sts, work 3rd part of PuffCl in next st, yo, pull through all lps on hk, ch 1 to tightly close PuffCl, sk next 2 sts, 1 sc in next st, sk next 2 sts, (1 Puff st, ch 2, 1 Puff st) in next st, sk next 2 sts, 1 sc in each of next 17 (20, 23) sts, join with a sl st to 1st sc: 41 (47, 53) sts. Note: The ch-2's made bet the Puff sts are not included in this stitch count.

Rnd 8: Ch 1, dec 1 over same sc as sl st and next sc, 1 sc in each of next 14 (17, 20) sc, sk next sc, sk next Puff st, (1 Puff st, ch 2, 1 Puff st) in next ch-2 sp, 1 sc in next Puff st; 1 PuffCl over next sc, next PuffCl, and next sc; 1 sc in next Puff st, (1 Puff st, ch 2, 1 Puff st) in next ch-2 sp, sk next Puff st, sk next sc, 1 sc in each of next 14 (17, 20) sc, dec 1 over next 2 sc, join with sl st to 1st st: 37 (43, 49) sts. Note: The ch-2's made bet the Puff sts are not included in this stitch count.

Rnd 9: Ch 1, dec 1 over same sc as sl st and next sc, 1 sc in each of next 13 (16, 19) sc, sk next Puff st, 4 sc in next ch-2 sp, sk next Puff st, 1 sc in next sc, 1 sc in next PuffCl, 1 sc in next sc, sk next Puff st, 4 sc in next ch-2 sp, sk next Puff st, 1 sc in each of next 13 (16, 19) sc, dec 1 over next 2 sc, join with a sl st to 1st st with B: 39 (45, 51) sts.

Rnd 10: With B, ch 1, beg in same sc as sl st, work 1 sc in each of next 13 (16, 19) sc, dec 1 over next 2 sc, 1 sc in next sc, 2 sc in next sc, 1 sc in next sc, dec 2 over next 3 sc, 1 sc in next sc, 2 sc in next sc, 1 sc in next sc, dec 1 over next 2 sc, 1 sc in each of next 13 (16, 19) sc, join with a sl st to 1st sc: 37 (43, 49) sts. Fasten off.

Finishing

Ties

With B, ch 25 (27, 29). Fasten off. Make 1 more tie same as the 1st.

Sew ties to 12 (15, 18)th sc on either side counting from center back heel.

Secure loose end of each tie with a tight overhand knot and trim yarn end. Weave in all loose ends. Block to shape as necessary.

Evening Scarf

Finished Size

Width: 6" (15 cm)

Length: 71" (180.5 cm), excluding fringe

Materials

A fine-weight mohair blend yarn: total yardage required: 444 yd (400 m).

Shown:

Karabella Gossamer (30% Kid Mohair, 52% Nylon, 18% Polyester; approx 222 yd [200 m] per 1¾ oz [50 g] ball): #6105 Baby Blue with Silver, 2 balls.

Size H/8 (5 mm) crochet hook or size to obtain gauge.

Notions

Yarn tapestry needle

Gauge

27 sts = 6" (15 cm) and 10 rows = 5¼" (12.5 cm) in lace pattern st using size H/8 (5 mm) crochet hook. Take time to check gauge.

Stitches and Techniques Used

(See pages 134–140)

Single crochet, double crochet,

LACE PATTERN STITCH

Repeat rows 2 and 3 for lace pattern stitch.

multiple stitches into 1 stitch, cluster st, working into an arch, fringe.

Note: To work a "Dc2Cl" (a 2-dc Cluster), work 1 dc in sp as instructed until 2 lps remain on hk, work 2nd dc in same sp until 3 lps remain on hk, yo, draw through all 3 lps on hk.

Scarf

Ch 30 and work in lace pattern st as follows:

Row 1: Sk 1st 3 ch, 1 dc in next ch, *ch 3, sk 3 ch, 1 sc in next ch, ch 4, sk 4 ch, 1 sc in next ch, ch 3, sk 3 ch*, (1 dc, ch 1, 1 dc) in next ch; rep from * to * once, 2 dc in last ch, turn.

Row 2: Ch 1, 1 sc in each of next 2 dc, ch 3, sk next ch-3 arch, *sk next sc, (1 Dc2Cl, ch 2, 1 Dc2Cl, ch 2, 1 Dc2Cl) in next ch-4 arch, ch 3, sk next sc, sk next ch-3 arch, 1 sc in next dc*, ch 3, sk next ch-1 sp, 1 sc in next dc, ch 3, sk next ch-3 arch; rep from * to * once, 1 sc in top of t-ch, turn.

Row 3: Ch 3, sk 1st sc, 1 dc in next sc, *ch 3, sk next ch-3 arch, sk next Dc2Cl, 1 sc in next ch-2 sp, ch 4, sk next Dc2Cl, 1 sc in next ch-2 sp, ch 3, sk next Dc2Cl, sk next ch-3 arch*, sk next sc, (1 dc, ch 1, 1 dc) in next ch-3 arch, sk next sc; rep from * to * once, 1 dc in each of last 2 sc, turn.

Rows 4 to 135: Rep rows 2 and 3 above 66 more times.

Fasten off.

Finishing

Cut 48 strands of yarn each 14" (35.5 cm) in length, for fringe. Using 3 strands for each fringe, attach fringe to each ch-3 and ch-4 sp along each end, and to each corner.

Weave in all loose ends.

~ i n s t r u c t i o n s ~

Level of Difficulty: **Advanced.** *While the stitch patterns are relatively simple, the shaping is quite involved. Count rows carefully.*

Shawl-Collared Wrap Cardigan

To Fit Bust Size

32-34 (35-36, 37-38, 39-41, 42-44)" [81.5-86.5 (89-91.5, 94-96.5, 99-104, 106.5-112) cm]

Finished Bust Size

34 (36½, 38½, 41, 43)" [86.5 (92.5, 98, 104, 109) cm]

Size 32"-34" shown.

Note: Instructions are given for smallest size, with larger sizes in parentheses. Where there is only one instruction, it applies to all sizes.

Materials

A medium worsted-weight yarn: total yardage required: 1364 (1364, 1488, 1488, 1612) yd [1243 (1243, 1356, 1356, 1469) m].

Shown:

Classic Elite Lush (50% Angora, 50% Wool; approx 124 yd [113 m] per 1 3/4 oz [50 g] ball):
#4474 Keys Green, 11 (11, 12, 12, 13) balls.

Size I/9 (5.5 mm) crochet hook or size to obtain gauge.

Notions

Sewing pins; yarn tapestry needle.

Gauge

8 (sc, ch 2, Dc2tog, ch 2) groups = 9" (23 cm) and 16 rows = 7" (18 cm) in open pattern st using size I/9 (5.5 mm) crochet hook. Take time to check gauge.

Stitches and Techniques Used

(See pages 134–140)

Single crochet, half double crochet, double crochet, multiple stitches into 1 stitch, working into an arch, working in back loop only, sewing pieces together.

Pattern Stitches

Open Pattern Stitch

Dc2tog—work 2 dc into st until 1 lp of each remains on hk, yo and pull through all 3 lps on hk.

Ch a multiple of 4 plus 2 extra.

Row 1: 1 sc in 2nd ch from hk, *ch 2, sk 1 ch, 1 Dc2tog in next ch, ch 2, sk 1 ch, 1 sc in next ch; rep from * to end, turn.

Row 2: Ch 5, *1 sc in next Dc2tog, ch 5; rep from * ending last rep with ch 2, 1 dc in last sc, turn.

Row 3: Ch 1, 1 sc in 1st dc, *ch 2, 1 Dc2tog in next sc, ch 2, 1 sc in next ch-5 arch; rep from * ending last rep with 1 sc in t-ch sp, turn.

Rep rows 2 and 3 for open pattern st.

Back

Ch 62 (66, 70, 74, 78).

1st Border Row: 1 sc in 2nd ch from hk, 1 sc in each of next ch to end, turn: 61 (65, 69, 73, 77) sc.

2nd Border Row: Ch 1, 1 sc in each of next sc to end, turn.

Change to open pattern st as follows:

Row 1 (RS): For this row only, insert hook in back lp only of each st. Work row 1 of open pattern st: 15 (16, 17, 18, 19) Dc2tog's.

Rows 2 to 7: Cont to follow open pattern st.

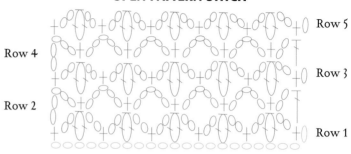

OPEN PATTERN STITCH

Row 5

Row 4

Row 3

Row 2

Row 1

Repeat rows 2 and 3 for open pattern stitch.

Begin dec to shape waist as follows:

Row 8: Ch 3, *1 sc in 1st Dc2tog, ch 5; rep from * ending with 1 dc in last sc, turn.

Row 9: Ch 3, sk 1st dc, 1 dc in next sc, *ch 2, 1 sc in next ch-5 arch, ch 2, 1 Dc2tog in next sc; rep from * to end, sk t-ch, turn.

Row 10: Ch 1, 1 sc in 1st Dc2tog, *ch 5, 1 sc in next Dc2tog; rep from * ending last rep with 1 sc in last dc, turn.

Row 11: Ch 3, 1 dc in 1st sc, *ch 2, 1 sc in next ch-5 arch, ch 2, 1 Dc2tog in next sc; rep from * to end, turn.

Row 12: Rep row 10.

Row 13: Ch 4, 1 sc in next ch-5 arch, *ch 2, 1 Dc2tog in next sc, ch 2, 1 sc in next ch-5 arch; rep from * to last sc, ch 1, 1 dc in last sc, turn.

Row 14: Ch 4, 1 sc in next Dc2tog, *ch 5, 1 sc in next Dc2tog; rep from * ending last rep with ch 4, 1 sc in t-ch sp, turn.

Row 15: Ch 2, 1 sc in 1st ch-4 arch, ch 2, 1 Dc2tog in next sc, *ch 2, 1 sc in next ch-5 arch, ch 2, 1 Dc2tog in next sc; rep from * to t-ch, ch 2, (1 sc, 1 dc) in t-ch sp, turn. Dec completed: 13 (14, 15, 16, 17) Dc2tog's.

Row 16: Ch 4, 1 sc in 1st Dc2tog, *ch 5, 1 sc in next Dc2tog; rep from * ending last rep with ch 4, 1 sc in top of t-ch, turn.

Rows 17 to 26: Rep rows 15 and 16 five more times.

Begin chest shaping as follows:

Row 27: Ch 4, 1 sc in 1st ch-4 arch, ch 2, 1 Dc2tog in next sc, *ch 2, 1 sc in next ch-5 arch, ch 2, 1 Dc2tog in next sc; rep from * to t-ch, ch 2, (1 sc, ch 1, 1 dc) in t-ch sp, turn.

Row 28: Ch 5, 1 sc in 1st Dc2tog, *ch 5, 1 sc in next Dc2tog; rep from * ending last rep with 1 sc in t-ch sp, turn.

Row 29: Ch 3, 1 dc in 1st sc, *ch 2, 1 sc in next ch-5 arch, ch 2, 1 Dc2tog in next sc; rep from * ending last rep with 1 Dc2tog in 1st ch of t-ch, turn.

Row 30: Ch 1, 1 sc in 1st Dc2tog, *ch 5, 1 sc in next Dc2tog; rep from * ending last rep with 1 sc in last dc, turn.

Row 31: Ch 3, 1 Dc2tog in 1st sc, *ch 2, 1 sc in next ch-5 arch, ch 2, 1 Dc2tog in next sc; rep from * to end, 1 dc in same sc as last Dc2tog, turn.

Row 32: Ch 4, sk 1st dc, 1 sc in 1st Dc2tog, * ch 5, 1 sc in next Dc2tog; rep from * ending with ch 2, 1 dc in t-ch, turn.

Row 33: Rep row 3 of open pattern st. Inc completed: 15 (16, 17, 18, 19) Dc2tog's.

Row 34: Rep row 2 of open pattern st.

Rows 35 to 38 (38, 38, 40, 40): Rep rows 3 and 2 of open pattern st 2 (2, 2, 3, 3) more times.

For Sizes X-Small, Small, and Medium Only

Begin armhole shaping as follows:

Row 39: Ch 1, 1 sc in 1st dc, *ch 2, 1 Dc2tog in next sc, ch 2, 1 sc in next ch-5 arch; rep from * to last sc, ch 2, 1 Dc2tog in last sc, 1 hdc in t-ch sp, turn.

Row 40: Ch 1, sl st in 1st Dc2tog, sl st in each of next 2 ch, ch 4, 1 sc in next Dc2tog, *ch 5, 1 sc in next Dc2tog; rep from * to last Dc2tog, ch 2, sk next ch-2 sp, sk next sc, 1 hdc in next ch-2 sp, sk last Dc2tog, sk last sc, turn.

Row 41: Ch 1, 1 sc in 1st hdc, *ch 2, 1 Dc2tog in next sc, ch 2, 1 sc in next ch-5 arch; rep from * ending with ch 2, 1 Dc2tog in last sc, 1 dc in t-ch sp, turn.

Row 42: Ch 1, sk 1st dc, 1 sc in first Dc2tog, *ch 5, 1 sc in next Dc2tog; rep from * to end, sk ch-1, sk last sc, turn. Dec completed: 12 (13, 14, —, —) ch-5 arches.

Row 43: Ch 3, 1 dc in 1st sc, *ch 2, 1 sc in next ch-5 arch, ch 2, 1 Dc2tog in next sc; rep from * to end.

Rows 44 to 53: Rep rows 42 and 43 five more times

Row 54: Rep row 42.

For Size Medium Only

Rows 55 to 56: Rep rows 43 and 42 one more time.

For Sizes X-Small, Small, and Medium Only

Row 55 (55, 57, —, —): Ch 3, 1 dc in 1st sc, *ch 2, 1 sc in next ch-5 arch, ch 2, 1 Dc2tog in next sc; rep from * 2 (2, 3, —, —) more times, ch 2, 1 sc in next ch-5 sp. Fasten off and cut yarn. Sk next 4 (5, 4, —, —) ch-5 arches for back neck, reattach yarn to next ch-5 arch, ch 1, 1 sc in same ch-5 arch, ch 2, 1 Dc2tog in next sc, [ch 2, 1 sc in next ch-5 arch, ch 2, 1 Dc2tog in next sc] 3 (3, 4, —, —) times. Fasten off.

For Sizes Large and X-Large Only

Begin armhole shaping as follows:

Row 41: Ch 1, 1 sc in 1st dc, *ch 2, 1 Dc2tog in next sc, ch 2, 1 sc in next ch-5 arch; rep from * to last sc, ch 2, 1 Dc2tog in last sc, 1 hdc in t-ch sp, turn.

Row 42: Ch 1, sl st in 1st Dc2tog, sl st in each of next 2 ch, ch 4, 1 sc in next Dc2tog, *ch 5, 1 sc in next Dc2tog; rep from * to last Dc2tog, ch 2, sk next ch-2 sp, sk next sc, 1 hdc in next ch-2 sp, sk last Dc2tog, sk last ch-2 sp, sk last sc, turn.

Row 43: Ch 1, 1 sc in 1st hdc, *ch 2, 1 Dc2tog in next sc, ch 2, 1 sc in next ch-5 arch; rep from * ending with ch 2, 1 Dc2tog in last sc, 1 dc in t-ch sp, turn.

Row 44: Ch 1, sk 1st dc, 1 sc in 1st Dc2tog, *ch 5, 1 sc in next Dc2tog; rep from * to last Dc2tog, ch 2, 1 dc in last Dc2tog, sk ch-2 sp, sk last sc, turn.

Row 45: Ch 1, 1 sc in 1st dc, *ch 2, 1 Dc2tog in next sc, ch 2, 1 sc in next ch-5 arch; rep from * to last sc, sk last sc, turn. Dec completed: — (—, —, 14, 15) Dc2tog's.

Row 46: Ch 5, 1 sc in 1st Dc2tog, *ch 5, 1 sc in next Dc2tog; rep from * ending last rep with ch 2, 1 dc in last sc, turn.

Row 47: Ch 1, 1 sc in 1st dc, *ch 2, 1 Dc2tog in next sc, ch 2, 1 sc in next ch-5 arch; rep from * ending last rep with 1 sc in t-ch sp, turn.

Rows 48 to 57: Rep rows 46 and 47 five more times.

Row 58: Rep row 46.

Row 59: Ch 1, 1 sc in 1st dc, *ch 2, 1 Dc2tog in next sc, ch 2, 1 sc in next ch-5 arch; rep from * 3 more times. Fasten off and cut yarn. Sk next — (—, —, 5, 6) ch-5 arches for back neck, reattach yarn to next ch-5 arch, ch 1, 1 sc in same ch-5 arch, [ch 2, 1 Dc2tog in next sc, ch 2, 1 sc in next ch-5 arch] 4 times. Fasten off.

Left Front

Ch 38 (38, 42, 42, 42).

1st Border Row: 1 sc in 2nd ch from hk, 1 sc in each of next ch to end, turn: 37 (37, 41, 41, 41) sc.

2nd Border Row: Ch 1, 1 sc in each of next sc to end, turn.

Change to open pattern st as follows:

Row 1 (RS): For this row only, insert

hook in back lp only of each st. Work row 1 of open pattern st: 9 (9, 10, 10, 10) Dc2tog's.

Inc to shape curve at bottom

Row 2: Ch 7, 1 sc in 1st Dc2tog, *ch 5, 1 sc in next Dc2tog; rep from * ending with ch 2, 1 dc in last sc, turn.

Row 3: Ch 1, 1 sc in 1st dc, *ch 2, 1 Dc2tog in next sc, ch 2, 1 sc in next ch-5 arch; rep from * ending last rep with 1 sc in t-ch sp, ch 2, (1 Dc2tog, ch 2, 1 sc) in 3rd ch of t-ch, turn: 10 (10, 11, 11, 11) Dc2tog's.

Row 4: Rep row 2.

For Sizes X-Small, Small, and Medium Only

Row 5: Rep row 3. Inc completed: 11 (11, 12, —, —) Dc2tog's.

Row 6: Ch 5, 1 sc in 1st Dc2tog, *ch 5, 1 sc in next Dc2tog; rep from * ending with ch 2, 1 dc in last sc, turn.

Row 7: Ch 1, 1 sc in 1st dc, *ch 2, 1 Dc2tog in next sc, ch 2, 1 sc in next ch-5 arch; rep from * ending last rep with 1 sc in t-ch sp, turn.

For Sizes Large and X-Large Only

Row 5: Rep row 3.

Row 6: Rep row 2.

Row 7: Rep row 3. Inc completed: 13 Dc2tog's.

For All Sizes

Beg dec to shape waist as follows:

Row 8: Ch 5, 1 sc in 1st Dc2tog, *ch 5, 1 sc in next Dc2tog; rep from * ending

with 1 dc in last sc, turn.

Row 9: Ch 3, sk 1st dc, 1 dc in 1st sc, *ch 2, 1 sc in next ch-5 arch, ch 2, 1 Dc2tog in next sc; rep from * ending with ch 2, 1 sc in t-ch sp, turn.

Row 10: Ch 5, 1 sc in 1st Dc2tog, *ch 5, 1 sc in next Dc2tog; rep from * ending last rep with 1 sc in last dc, turn.

Row 11: Rep row 9.

Row 12: Rep row 10.

Row 13: Ch 4, 1 sc in 1st ch-5 arch, *ch 2, 1 Dc2tog in next sc, ch 2, 1 sc in next ch-5 arch; rep from * ending with ch 2, 1 Dc2tog in next sc, ch 2, 1 sc in t-ch sp, turn.

Row 14: Ch 5, 1 sc in 1st Dc2tog, *ch 5, 1 sc in next Dc2tog; rep from * ending last rep with ch 4, 1 sc in t-ch sp, turn.

Row 15: Ch 2, 1 sc in 1st ch-4 arch, *ch 2, 1 Dc2tog in next sc, ch 2, 1 sc in next ch-5 arch; rep from * ending with ch 2, 1 Dc2tog in next sc, ch 2, 1 sc in t-ch sp, turn. Dec completed: 10 (10, 11, 12, 12) Dc2tog's.

Row 16: Ch 5, 1 sc in 1st Dc2tog, *ch 5, 1 sc in next Dc2tog; rep from * ending last rep with ch 4, 1 sc in top of t-ch, turn.

Rows 17 to 26: Rep rows 15 and 16 five more times.

Dec to shape neckline and inc to shape bust as follows:

Row 27: Ch 4, 1 sc in 1st ch-4 arch, *ch 2, 1 Dc2tog in next sc, ch 2, 1 sc in next ch-5 arch; rep from * ending last rep with 1 sc in t-ch sp, turn.

Row 28: Ch 3, 1 sc in 1st Dc2tog, *ch 5, 1 sc in next Dc2tog; rep from * ending

last rep with 1 sc in t-ch sp, turn.

Row 29: Ch 3, 1 dc in 1st sc, *ch 2, 1 sc in next ch-5 arch, ch 2, 1 Dc2tog in next sc; rep from * to last ch-5 arch, 1 dc in 3rd ch of last ch-5 arch, sk last sc, sk t-ch, turn: 9 (9, 10, 11, 11) Dc2tog's (not counting ch 3, 1 dc at beg as a Dc2tog).

Row 30: Ch 1, 1 sc in 1st Dc2tog, *ch 5, 1 sc in next Dc2tog; rep from * ending last rep with 1 sc in last dc, turn.

Row 31: Ch 3, 1 Dc2tog in 1st sc, *ch 2, 1 sc in next ch-5 arch, ch 2, 1 Dc2tog in next sc; rep from * to last ch-5 arch, 1 dc in 3rd ch of last ch-5 arch, sk last sc, turn: 9 (9, 10, 11, 11) Dc2tog's.

Row 32: Ch 1, 1 sc in 1st Dc2tog, *ch 5, 1 sc in next Dc2tog; rep from * ending with ch 1, 1 dc in top of t-ch, turn.

Row 33: Ch 1, 1 sc in 1st dc, *ch 2, 1 Dc2tog in next sc, ch 2, 1 sc in next ch-5 arch; rep from * to last ch-5 arch, ch 2, 1 Dc2tog in next sc, 1 dc in 3rd ch of last ch-5 arch, sk last sc, turn: 8 (8, 9, 10, 10) Dc2tog's.

Row 34: Ch 1, 1 sc in 1st Dc2tog, *ch 5, 1 sc in next Dc2tog; rep from * ending with ch 2, 1 dc in last sc, turn.

Row 35: Rep row 33: 7 (7, 8, 9, 9) Dc2tog's.

Rows 36 and 38: Rep row 34.

Row 37: Rep row 33: 6 (6, 7, 8, 8) Dc2tog's.

Row 39: Rep row 33: 5 (5, 6, 7, 7) Dc2tog's.

For Sizes X-Small, Small, and Medium Only

Dec for armhole shaping, while cont to dec to shape neckline as follows:

Row 40: Ch 1, 1 sc in 1st Dc2tog, *ch 5, 1 sc in next Dc2tog; rep from * to last Dc2tog, ch 2, sk next ch-2 sp, sk next sc, 1 hdc in next ch-2 sp, sk last Dc2tog, sk last ch-2 sp, sk last sc, turn.

Row 41: Ch 1, 1 sc in 1st hdc, ch 1, 1 Dc2tog in next sc, [ch 2, 1 sc in next ch-5 arch, ch 2, 1 Dc2tog in next sc] 2 times, ch 2, 1 sc in next ch-5 arch, ch 1, 1 dc in last sc, turn: 3 (3, 4, —, —) Dc2tog's.

Row 42: Ch 5, 1 sc in 1st Dc2tog, [ch 5, 1 sc in next Dc2tog] 2 times, sk next ch-1 sp, sk last sc, turn.

Work even to shoulder:

Row 43: Ch 3, 1 dc in 1st sc, [ch 2, 1 sc in next ch-5 arch, ch 2, 1 Dc2tog in next sc] 2 times, ch 2, 1 sc in t-ch sp, turn: 3 (3, 4, —, —) Dc2tog's (counting ch 3, 1 dc at beg as a Dc2tog).

Rows 44 to 55: Rep rows 42 and 43 six more times.

For Sizes X-Small and Small Only

Fasten off.

For Size Medium Only

Rows 56 to 57: Rep rows 42 and 43 once more.

Fasten off.

For Sizes Large and X-Large Only

Cont dec to shape neckline as follows:

Row 40: Ch 1, 1 sc in 1st Dc2tog, *ch 5, 1 sc in next Dc2tog; rep from * ending last rep with ch 2, 1 dc in last sc, turn.

Dec for armhole shaping, while cont to dec to shape neckline as follows:

Row 41: Ch 1, 1 sc in 1st dc, *ch 2, 1 Dc2tog in next sc, ch 2, 1 sc in next ch-5 arch; rep from * to last sc, ch 1, 1 dc in last sc, turn: 6 Dc2tog's.

Row 42: Ch 5, 1 sc in 1st Dc2tog, [ch 5, 1 sc in next Dc2tog] 4 times, ch 2, sk next ch-2 sp, sk next sc, 1 hdc in next ch-2 sp, sk last Dc2tog, sk last ch-2 sp, sk last sc, turn.

Row 43: Ch 1, 1 sc in 1st hdc, *ch 2, 1 Dc2tog in next sc, ch 2, 1 sc in next ch-5 arch; rep from * ending last rep with 1 sc in t-ch sp, turn: 5 Dc2tog's.

Row 44: Ch 5, 1 sc in 1st Dc2tog, [ch 5, 1 sc in next Dc2tog] 3 times, ch 2, 1 dc in last Dc2tog, sk last ch-2 sp, sk last sc, turn.

Row 45: Ch 1, 1 sc in 1st dc, *ch 2, 1 Dc2tog in next sc, ch 2, 1 sc in next ch-5 sp; rep from * ending last rep with 1 sc in t-ch sp, turn: 4 Dc2tog's.

Row 46: Ch 5, 1 sc in 1st Dc2tog, *ch 5, 1 sc in next Dc2tog; rep from * ending last rep with ch 2, 1 dc in last sc, turn.

Rows 47 to 58: Rep rows 45 and 46 six more times.

Row 59: Rep row 45.

Fasten off.

Right Front

Ch 38 (38, 42, 42, 42).

1st Border Row: 1 sc in 2nd ch from hk, 1 sc in each of next ch to end, turn: 37 (37, 41, 41, 41) sc.

2nd Border Row: Ch 1, 1 sc in each of next sc to end, turn.

Change to open pattern st as follows:

Row 1 (RS): For this row only, insert hook in back lp only of each st. Work row 1 of open pattern st: 9 (9, 10, 10, 10) Dc2tog's.

Inc to shape curve at bottom:

Row 2: Ch 5, 1 sc in 1st Dc2tog, *ch 5, 1 sc in next Dc2tog; rep from * ending with ch 5, 1 dc in last sc, turn.

Row 3: Ch 5, 1 Dc2tog in 1st dc, *ch 2, 1 sc in next ch-5 arch, ch 2, 1 Dc2tog in next sc; rep from * ending with ch 2, 1 sc in t-ch sp, turn: 10 (10, 11, 11, 11) Dc2tog's.

Row 4: Ch 5, 1 sc in 1st Dc2tog, *ch 5, 1 sc in next Dc2tog; rep from * ending with ch 5, 1 dc in 3rd ch of t-ch, turn.

For Sizes X-Small, Small, and Medium Only

Row 5: Rep row 3. Inc completed: 11 (11, 12, —, —) Dc2tog's.

Row 6: Ch 5, 1 sc in 1st Dc2tog, *ch 5, 1 sc in next Dc2tog; rep from * ending with ch 2, 1 tr in 3rd ch of t-ch, turn.

Row 7: Ch 1, 1 sc in 1st tr, *ch 2, 1 Dc2tog in next sc, ch 2, 1 sc in next ch-5 arch; rep from * ending last rep with 1 sc in t-ch sp, turn.

Beg dec to shape waist as follows:

Row 8: Ch 3, 1 sc in 1st Dc2tog, *ch 5, 1

sc in next Dc2tog; rep from * ending with ch 2, 1 dc in last sc, turn.

For Sizes Large and X-Large Only

Row 5: Rep row 3.

Row 6: Rep row 4.

Row 7: Rep row 5. Inc completed: 13 Dc2tog's.

Beg dec to shape waist as follows:

Row 8: Ch 3, 1 sc in 1st Dc2tog, *ch 5, 1 sc in next Dc2tog; rep from * ending with ch 1, 1 tr in 3rd ch of t-ch, turn.

For All Sizes

Cont dec to shape waist as follows:

Row 9: Ch 1, 1 sc in 1st dc, *ch 2, 1 Dc2tog in next sc, ch 2, 1 sc in next ch-5 arch; rep from * ending with ch 2, 1 Dc2tog in last sc, turn.

Row 10: Ch 1, 1 sc in 1st Dc2tog, *ch 5, 1 sc in next Dc2tog; rep from * ending with ch 2, 1 dc in last sc, turn.

Row 11: Rep row 9.

Row 12: Rep row 10.

Row 13: Ch 1, 1 sc in 1st dc, *ch 2, 1 Dc2tog in next sc, ch 2, 1 sc in next ch-5 arch; rep from * ending with ch 1, 1 dc in last sc, turn.

Row 14: Ch 4, 1 sc in 1st Dc2tog, *ch 5, 1 sc in next Dc2tog; rep from * ending with ch 2, 1 dc in last sc, turn.

Row 15: Ch 1, 1 sc in 1st dc, *ch 2, 1 Dc2tog in next sc, ch 2, 1 sc in next ch-5 arch; rep from * ending last rep with (1 sc, 1 hdc) in t-ch sp, turn: 10 (10, 11, 12, 12) Dc2tog's.

Row 16: Ch 4, 1 sc in 1st Dc2tog, *ch 5, 1 sc in next Dc2tog; rep from * ending

with ch 2, 1 dc in last sc, turn.

Rows 17 to 24: Rep rows 15 and 16 four more times.

Row 25: Rep row 15.

Dec to shape neckline and inc to bust as follows:

Row 26: Ch 4, 1 sc in 1st Dc2tog, *ch 5, 1 sc in next Dc2tog; rep from * ending with 1 dc in last sc, turn.

Row 27: Ch 3, sk 1st dc, 1 Dc2tog in next sc, *ch 2, 1 sc in next ch-5 arch, ch 2, 1 Dc2tog in next sc; rep from * ending with ch 2, (1sc, ch 1, 1 dc) in t-ch sp, turn: 10 (10, 11, 12, 12) Dc2tog's.

Row 28: Ch 5, 1 sc in 1st Dc2tog, *ch 5, 1 sc in next Dc2tog; rep from * to last Dc2tog, ch 1, 1 dc in last Dc2tog, turn.

Row 29: Ch 2, sk 1st dc, 1 Dc2tog in next sc, *ch 2, 1 sc in next ch-5 arch, ch 2, 1 Dc2tog in next sc; rep from * ending last rep with 1 Dc2tog in 1st ch of t-ch, turn.

Row 30: Ch 1, 1 sc in 1st Dc2tog, *ch 5, 1 sc in next Dc2tog; rep from * to last Dc2tog, ch 1, 1 dc in last Dc2tog, turn.

Row 31: Ch 2, 1 Dc2tog in 1st sc, *ch 2, 1 sc in next ch-5 arch, ch 2, 1 Dc2tog in next sc; rep from * ending with 1 dc in top of t-ch, turn: 9 (9, 10, 11, 11) Dc2tog's.

Row 32: Ch 4, 1 sc in 1st Dc2tog, *ch 5, 1 sc in next Dc2tog; rep from * to last Dc2tog, ch 1, 1 dc in last Dc2tog, turn.

Row 33: Ch 2, 1 Dc2tog in 1st sc, *ch 2, 1 sc in next ch-5 arch, ch 2, 1 Dc2tog in next sc; rep from * ending with ch 2, 1 sc in t-ch sp, turn: 8 (8, 9, 10, 10) Dc2tog's.

Row 34: Ch 5, 1 sc in 1st Dc2tog, *ch 5, 1

sc in next Dc2tog; rep from * to last Dc2tog, ch 1, 1 dc in last Dc2tog, turn.

Row 35: Rep row 33: 7 (7, 8, 9, 9) Dc2tog's.

Row 36: Rep row 34.

Row 37: Rep row 33: 6 (6, 7, 8, 8) Dc2tog's.

Row 38: Ch 5, 1 sc in 1st Dc2tog, *ch 5, 1 sc in next Dc2tog; rep from * to last Dc2tog, ch 2, 1 dc in last Dc2tog, turn.

For Sizes X-Small, Small, and Medium Only

Dec for armhole shaping, while cont dec to shape neckline as follows:

Row 39: Ch 1, 1 sc in 1st dc, *ch 2, 1 Dc2tog in next sc, ch 2, 1 sc in next ch-5 arch; rep from * to last sc, ch 2, 1 Dc2tog in next sc, 1 hdc in t-ch sp, turn: 5 (5, 6, —, —) Dc2tog's.

Row 40: Ch 1, sk hdc, sl st in 1st Dc2tog, sl st in each of next 2 ch, ch 4, 1 sc in next Dc2tog, *ch 5, 1 sc in next Dc2tog; rep from * to end, sk last sc, turn.

Row 41: Ch 3, 1 Dc2tog in 1st sc, [ch 2, 1 sc in next ch-5 arch, ch 2, 1 Dc2tog in next sc] 3 times, 1 dc in t-ch sp, turn: 4 (4, 5, —, —) Dc2tog's.

Row 42: Ch 1, 1 sc in 1st Dc2tog, [ch 5, 1 sc in next Dc2tog] 2 times, ch 2, 1 hdc in last Dc2tog, turn.

Work even to shoulder:

Row 43: Ch 1, 1 sc in 1st hdc, [ch 2, 1 Dc2tog in next sc, ch 2, 1 sc in next ch-5 arch] 2 times, ch 2, 1 Dc2tog in last sc, turn: 3 (3, 4, —, —) Dc2tog's.

Row 44: Ch 1, 1 sc in 1st Dc2tog, [ch 5, 1 sc in next Dc2tog] 2 times, ch 2, 1 dc in last sc, turn.

Row 45: Ch 1, 1 sc in 1st dc, [ch 2, 1 Dc2tog in next sc, ch 2, 1 sc in next ch-5 arch] 2 times, ch 2, 1 Dc2tog in last sc, turn.

Rows 46 to 55: Rep rows 44 and 45 five more times.

For Sizes X-Small and Small Only

Fasten off.

For Size Medium Only

Rows 56 to 57: Rep rows 44 and 45. Fasten off.

For Sizes Large and X-Large Only

Cont dec to shape neckline as follows:

Row 39: Ch 1, 1 sc in 1st dc, *ch 2, 1 Dc2tog in next sc, ch 2, 1 sc in next ch-5 arch; rep from * ending last rep with 1 sc in t-ch sp, turn.

Row 40: Ch 5, 1 sc in 1st Dc2tog, *ch 5, 1 sc in next Dc2tog; rep from * to end, sk last ch-2 sp, sk last sc, turn.

Dec for armhole shaping, while cont dec to shape neckline as follows:

Row 41: Ch 3, 1 Dc2tog in 1st sc, ch 2, 1 sc in next ch-5 arch, *ch 2, 1 Dc2tog in next sc, ch 2, 1 sc in next ch-5 arch; rep from * ending last rep with 1 hdc in t-ch sp, turn: 7 Dc2tog's.

Row 42: Ch 1, sk hdc, sl st in 1st Dc2tog, sl st in each of next 2 ch, ch 4, 1 sc in next Dc2tog, *ch 5, 1 sc in next Dc2tog; rep from * ending last rep with ch 2, 1 hdc in last Dc2tog, turn.

Row 43: Ch 1, 1 sc in 1st dc, *ch 2, 1 Dc2tog in next sc, ch 2, 1 sc in next ch-5 arch; rep from * ending with 1 dc in t-ch sp, turn: 5 Dc2tog's.

Row 44: Ch 1, 1 sc in 1st Dc2tog, *ch 5, 1 sc in next Dc2tog; rep from * ending last rep with ch 2, 1 dc in last sc, turn. Work even to shoulder:

Row 45: Ch 1, 1 sc in 1st dc, *ch 2, 1 Dc2tog in next sc, ch 2, 1 sc in next ch-5 arch; rep from * ending last rep with 1 sc in t-ch sp, turn: 4 Dc2tog's.

Row 46: Ch 5, 1 sc in 1st Dc2tog, *ch 5, 1 sc in next Dc2tog; rep from * ending last rep with ch 2, 1 dc in last sc, turn.

Rows 47 to 58: Rep rows 45 and 46 six more times.

Row 59: Rep row 45. Fasten off.

Sleeves

Ch 30 (30, 34, 38, 38).

Work open pattern st for 6 rows: 7 (7, 8, 9, 9) Dc2tog's.

Row 7 (Inc row): Ch 4, 1 sc in 1st dc, *ch 2, 1 sc in next ch-5 arch, ch 2, 1 Dc2tog in next sc; rep from * ending with ch 2, (1 sc, ch 2, 1 dc) in t-ch sp, turn.

Row 8: Ch 1, 1 sc in 1st dc, *ch 5, 1 sc in next Dc2tog; rep from * ending last rep with 1 sc in ch-4 t-ch sp, turn.

Row 9: Ch 3, 1 dc in 1st sc, *ch 2, 1 sc in next ch-5 arch, ch 2, 1 Dc2tog in next sc; rep from * to end, turn. Inc completed: 9 (9, 10, 11, 11) Dc2tog's (counting beg ch 3 and 1 dc as a Dc2tog).

Row 10: Ch 1, 1 sc in 1st Dc2tog, *ch 5, 1 sc in next Dc2tog; rep from * ending last rep with 1 sc in last dc, turn.

Rows 11 and 13: Rep row 9.

Row 12: Rep row 10.

Row 14 (Inc row): Ch 4, 1 sc in 1st Dc2tog, *ch 5, 1 sc in next Dc2tog; rep from * ending last rep with 1 sc in last dc, 1 dc in same dc, turn.

Row 15: Ch 4, sk 1st dc, 1 Dc2tog in next sc, *ch 2, 1 sc in next ch-5 arch, ch 2, 1 Dc2tog in next sc; rep from * ending with ch 2, 1 sc in t-ch sp, turn: 9 (9, 10, 11, 11) complete Dc2tog's.

Row 16: Ch 5, 1 sc in 1st Dc2tog, *ch 5, 1 sc in next Dc2tog; rep from * to end, ch 2, 1 dc in t-ch sp, turn.

Row 17: Ch 1, 1 sc in 1st dc, *ch 2, 1 Dc2tog in next sc, ch 2, 1 sc in next ch-5 arch; rep from * ending last rep with 1 sc in t-ch sp, turn.

Rows 18 and 20: Rep row 16.

Row 19: Rep row 17.

Rows 21 to 27: Rep rows 7 to 13: 11 (11, 12, 13, 13) Dc2tog's (counting beg ch 3 and 1 dc as a Dc2tog).

Rows 28 to 32: Rep rows 14 to 18: 11 (11, 12, 13, 13) complete Dc2tog's.

For Size Medium Only

Rows 33 and 34: Rep rows 17 and 18.

For Sizes X-Small, Small, and Medium Only

Begin shaping sleeve cap as follows:

Row 33 (33, 35, —, —): Ch 1, 1 sc in 1st dc, *ch 2, 1 Dc2tog in next sc, ch 2, 1 sc in next ch-5 arch; rep from * to last sc, ch 2, 1 Dc2tog in last sc, 1 hdc in 3rd ch of t-ch, turn.

Row 34 (34, 36, —, —): Ch 1, sl st in 1st 2 sts, sl st in each of next 2 ch, ch 4, 1 sc in next Dc2tog, *ch 5, 1 sc in next Dc2tog; rep from * to last Dc2tog, ch 2, sk next ch-2 sp, sk next sc, 1 hdc in next ch-2 sp, sk last Dc2tog, sk last ch-2 sp, sk last sc, turn.

Row 35 (35, 37, —, —): Ch 1, 1 sc in 1st hdc, ch 2, 1 Dc2tog in next sc, *ch 2, 1 sc in next ch-5 arch, ch 2, 1 Dc2tog in next sc; rep from * ending with 1 dc in 3rd ch of t-ch, turn.

Row 36 (36, 38, —, —): Ch 1, sk 1st dc, 1 sc in next Dc2tog, *ch 5, 1 sc in next Dc2tog; rep from * to end, sk next ch-2 sp, sk last sc, turn.

Row 37 (37, 39, —, —): Ch 3, 1 dc in 1st sc, *ch 2, 1 sc in next ch-5 sp, ch 2, 1 Dc2tog in next sc; rep from * to end, turn: 9 (9, 10, —, —) Dc2tog's (counting beg ch 3 and 1 dc as a Dc2tog).

Row 38 (38, 40, —, —): Ch 1, 1 sc in 1st Dc2tog, *ch 5, 1 sc in next Dc2tog; rep from * ending last rep with ch 2, 1 dc in last dc, turn.

Row 39 (39, 41, —, —): Ch 1, 1 sc in first dc, *ch 2, 1 Dc2tog in next sc, ch 2, 1 sc in next ch-5 arch; rep from * to end, sk last sc, turn: 7 (7, 8, —, —) Dc2tog's.

Row 40 (40, 42, —, —): Ch 5, *1 sc in next Dc2tog, ch 5; rep from * ending with ch 2, 1 dc in last sc, turn.

Row 41 (41, 43, —, —): Ch 1, 1 sc in 1st dc, *ch 2, 1 Dc2tog in next sc, ch 2, 1 sc in next ch-5 arch; rep from * ending last rep with 1 sc in t-ch sp, turn.

Row 42 (42, 44, —, —): Rep row 40 (40, 42, —, —).

Row 43 (43, 45, —, —): Ch 1, 1 sc in 1st dc, ch 2, 1 Dc2tog in next sc, *ch 2, 1 sc in next ch-5 arch, ch 2, 1 Dc2tog in next

sc; rep from * ending with 1 dc in t-ch sp, turn.

Row 44 (44, 46, —, —): Ch 1, 1 sc in 1st Dc2tog, *ch 5, 1 sc in next Dc2tog; rep from * to end, sk next ch-2 sp, sk last sc, turn.

Row 45 (45, 47, —, —): Ch 3, 1 dc in 1st sc, *ch 2, 1 sc in next ch-5 arch, ch 2, 1 Dc2tog in next sc; rep from * to end, turn: 8 (8, 9, —, —) Dc2tog's (counting beg ch 3 and 1 dc as a Dc2tog).

Row 46 (46, 48, —, —): Ch 1, 1 sc in 1st Dc2tog, *ch 5, 1 sc in next Dc2tog; rep from * to last dc, ch 2, 1 dc in last dc, turn.

Row 47 (47, 49, —, —): Ch 1, 1 sc in 1st dc, *ch 2, 1 Dc2tog in next sc, ch 2, 1 sc in next ch-5 arch; rep from * to end, sk last sc: 5 (5, 6, —, —) Dc2tog's.
Fasten off.
Make second sleeve same as the first.

For Sizes Large and X-Large Only

Rows 33 to 36: Rep rows 17 and 18 two more times.

Begin shaping sleeve cap as follows:

Row 37: Ch 1, 1 sc in 1st dc, *ch 2, 1 Dc2tog in next sc, ch 2, 1 sc in next ch-5 arch; rep from * to last sc, ch 2, 1 Dc2tog in last sc, 1 hdc in 3rd ch of t-ch, turn.

Row 38: Ch 1, sl st in 1st 2 sts, sl st in each of next 2 ch, ch 4, 1 sc in next Dc2tog, *ch 5, 1 sc in next Dc2tog; rep from * to last Dc2tog, ch 2, sk next ch-2 sp, sk next sc, 1 hdc in next ch-2 sp, sk last Dc2tog, sk last ch-2 sp, sk last sc, turn.

Row 39: Ch 1, 1 sc in 1st hdc, ch 2, 1 Dc2tog in next sc, *ch 2, 1 sc in next ch-5 arch, ch 2, 1 Dc2tog in next sc; rep from * ending with 1 dc in 3rd ch of t-ch, turn.

Row 40: Ch 1, sk 1st dc, 1 sc in next Dc2tog, *ch 5, 1 sc in next Dc2tog; rep from * to end, sk next ch-2 sp, sk last sc, turn.

Row 41: Ch 3, 1 dc in 1st sc, *ch 2, 1 sc in next ch-5 sp, ch 2, 1 Dc2tog in next sc; rep from * to end, turn: 11 Dc2tog's (counting beg ch 3 and 1 dc as a Dc2tog).

Row 42: Ch 1, 1 sc in 1st Dc2tog, *ch 5, 1 sc in next Dc2tog; rep from * ending with ch 2, 1 dc in last dc, turn.

Row 43: Ch 1, 1 sc in 1st dc, *ch 2, 1 Dc2tog in next sc, ch 2, 1 sc in next ch-5 arch; rep from * to end, sk last sc, turn: 9 Dc2tog's.

Row 44: Ch 5, *1 sc in next Dc2tog, ch 5; rep from * ending with ch 2, 1 dc in last sc, turn.

Row 45: Ch 1, 1 sc in first dc, *ch 2, 1 Dc2tog in next sc, ch 2, 1 sc in next ch-5 arch; rep from * ending last rep with 1 sc in t-ch sp, turn.

Row 46: Rep row 44.

Row 47: Ch 1, 1 sc in 1st dc, ch 2, 1 Dc2tog in next sc, *ch 2, 1 sc in next ch-5 arch, ch 2, 1 Dc2tog in next sc; rep from * ending with 1 dc in t-ch sp, turn.

Row 48: Ch 1, 1 sc in 1st Dc2tog, *ch 5, 1 sc in next Dc2tog; rep from * ending last rep with ch 2, 1 dc in last Dc2tog, sk last ch-2 sp, sk last sc, turn.

Row 49: Ch 1, 1 sc in 1st dc, ch 2, 1

Dc2tog in next sc, *ch 2, 1 sc in next ch-5 arch, ch 2, 1 Dc2tog in next sc; rep from * to last sc, sk last sc, turn: 7 Dc2tog's.

Row 50: Ch 5, *1 sc in next Dc2tog, ch 5; rep from * ending with ch 2, 1 dc in last sc, turn.

Row 51: Ch 2, 1 Dc2tog in next sc, *ch 2, 1 sc in next ch-5 arch, ch 2, 1 Dc2tog in next sc; rep from * ending with 1 dc in t-ch sp: 7 Dc2tog's.

Fasten off.

Make second sleeve same as the first.

Left Front Edging and Shawl Collar

Note: Work ALL rows of collar by inserting hk in back lp only of each st.
Ch 3.

Row 1: 1 sc in 2nd ch from hk, 1 sc in next ch, turn: 2 sc.

Row 2: Ch 1, 1 sc in 1st sc, 2 sc in next sc, turn: 3 sc.

Row 3: Ch 1, 2 sc in 1st sc, 1 sc in each of next 2 sc, turn: 4 sc.

Row 4: Ch 1, 1 sc in each sc to last sc, 2 sc in last sc, turn: 5 sc.

Row 5: Ch 1, 2 sc in 1st sc, 1 sc in each of next sc to end, turn: 6 sc.

Row 6: Rep row 4: 7 sc.

Row 7: Rep row 5: 8 sc.

Row 8: Rep row 4: 9 sc.

Row 9: Rep row 5: 10 sc.

Row 10: Rep row 4: 11 sc.

Row 11: Rep row 5: 12 sc.

Row 12: Ch 1, 1 sc in each sc to end, turn.

Row 13: Rep row 5: 13 sc.

For Sizes X-Small, Small, and Medium Only

Work even to beg of neck shaping:

Rows 14 to 49: Rep row 12.

Inc to shape collar:

Row 50: Rep row 4: 14 sc.

Rows 51, 53, 54, 56, 57, 59, 60, 62, 63, 64: Rep row 12.

Row 52: Rep row 4: 15 sc.

Row 55: Rep row 5: 16 sc.

Row 58: Rep row 4: 17 sc.

Row 61: Rep row 5: 18 sc.

Row 65: Rep row 5: 19 sc.

Rep row 12 (work even) until 128 (130, 133, —, —) rows total or collar is long enough to border curved edge of left front and half of back neckline.

Fasten off.

For Sizes Large and X-Large Only

Row 14: Rep row 4: 14 sc.

Row 15: Rep row 5: 15 sc.

Work even to beg of neck shaping:

Rows 16 to 53: Rep row 12.

Inc to shape collar:

Row 54: Rep row 4: 16 sc.

Rows 55, 57, 58, 60, 61, 63, 64, 66, 67, 68: Rep row 12.

Row 56: Rep row 4: 17 sc.

Row 59: Rep row 5: 18 sc.

Row 62: Rep row 4: 19 sc.

Row 65: Rep row 5: 20 sc.

Row 69: Rep row 5: 21 sc.

Rep row 12 (work even) until 138 rows total or collar is long enough to border curved edge of left front and half of back neckline.

Fasten off.

Right Front Edging and Shawl Collar

Work same as for the left front edging and shawl collar.

Belt

Note: Work ALL rows by inserting hk in BOTH lps of each st as usual.
Ch 235 (235, 240, 245, 245).

Row 1: 1 sc in 2nd ch from hk, 1 sc in each ch across, turn: 234 (234, 239, 244, 244) sc.

Row 2: Ch 1, 2 sc in 1st sc, 1 sc in each of next sc to last sc, 2 sc in last sc, turn: 236 (236, 241, 246, 246) sc.

Row 3: Rep row 2: 238 (238, 243, 248, 248) sc.

Row 4: Ch 1, 1 sc in each sc across, turn.

Row 5: Ch 1, dec 1 sc over next 2 sc, 1 sc in each of next sc to last 2 sc, dec 1 sc over next 2 sc, turn: 236 (236, 241, 246, 246) sc.

Row 6: Rep row 5: 234 (234, 239, 244, 244) sc.

Row 7: Rep row 4.

Fasten off.

Cuffs

Note: Work ALL rows by inserting hk in back lp only of each st.
Ch 21 (21, 23, 25, 25).

Row 1: 1 sc in 2nd ch from hk, 1 sc in each ch across, turn: 20 (20, 22, 24, 24) sc.

Row 2: Ch 1, 1 sc in each sc across, turn.

Rows 3 to 27 (27, 30, 34, 34): Rep row 2.

Fasten off. Make second cuff same as the first.

Patch Pocket

Note: Work ALL rows by inserting hk in back lp only of each st.

Ch 17.

Row 1: 1 sc in 2nd ch from hk, 1 sc in each ch across, turn: 16 sc.

Row 2: Ch 1, 1 sc in each sc to last sc, 2 sc in last sc, turn: 17 sc.

Row 3: Ch 1, 2 sc in 1st sc, 1 sc in each of next sc to last sc, 2 sc in last sc, turn: 19 sc.

Rows 4 to 7: Rep row 2: 23 sc.

Rows 8 to 11: Ch 1, 1 sc in each sc to end, turn: 23 sc.

Row 12: Ch 1, dec 1 sc over next 2 sc, 1 sc in each of next sc to end, turn: 22 sc.

Rows 13 to 15: Rep row 12: 19 sc.

Row 16: Ch 1, dec 1 sc over next 2 sc, 1 sc in each of next sc to last 2 sc, dec 1 sc over next 2 sc, turn: 17 sc.

Row 17: Rep row 12: 16 sc.

Row 18: Rep row 8.

Fasten off. Cut yarn, leaving a 30" (76 cm) tail for sewing.

Finishing

Sew side and shoulder seams. Sew sleeve seams and set-in sleeves, easing in any fullness evenly around armhole. Pin left front edging and shawl collar along front edge of left front and left back collar evenly, matching straight edge of edging/collar piece to shaped edges of cardigan. Whip stitch into place. Pin right front edging and shawl collar along front edge of right front and right back collar evenly. Whip stitch into place. Sew ends of collar together at back neck. Sew one edge of each cuff to bottom edge of each sleeve. Seam cuffs along 1st third of openings, leaving ⅔ unseamed for open fold-back cuffs.

Sew patch pocket to right front as shown in photo. Use the 30" (76 cm) tail and whip stitch into place, beg at top right corner, along right edge, along bottom, then up left edge. Fold top flap down. Belt loops: Ch 10. Fasten off. Make second belt loop same as the first. Sew belt loops to side seams. Weave in all loose ends. Gently steam press cardigan to flatten all seams, pocket flap, belt, and fold-back cuffs.

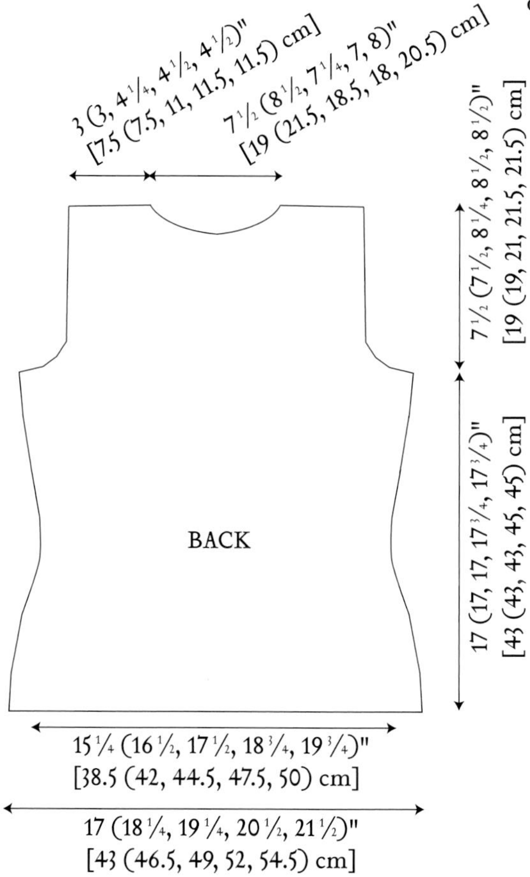
3 (3, 4¼, 4½, 4½)"
[7.5 (7.5, 11, 11.5, 11.5) cm]
7½ (8½, 7¼, 7, 8)"
[19 (21.5, 18.5, 18, 20.5) cm]
7½ (7½, 8¼, 8½, 8½)"
[19 (19, 21, 21.5, 21.5) cm]
17 (17, 17, 17¾, 17¾)"
[43 (43, 43, 45, 45) cm]
BACK
15¼ (16½, 17½, 18¾, 19¾)"
[38.5 (42, 44.5, 47.5, 50) cm]
17 (18¼, 19¼, 20½, 21½)"
[43 (46.5, 49, 52, 54.5) cm]

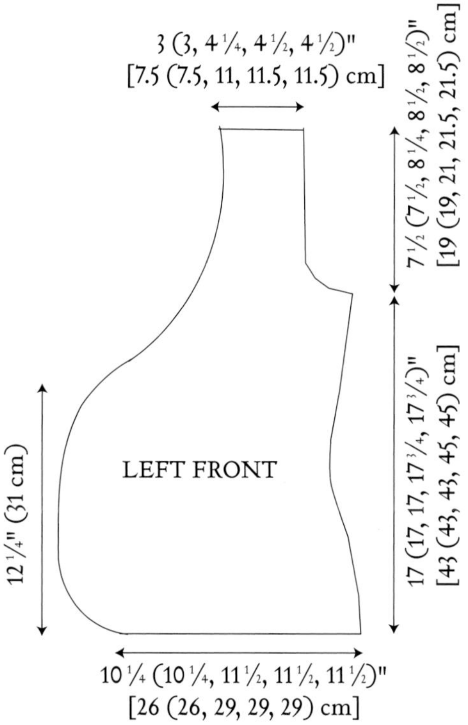
3 (3, 4¼, 4½, 4½)"
[7.5 (7.5, 11, 11.5, 11.5) cm]
7½ (7½, 8¼, 8½, 8½)"
[19 (19, 21, 21.5, 21.5) cm]
17 (17, 17, 17¾, 17¾)"
[43 (43, 43, 45, 45) cm]
12¼" (31 cm)
LEFT FRONT
10¼ (10¼, 11½, 11½, 11½)"
[26 (26, 29, 29, 29) cm]

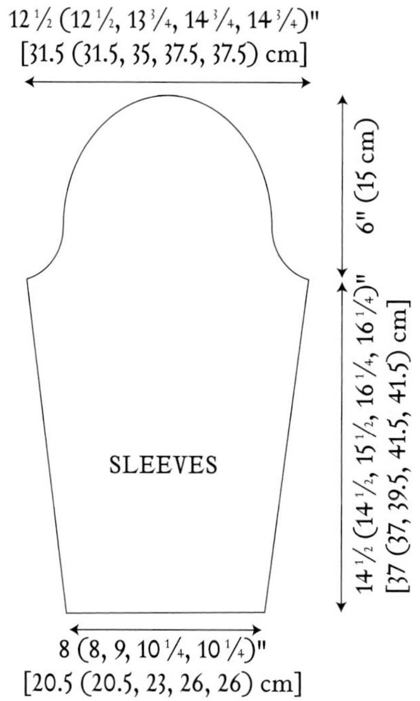
12½ (12½, 13¾, 14¾, 14¾)"
[31.5 (31.5, 35, 37.5, 37.5) cm]
6" (15 cm)
14½ (14½, 15½, 16¼, 16¼)"
[37 (37, 39.5, 41.5, 41.5) cm]
SLEEVES
8 (8, 9, 10¼, 10¼)"
[20.5 (20.5, 23, 26, 26) cm]

Textured Cloche Hat

To Fit Head Size
20–22" (51–56 cm)

Finished Hat Size (circumference)
22" (56 cm). One size fits most.

Materials

For A, a light DK-weight wool blend yarn (double strand used throughout): total yardage required: 218 yd (200 m); or 109 yd (100 m) of a bulky-weight wool blend yarn (used as a single strand throughout).

For B, a medium worsted-weight mohair blend yarn (single strand used throughout): total yardage required: 90 yd (82 m).

Shown:

Classic Elite Wings (55% Alpaca, 23% Silk, 22% Wool; approx 109 yd [100 m] per 1¾ oz [50 g] ball):
Color A: #2321 Ash Leaf, 2 balls.

Classic Elite La Gran Mohair (76.5% Mohair, 17.5% Wool, 6% Nylon; approx 90 yd [82 m] per 1½ oz [42 g] ball):
Color B: #6570 Jade Green, 1 ball.

Size L/11 (8 mm) crochet hook or size to obtain gauge.

Notions

Yarn tapestry needle, stitch marker.

Gauge

17 sts = 8" (20.5 cm) and 8 rows = 4" (10 cm) in textured pattern st using size L/11 (8 mm) crochet hook and 2 strands of A held together. Take time to check gauge.

Stitches and Techniques Used

(See pages 134–140)

Slip st, single crochet, double crochet, multiple stitches into 1 stitch, forming ring, working in the round, joining in the round.

Pattern Stitches

Textured Pattern Stitch

Ch a multiple of 2 plus 2 extra.

Row 1: Sk 3 ch (counts as 1 dc), *1 sc in next ch, 1 dc in next ch; rep from * ending with 1 sc in last ch, turn.

Row 2: Ch 3 (counts as 1 dc), sk 1st st, *1 sc in next dc, 1 dc in next sc; rep from * ending with 1 sc in top of t-ch, turn. Rep row 2 for textured pattern st.

Notes:

1. Hat is worked in the rnd with the RS facing for the first 5 rnds. After that, the hat is still worked in the rnd, but most of the rnds are turned to alternate working on the RS and WS. All turns are indicated.

2. Use 2 strands of A held together throughout. Use 1 strand of B only throughout.

3. When changing yarns, use the new yarn to work the sl st joining the previous rnd.

TEXTURED PATTERN STITCH

Repeat row 2 for textured pattern stitch.

Hat

Starting at the top of the hat, with 2 strands of A held together, wind yarn around fingers to form a ring.

Rnd 1 (RS): Ch 1, work 6 sc into ring. Do not join rnd with a sl st. Mark beg of rnd.

Rnd 2: 2 sc in each sc around: 12 sc.

Rnd 3: *1 sc in next sc, 2 sc in next sc; rep from * around: 18 sc.

Rnd 4: *1 sc in each of next 2 sc, 2 sc in next sc; rep from * around: 24 sc.

Rnd 5: *1 sc in each of next 3 sc, 2 sc in next sc; rep from * around, join rnd with a sl st to 1st sc using B, turn: 30 sc.

Rnd 6 (WS): With B, ch 3, *1 dc in next sc, 1 sc in next sc; rep from * around, join rnd with a sl st to top of ch-3 using A, turn: 30 sts (not counting ch-3 at beg).

Rnd 7 (RS): With A, ch 3, *2 dc in next st, [1 sc in next st, 1 dc in next st] 2 times, 1 sc in next st; rep from * around, join rnd with a sl st to top of ch-3, turn: 35 sts

Rnd 8: With A, ch 3, *[1 dc in next sc, 1 sc in next dc] 3 times, (1 dc, 1 sc) in next dc; rep from * around, join rnd with a sl st to top of ch-3 using B, turn: 40 sts.

Rnd 9: With B, ch 3, [1 dc in 1st sc, 1 sc in next dc] 2 times, *2 dc in next sc, [1 sc in next dc, 1 dc in next sc] 2 times, 1 sc in next dc; rep from * around, join rnd with a sl st to top of ch-3 using A, turn: 46 sts.

Work even to continue as follows:

Rnd 10: With A, ch 3, *1 dc in next st, 1 sc in next st; rep from * around, join rnd with a sl st to top of ch-3, turn.

Rnd 11: With A, ch 3, *1 dc in next sc, 1 sc in next dc; rep from * around, join rnd with a sl st to top of ch-3 using B, turn.

Rnd 12: With B, rep row 11, ending with sl st in B.

Rnd 13: With B, rep row 11, ending with the sl st in A.

Rnds 14, 15, and 16: With A, rep row 11, ending with sl st in A.

Rnd 17 (RS): With A, ch 1, 1 sc in 1st sc, 1 sc in each st around, join rnd with a sl st to ch-1, do not turn: 46 sc.

Work scallop brim as follows:

Rnd 18 (RS): With A, Ch 3, 4 dc in 1st sc, [sk 2 sc, 1 sc in next sc, sk 1 sc, 5 dc in next sc] 7 times, sk 2 sc, 1 sc in next sc, sk 2 sc, 5 dc in next sc, sk 1 sc, 1 sc in next sc, sk 2 sc, join with a sl st to top of ch-3, turn: 9 scallops.

Rnd 19 (WS): With A, Ch 3, 5 dc in 1st sc, *sk 2 dc, 1 sc in next dc, sk 2 dc, 6 dc in next sc; rep from * ending with sk 2 dc, 1 sc in next dc, sk 1 dc, join rnd with a sl st to top of ch-3 using B, turn.

Rnd 20 (RS): With B, ch 1, 1 sc in each st around, join rnd with a sl st to 1st sc. Fasten off.

Finishing

Weave in all loose ends to wrong side of work. Block to shape as necessary.

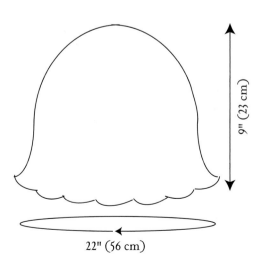

9" (23 cm)

22" (56 cm)

Tortoise-Handled Purse

Finished Size
Approx. 7½" (19 cm) high x 12" (30.5 cm) wide
(at lower edge)

Materials

For A, a light DK-weight cotton and
viscose blend yarn: total yardage required: 360 yd (329 m).
For B, a bulky-weight wool blend yarn:
total yardage required: 110 yd (100 m).

Shown:

Filatura Di Crosa Brilla (42% Cotton,
58% Viscose; approx 120 yd [110 m]
per 1¾ oz [50 g] per ball):
Color A: #307 Orange, 3 balls.
Filatura Di Crosa Love (30% Merino,
extra fine, 30% Acrylic, 20% Nylon;
approx 110 yd [100 m] per 1¾ oz
[50 g] ball):
Color B: #6 Pumpkin, 1 ball.

Size I/9 (5.5 mm) crochet hook or size
to obtain gauge.

Notions

2 acrylic purse handles: 2½" (6.5 cm)
high x 7⅝" (19.5 cm) wide; yarn tapestry
needle; lining fabric, approx. 20" x 15"
(51 x 38 cm); sewing pins; sewing
thread to match A; sewing needle.

Shown:

Style #30520 Acrylic Handles in
Golden Brown Tortoise from MJ
Trim; satin lining fabric.

Gauge

18 sts = 5" (12.5 cm) and 5 rows = 2"
(5 cm) in spray pattern st using size
I/9 (5.5 mm) crochet hook. Take time
to check gauge.

Stitches and Techniques Used

(See pages 134–140)

Slip st, single crochet, half double crochet, double crochet, treble, multiple
stitches into 1 stitch, picot, working
into an arch, forming ring, working in
the round, joining in the round,
sewing pieces together.

Pattern Stitches

Spray Pattern Stitch

Ch a multiple of 3 plus 3 extra.
Row 1: 2 dc into 3rd ch from hk, *sk 2 ch,
(1 sc, 2 dc) in next ch; rep from * to
last 3 ch, sk 2 ch, 1 sc in last ch, turn.
Row 2: Ch 2, 2 dc in 1st sc, *sk 2 dc, (1
sc, 2 dc) in next sc; rep from * ending
with sk 2 dc, 1 sc in top of t-ch, turn.
Rep row 2 for spray pattern st.

SPRAY PATTERN STITCH

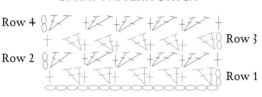

Row 4, Row 3, Row 2, Row 1

Repeat row 2 for spray pattern stitch.

Flower

Ch 6, join with a sl st to form ring.
Rnd 1: Ch 3, 15 dc in ring, join with a sl
st to top of ch-3.
Rnd 2: *Ch 5, sk next dc, sl st in next dc;
rep from * around, join with a sl st in
1st sl st.
Rnd 3: Ch 3, (7 dc, 1 ch-3 picot, 7 dc) in
each ch-5 arch, join with a sl st to top
of ch-3.
Fasten off.

Flower Center

Ch 3, join with a sl st to form ring.
Rnd 1: [Ch 5, 1 sl st in ring] 7 times.
Fasten off.

Leaves (Optional)

First leaf: Ch 10.
Row 1: 1 sc in 2nd ch from hk, 1 hdc in
next ch, 1 dc in each of next 2 ch, 1 tr
in each ch to end. Do not fasten off.
Second leaf: Ch 10. Rep row 1.
Fasten off.

Purse Body

Note: The purse is made as a rectangle, and the shaping occurs when the fabric is attached to the handles.

With A, ch 63.

Rows 1 to 5: Work in spray pattern st: 61 sts (counting ch-2 as 1 st). Change to B at end of row 5.

Row 6: With B, ch 1, 1 sc in 1st sc, 1 sc in each st to end, 1 sc in top of t-ch, turn: 61 sts.

Row 7: Ch 1, 1 sc in each sc across, sk t-ch, change to A, turn.

Row 8: With A, ch 2, 2 dc in 1st sc, *sk 2 sc, (1 sc, 2 dc) in next sc; rep from * to last 3 sc, sk 2 sc, 1 sc in last sc, turn: 61 sts.

Rows 9 to 12: Rep row 2 of spray pattern st. Rep rows 6 to 12 three more times. Fasten off.

Finishing

With A, make 1 flower. With B, make 1 flower center and 1 pair of leaves.

Fold purse piece in half with right sides together and WS facing outward, sew seam sides, leaving 4 (1 sc, 2 dc) groups on either edge (at top of purse) un-seamed. Turn right side out.

Attach a handle by folding unseamed edge of purse piece over bottom bar of a handle. The purse fabric is wider than the handle bar, so ease the fabric together slightly while sewing; this will form the purse shape. Using yarn and yarn needle, stitch in place on WS. Stitch second handle to other edge of purse piece in the same way.

Sew flower center to center of flower. Sew leaves and flower to one side of purse near top as shown.

Weave in all loose ends.

Cut a 14½" x 12¼" (37 x 31 cm) lining fabric. Fold as shown in diagram. Sew side seams with sewing thread by hand or machine, keeping a ¼" (6 mm) seam allowance and leaving approx 1¼" (3 cm) un-seamed at top. Insert lining in purse with WS of lining facing WS of purse, and fold top edges down so that the top edges align with the crocheted fabric where it is folded over the bottom bar of handle (so lining will cover stitching of crocheted fabric to the handles). Pin in place. Using sewing needle and thread, stitch into place by hand.

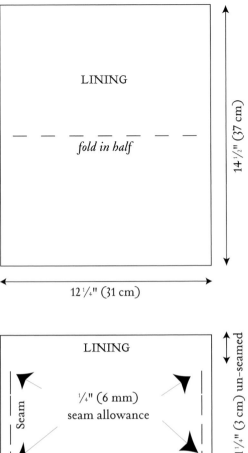

LINING

fold in half

14½" (37 cm)

12¼" (31 cm)

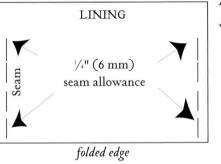

LINING

Seam

¼" (6 mm) seam allowance

1¼" (3 cm) un-seamed

folded edge

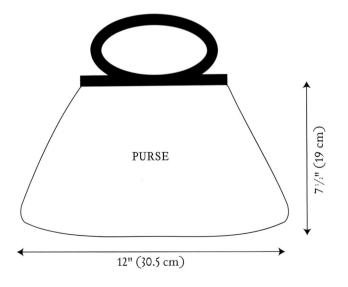

PURSE

7½" (19 cm)

12" (30.5 cm)

Elegant Rectangular Stole

Finished Size
Width: 20½" (52 cm)
Length: 74½" (189 cm), excluding fringe

Materials
A light-weight wool and blend yarn:
total yardage required: 1224 yd (1120 m).

Shown:
Lana Gatto Feeling (70% Merino
Wool, 20% Silk, 10% Cashmere; 153 yd
[140 m] per 1¾ oz [50 g] ball): #12246
Raven, 8 balls.

Size I/9 (5.5 mm) crochet hook or
size to obtain gauge.

Notions
Yarn tapestry needle

Gauge
Each larger motif measures 6¾" (17 cm)
from point to opposite point using
size I/9 (5.5 mm) crochet hook. Take
time to check gauge.

Stitches and Techniques Used
(See pages 134–140)
Slip st, single crochet, half double cro-
chet, double crochet, treble, multiple

FLOWER MOTIF
When attaching flower motifs, work slip st
to next motif instead of making 2nd ch of ch-3.

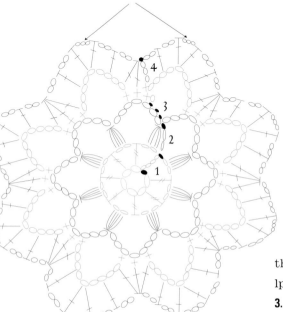

SMALL MOTIF
Follow text instructions for joining small motifs at red slip sts.

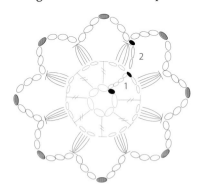

stitches into 1 stitch, cluster st, puff
st, picot, working into an arch, forming ring, working in the round, joining
in the round, joining motifs, fringe.

Notes:
1. To work a "Hdc4tog" (Puff st), (yo,
insert hk in sp indicated, yo, draw 1 lp
through) 4 times, yo, pull through all
lps on hk, ch 1 to close Puff st.
2. To work a "Hdc5tog" (Puff st), (yo,
insert hk in sp indicated, yo, draw 1 lp
through) 5 times, yo, pull through all
lps on hk, ch 1 to close Puff st.
3. To work a "Dc2Cl," work 2 dc in sps
indicated, leaving last lp of each dc on
hk, yo, pull through all 3 lps on hook.
4. To work a "Dc3Cl," work 3 dc in sps
indicated, leaving last lp of each dc on
hk, yo, pull through all 4 lps on hook.

Large Flower Motif
Ch 6. Join with a sl st to form ring.
Rnd 1: Ch 6 (counts as 1 tr and ch-2), [1
tr in ring, ch 2] 7 times, join with a sl
st to 4th ch of ch-6: 8 spaces.
Rnd 2: Ch 2, Hdc4tog in 1st ch-2 sp
(counts as Hdc5tog), [ch 7, Hdc5tog

● Sl st to join motifs   Small motif   Large flower motif

in next sp] 7 times, ch 7, join with sl st to top of 1st Hdc4tog.

Rnd 3: 1 sl st in each of next 3 ch, ch 1, 3 sc in same ch-7 arch, [ch 9, 3 sc in next ch-7 arch] 7 times, ch 9, join with 1 sc in 1st sc.

Rnd 4: Ch 3, sk 1st sc; work 1st dc of Dc2Cl in next sc, sk next sc, work 2nd dc in next ch, yo, pull through 3 lps on hk; [ch 2, sk next ch, 1 dc in next ch, ch 2, sk next ch, (1 dc, ch 3, 1 dc) in next ch, ch 2, sk next ch, 1 dc in next ch, ch 2, sk next ch; work 1st dc of Dc3Cl in next ch, sk next sc, work 2nd dc in next sc, sk next sc, work 3rd dc in next ch, yo, pull through 4 lps on hk] 7 times, ch 2, sk next ch, 1 dc in next ch, ch 2, sk next ch, (1 dc, ch 3, 1

dc) in next ch, ch 2, sk next ch, 1 dc in next ch, ch 2, sk next ch, join with a sl st to top of 1st Dc2Cl.

Stole

First strip of 11 flower motifs:
Make 1st flower motif. Fasten off.

Work 3 rnds of 2nd motif. Join to 1st motif during rnd 4 as follows:

Rnd 4: Ch 3, sk 1st sc; work 1st dc of Dc2Cl in next sc, sk next sc, work 2nd dc in next ch, yo, pull through 3 lps on hk; [ch 2, sk next ch, 1 dc in next ch, ch 2, sk next ch, 1 dc in next ch, ch 1, sl st to 2nd ch of corresponding ch-3 point of 1st flower motif, ch 1, 1 dc in same ch as last dc, ch 2, sk next ch, 1

dc in next ch, ch 2, sk next ch; work 1st dc of Dc3Cl in next ch, sk next sc, work 2nd dc in next sc, sk next sc, work 3rd dc in next ch, yo, pull through 4 lps on hk] 2 times; [ch 2, sk next ch, 1 dc in next ch, ch 2, sk next ch, (1 dc, ch 3, 1 dc) in next ch, ch 2, sk next ch, 1 dc in next ch, ch 2, sk next ch; work 1st dc of Dc3Cl in next ch, sk next sc, work 2nd dc in next sc, sk next sc, work 3rd dc in next ch, yo, pull through 4 lps on hk] 5 times; ch 2, sk next ch, 1 dc in next ch, ch 2, sk next ch, (1 dc, ch 3, 1 dc) in next ch, ch 2, sk next ch, 1 dc in next ch, ch 2, sk next ch, join with a sl st to top of 1st Dc2Cl.

Referring to assembly diagram (opposite) for joining order, make 3rd motif, joining to 2nd motif at 2 points directly opposite the 2 points used to join to 1st motif. Continue, working and joining a total of 11 motifs.

Second strip of motifs:
Make 12th motif, joining to 2 side points of 1st motif.
Make 13th motif, joining to 2 side points of 2nd motif first, then next 2 points of motif 12 in the same way. Continue to create 3 rows of 11 motifs, referring to diagram for joining order.

Smaller Motifs

Smaller motifs are used to fill in the large holes between the 3 long rows of the larger flower motifs.

Begin a smaller motif by working a flower motif through Rnd 1.
Rnd 2: Ch 2, Hdc4tog in 1st ch-2 sp, *ch 3, sl st to next sl st joining 2 larger flower motifs, ch 3, Hdc5tog in next ch-2 sp, ch 3, sl st to next Dc3Cl counter-clockwise from last join, ch 3, Hdc5tog in next ch-2 sp; rep from * 2 times, ch 3, sl st to next sl st joining 2 larger flower motifs, ch 3, Hdc5tog in next ch-2 sp, ch 3, sl st to next Dc3Cl counter-clockwise from last join, ch 3, join with a sl st to top of 1st Hdc4tog. Fasten off.

Make a total of 20 smaller motifs joining as instructed above. Refer to assembly diagram (opposite) for joining as you work.

Finishing

Edging

Attach yarn to any dc along outer edge.
Rnd 1: Ch 1, 1 sc in same dc, continue by working 1 sc in each st, 2 sc in each ch-2 sp, and 3 sc in each ch-3 sp around. Work 1 sc in each sp on either side of motif joins. Join with a sl st to first sc. Fasten off.

Fringe

Cut 12" (30.5 cm) lengths of yarn for fringe. Using 3 strands for each fringe, attach 1 fringe to each ch-3 and ch-2 sp on each end of stole.

Weave in all loose ends.

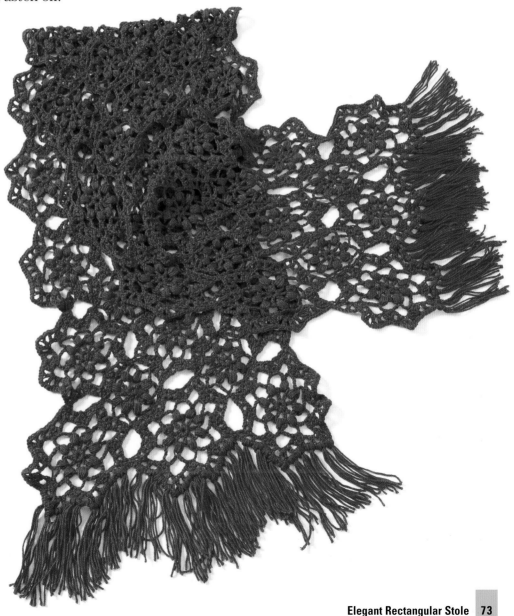

Lush Cowl-Neck Sweater

To Fit Bust Size

33-34 ½ (36 ½-38, 40-41 ½)" [84-87.5 (92.5-96.5, 101.5-105.5) cm]

Finished Bust Size

32 ½ (36, 39 ½)" [82.5 (91.5, 100.5) cm]
Sizes: Small, Medium, and Large
Size Small shown.

Note: Instructions are given for smallest size, with larger sizes in parentheses. Where there is only one instruction, it applies to all sizes.

Materials

A light-weight mohair blend yarn:
total yardage required: 755 (906, 906) yd [690 (828, 828) m].

Shown:

GGH Soft-Kid (70% Super Kid Mohair, 25% Nylon, 5% Wool; approx 151 yd [138 m] per .875 oz [25 g] ball): #032 Amethyst, 5 (6, 6) balls.

Size J/10 (6 mm) crochet hook or size to obtain gauge.
Size K/10.5 (7 mm) hook or size to obtain gauge.

Notions

Yarn tapestry needle

Gauge

7 sc = 2" (5 cm) and 22 rows = 7" (18 cm) in sc using size J/10 (6 mm) crochet hook. 17 sts = 5" (12.5 cm) and 4 rows = 3" (7.5 cm) in lace pattern st using size K/10.5 (7 mm) crochet hook. Take time to check gauge.

Stitches and Techniques Used

(See page 134–140)

Slip st, single crochet, double crochet, multiple stitches into 1 stitch, working into an arch, working in back loop only, working in the round, joining in the round, sewing pieces together.

Pattern Stitches

Lace Pattern Stitch

Ch a multiple of 6 plus 4 extra.

Row 1 (RS): (1 dc, ch 1, 1 dc, ch 1, 1 dc) in 7th ch from hk, *sk 2 ch, 1 dc in next ch, sk 2 ch, (1 dc, ch 1, 1 dc, ch 1, 1 dc) in next ch; rep from * ending with sk 2 ch, 1 dc in next ch, turn.

Row 2: Ch 4, 1 dc in 1st dc, sk next dc, sk next ch-1 sp, 1 dc in next dc, *sk next ch-1 sp, sk next dc, (1 dc, ch 1, 1 dc, ch 1, 1 dc) in next dc, sk next dc, sk next ch-1 sp, 1 dc in next dc; rep from * to last ch-1 sp, sk ch-1 sp, sk dc, (1 dc, ch 1, 1 dc) in top of t-ch, turn.

Row 3: Ch 3, sk 1st dc, *sk next ch-1 sp, sk next dc, (1 dc, ch 1, 1 dc, ch 1, 1 dc) in next dc, sk next dc, sk next ch-1 sp, 1 dc in next dc; rep from * ending last rep with last dc in 3rd ch of t-ch, turn. Rep rows 2 and 3 for lace pattern st.

Back

Begin waist ribbing, which is worked from side to side.

With smaller crochet hook, ch 24 (26, 28).

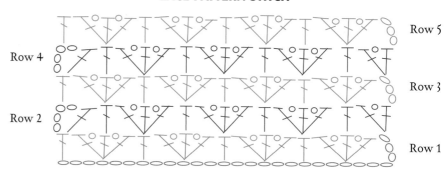

LACE PATTERN STITCH

Row 5

Row 4

Row 3

Row 2

Row 1

Repeat rows 2 and 3 for lace pattern stitch.

Row 1: 1 sc in 2nd ch from hk, 1 sc in each ch across, turn: 23 (25, 27) sc.

Row 2: Ch 1, 1 sc in each sc across in back loops only, turn.

Rep row 2 for a total of 44 (47, 50) rows. Turn waist piece counter-clockwise to begin working along side edge. Change to larger crochet hook.

For Size Small Only

Row 1 (RS): Ch 3, [(1 dc, ch 1, 1 dc, ch 1, 1 dc) in edge of next row, sk 2 rows, 1 dc in edge of next row, sk 2 rows] 2 times, *(1 dc, ch 1, 1 dc, ch 1, 1 dc) in edge of next row, sk 1 row, 1 dc in edge of next row, sk 2 rows, (1 dc, ch 1, 1 dc, ch 1, 1 dc) in edge of next row, sk 2 rows, 1 dc in edge of next row, sk 2 rows; rep from * 2 more times, turn: 49 sts (counting ch-3 as 1 st and ch-1 sps as 1 st).

For Size Medium Only

Row 1 (RS): Ch 3, [sk 2 rows, (1 dc, ch 1, 1 dc, ch 1, 1 dc) in edge of next row, sk 1 row, 1 dc in edge of next row] 4 times, sk 2 rows, (1 dc, ch 1, 1 dc, ch 1, 1 dc) in edge of next row, sk 2 rows, 1 dc in edge of next row, [sk 2 rows, (1 dc, ch 1, 1 dc, ch 1, 1 dc) in edge of next row, sk 1 row, 1 dc in edge of next row] 4 times, turn: 55 sts (counting ch-3 as 1 st and ch-1 sps as 1 st).

For Size Large Only

Row 1 (RS): Ch 3, [sk 2 rows, (1 dc, ch 1, 1 dc, ch 1, 1 dc) in edge of next row, sk 1 row, 1 dc in edge of next row] 9 times, sk 1 row, (1 dc, ch 1, 1 dc, ch 1, 1 dc) in edge of next row, sk 1 row, 1 dc in edge of next row, turn: 61 sts (counting ch-3 as 1 st and ch-1 sps as 1 st).

For All Sizes

Row 2 (WS): Work row 2 of lace pattern st.

Row 3: Work row 3 of lace pattern st. Increase to bust width as follows:

Row 4 (Inc row): Ch 4, (1 dc, ch 1, 1 dc) in 1st dc, sk next dc, sk next ch-1 sp, 1 dc in next dc, *sk next ch-1 sp, sk next dc, (1 dc, ch 1, 1 dc, ch 1, 1 dc) in next dc, sk next dc, sk next ch-1 sp, 1 dc in next dc; rep from * to last ch-1 sp, sk ch-1 sp, sk dc, (1 dc, ch 1, 1 dc, ch 1, 1 dc) in top of t-ch, turn: 53 (59, 65) sts (counting ch-4 as 2 sts and ch-1 sps as 1 st).

Row 5 (Inc row): Ch 4, 1 dc in 1st dc, sk next ch-1 sp, 1 dc in next dc, *sk next ch-1 sp, sk next dc, (1 dc, ch 1, 1 dc, ch 1, 1 dc) in next dc, sk next dc, sk next ch-1 sp, 1 dc in next dc; rep from * to t-ch, (1 dc, ch 1, 1 dc) in 3rd ch of t-ch, turn: 55 (61, 67) sts (counting ch-4 as 2 sts and ch-1 sps as 1 st).

Note: Rows 2 and 3 of lace patt were worked as even (row 2) and odd-numbered (row 3) rows above; because the increased number of sts change the row beginning, to stay in patt row 3 is worked as even-numbered row, and row 2 as odd-numbered row below.

Row 6: Work row 3 of lace pattern st
Row 7: Work row 2 of lace pattern st.

For Sizes Medium and Large Only

Row 8: Work row 3 of lace pattern st.
Row 9: Work row 2 of lace pattern st.

For All Sizes

Increase to make attached sleeves as follows:
Row 8 (10, 10): Ch 21 (21, 27), (1 dc, ch 1, 1 dc, ch 1, 1 dc) in 7th ch from hk, [sk 2 ch, 1 dc in next ch, sk 2 ch, (1 dc, ch 1, 1 dc, ch 1, 1 dc) in next ch] 2 (2, 3) times, sk 2 ch, 1 dc in next dc, cont to end of row as established in lace pattern st, do not turn.
Add more sts to the end of row 8 (10, 10) as follows:
With a separate ball of yarn and larger hook, ch 18 (18, 24) and fasten off. Attach to end of row 8 by working along this ch as a base ch as follows:
[Sk 2 ch, (1 dc, ch 1, 1 dc, ch 1, 1 dc) in next ch, sk 2 ch, 1 dc in next dc] 3 (3, 4) times, turn: 91 (97, 115) sts.
Row 9 (11, 11): Ch 28, 1 dc in 5th ch from hk, sk 2 ch, 1 dc in next ch, [sk 2 ch, (1 dc, ch 1, 1 dc, ch 1, 1 dc) in next ch, sk

2 ch, 1 dc in next ch] 3 times, sk 2 ch, (1 dc, ch 1, 1 dc, ch 1, 1 dc) in next dc, cont to end of row as established in lace pattern st, ending with ch 1, 1 dc in same ch as last dc, do not turn.
Add more sts to the end of row 9 (11, 11) as follows:
With a separate ball of yarn and larger hook, ch 24 and fasten off. Attach to end of row 9 by working along this ch as a base ch as follows:
Sk 2 ch, 1 dc in next ch, [sk 2 ch, (1 dc, ch 1, 1 dc, ch 1, 1 dc) in next ch, sk 2 ch, 1 dc in next dc] 3 times, sk 2 ch, (1 dc, ch 1, 1 dc) in last ch, turn: 139 (145, 163) sts.
Row 10 (12, 12): Work row 3 of lace pattern st.
Rows 11 (13, 13) to 16 (18, 20): Work rows 2 and 3 of lace pattern st.

For Sizes Small and Large Only

Fasten off.
Shape shoulders and neck opening:
With WS of row 16 (—, 20) facing, sk 1st 8 (—, 9) complete groups of (1 dc, ch 1, 1 dc, ch 1, 1 dc). In next group, attach yarn to middle dc using larger crochet hook.
Row 1: Ch 3, [sk next ch-1 sp, sk next dc, (1 dc, ch 1, 1 dc, ch 1, 1 dc) in next dc, sk next dc, sk next ch-1 sp, 1 dc in next dc] 6 (—, 8) times, turn: 37 (—, 49) sts.
Row 2: Ch 3, sk 1st 2 dc, sk next ch-1 sp, 1 dc in next dc, [sk next ch-1 sp, sk next dc, (1 dc, ch 1, 1 dc, ch 1, 1 dc) in next dc, sk next dc, sk next ch-1 sp, 1

dc in next dc] 5 (—, 7) times, sk next ch-1 sp, sk next dc, 1 dc in top of t-ch: 33 (—, 45) sts.
Fasten off.

For Size Medium Only

Row 19: Work row 2 of lace pattern st.
Fasten off.

Shape shoulders and neck opening:
With WS of row 19 facing, sk 1st 8 complete groups of (1 dc, ch 1, 1 dc, ch 1, 1 dc). In next dc, attach yarn using larger crochet hook.

Row 1: Ch 4, 1 dc in same dc, sk next dc, sk next ch-1 sp, 1 dc in next dc, [sk next ch-1 sp, sk next dc, (1 dc, ch 1, 1 dc, ch 1, 1 dc) in next dc, sk next dc, sk next ch-1 sp, 1 dc in next dc] 6 times, sk next ch-1 sp, sk next dc, (1 dc, ch 1, 1 dc) in next dc, turn: 43 sts.
Row 2: Ch 3, sk 1st dc, sk next ch-1 sp, sk next dc, (1dc, ch 1, 1 dc) in next dc, sk next dc, sk next ch-1 sp, 1 dc in next dc, [sk next ch-1 sp, sk next dc, (1 dc, ch 1, 1 dc, ch 1, 1 dc) in next dc, sk next dc, sk next ch-1 sp, 1 dc in next dc] 5 times, sk next ch-1 sp, sk next dc, (1dc, ch 1, 1 dc) in next dc, sk next dc, sk next ch-1 sp, 1 dc in 3rd of t-ch: 39 sts.
Fasten off.

Front

Work same as for BACK.

Finishing

Sew side seams and sleeve seams. Sew seams at top of sleeves along shoulders and to neck opening.

Cowl Neck

With RS facing and larger crochet hook, attach yarn at one edge of neck opening.

Rnd 1: Ch 3, 1 dc in each st and in each ch-1 sp across neckline of back and front, join with a sl st to top of ch-3: 66 (78, 90) sts (counting ch-3 as 1 dc).

Rnd 2 (Inc rnd): Ch 3, 1 dc in same sp as sl st, 1 dc in each of next 31 (37, 43) dc, 2 dc in each of next 2 dc, 1 dc in each of next 31 (37, 43) dc, 2 dc in last dc, join with a sl st to top of ch-3: 70 (82, 94) dc (counting ch-3 as 1 dc).

Rnd 3: Ch 3, 1 dc in each dc around, join with a sl st to top of ch-3.

Rnd 4 (Inc rnd): Ch 3, 1 dc in same sp as sl st, 1 dc in each of next 33 (39, 45) dc, 2 dc in each of next 2 dc, 1 dc in each of next 33 (39, 45) dc, 2 dc in last dc, join with a sl st to top of ch-3: 74 (86, 98) dc (counting ch-3 as 1 dc).

Rnds 5 to 7: Ch 3, 1 dc in each dc around, join with a sl st to top of ch-3.

Rnd 8 (Inc rnd): Ch 3, 1 dc in same sp as sl st, 1 dc in each of next 35 (41, 47) dc, 2 dc in each of next 2 dc, 1 dc in each of next 35 (41, 47) dc, 2 dc in last dc, join with a sl st to top of ch-3: 78 (90, 102) dc (counting ch-3 as 1 dc).

Rnds 9 to 11: Ch 3, 1 dc in each dc around, join with a sl st to top of ch-3. Fasten off.

Cuffs

With smaller crochet hook, ch 21 (23, 19).

Row 1: 1 sc in 2nd ch from hk, 1 sc in each ch across, turn: 20 (22, 18) sc.

Row 2: Ch 1, 1 sc in each sc across in back loops only, turn.

Rep row 2 for a total of 27 (31, 34) rows. Fasten off. Make second cuff same as the first.

Sew cuffs to ends of sleeves, easing in any sleeve fullness evenly.

Weave in all loose ends. Block to shape as necessary.

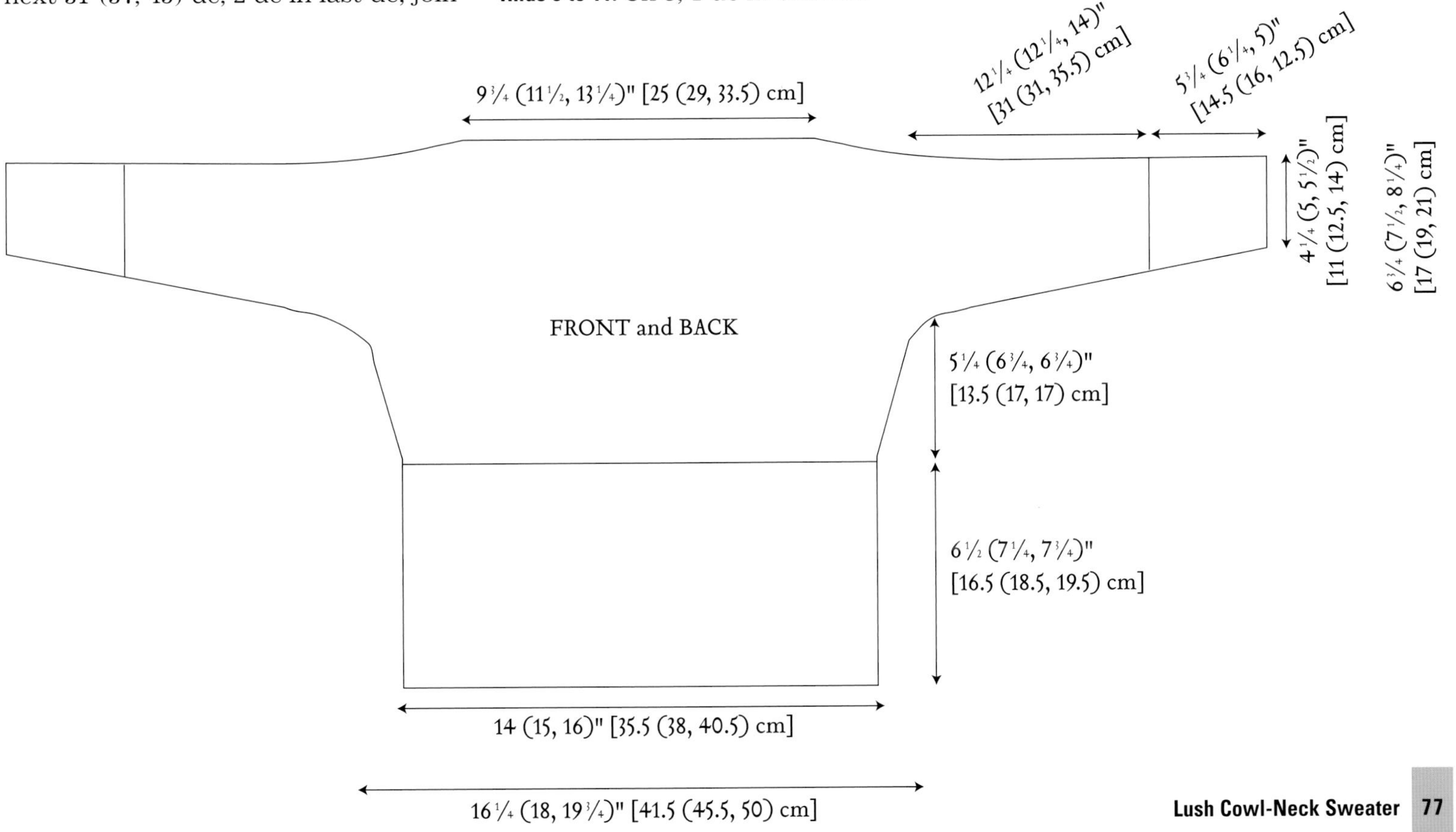

9 3/4 (11 1/2, 13 1/4)" [25 (29, 33.5) cm]
12 1/4 (12 1/4, 14)" [31 (31, 35.5) cm]
5 3/4 (6 1/4, 5)" [14.5 (16, 12.5) cm]
4 1/4 (5, 5 1/2)" [11 (12.5, 14) cm]
6 3/4 (7 1/2, 8 1/4)" [17 (19, 21) cm]
FRONT and BACK
5 1/4 (6 3/4, 6 3/4)" [13.5 (17, 17) cm]
6 1/2 (7 1/4, 7 3/4)" [16.5 (18.5, 19.5) cm]
14 (15, 16)" [35.5 (38, 40.5) cm]
16 1/4 (18, 19 3/4)" [41.5 (45.5, 50) cm]

Chunky Flower Hat

To Fit Head Size
20-22" (51-56 cm)

Finished Hat Size (circumference)
18¾" (47.5 cm) not stretched. One size fits most.

Materials

A bulky-weight wool and acrylic blend yarn: Color A total yardage required: 62 yd (57 m);

Color B total yardage required: 62 yd (57 m);

Color C total yardage required: 62 yd (57 m).

Shown:

GGH Aspen (50% Merino Wool, 50% Acrylic; approx 62 yd [57 m] per 1¾ oz [50 g] ball):

Color A: #4 Red, 1 ball;

Color B: #5 Dark Red, 1 ball;

Color C: #14 Rose, 1 ball.

Size L/11 (8 mm) crochet hook or size to obtain gauge.

Notions

Yarn tapestry needle

Gauge

12 dc = 5" (12.5 cm) and 8 rows = 7" (18 cm) in pattern st using size L/11 (8 mm) crochet hook. Take time to check gauge.

Stitches and Techniques Used

(See page 134–140)

Slip st, single crochet, half double crochet, double crochet, multiple stitches into 1 stitch, cluster st, working into an arch, forming ring, working in the round, joining in the round.

Notes:

1. To change colors at the end of a rnd, drop the old color while there are still 2 lps on hk for last st. Yo with the new color and draw through the 2 lps to finish the last st.

2. To work a "Dc2Cl"(a 2-dc cluster), work 1 dc in st/sp as instructed until 2 lps remain on hk, work 2nd dc in same st/sp until 3 lps remain on hk, yo, draw through 3 lps on hk.

3. To work a "Dc3Cl"(a 3-dc cluster), work 1 dc in st/sp as instructed until 2 lps remain on hk, work 2nd dc in same st/sp until 3 lps remain on hk, work

3rd dc in same st/sp until 4 lps remain on hk, yo, draw through 4 lps on hk.

Pattern Stitches

Striped Pattern Stitch

Same as for Chunky Striped Car Coat, page 80, only the flower hat is worked in the round; follow specific instructions below.

Flower Hat

With A, ch 4, join with a sl st to 1st ch to form ring.

Rnd 1: Ch 3, 1 Dc2Cl in ring, ch 2, [1 Dc3Cl in ring, ch 2] 5 times, join with a sl st to 1st Dc2Cl: 6 clusters.

Rnd 2: Ch 3, 1 Dc2Cl in same sp as sl st, ch 2, [1 Dc3Cl in next ch-2 sp, ch 2, 1 Dc3Cl in next Dc3Cl, ch 2] 5 times, 1 Dc3Cl in next ch-2 sp, ch 2, join with a sl st to 1st Dc2Cl with B: 12 clusters.

Rnd 3: With B, Ch 3, sk 1st Dc2Cl, *2 dc in next ch-2 sp, 1 dc in next Dc3Cl; rep from * around, 2 dc in next ch-2 sp, join with a sl st to top of ch-3 with C: 36 dc (counting ch-3 as 1 dc).

Rnd 4: With C, ch 3, 1 dc in each of next 7 dc, 2 dc in next dc, [1 dc in each of next 8 dc, 2 dc in next dc] 3 times, join with a sl st to top of ch-3 with A: 40 dc (counting ch-3 as 1 dc).

Rnd 5: With A, ch 3, 1 Dc2Cl in same sp as sl st, [ch 2, sk 2 dc, 1 Dc3Cl in next dc] 3 times, ch 2, sk 1 dc, 1 Dc3Cl in next dc, [ch 2, sk 2 dc, 1 Dc3Cl in next dc] 4 times, ch 2, sk 1 dc, 1 Dc3Cl in next dc, [ch 2, sk 2 dc, 1 Dc3Cl in next dc] 3 times, [ch 2, sk 1 dc, 1 Dc3Cl in next dc] 2 times, ch 2, sk next dc, join with a sl st to top of ch-3 with B: 15 clusters.

Rnd 6: With B, ch 3, sk 1st Dc2cl, *2 dc in next ch-2 sp, 1 dc in next Dc3Cl; rep from * around, 2 dc in next ch-2 sp, join with a sl st to top of ch-3 with C: 45 dc (counting ch-3 as 1 dc).

Rnd 7: With C, ch 3, 1 dc in each dc around, join with a sl st to top of ch-3 with A: 45 dc (counting ch-3 as 1 dc).

Rnd 8: With A, ch 3, 1 dc in each dc around, join with a sl st to top of ch-3 with B: 45 dc (counting ch-3 as 1 dc).

Rnd 9: With B, ch 1, 1 sc in each dc around, join with a sl st to ch-1: 45 sc (counting ch-1 as 1 sc).

Fasten off.

Flower

With C, ch 5, join with a sl st to 1st ch to form ring.

Rnd 1: [1 sc in ring, ch 3] 5 times, join with a sl st to 1st sc.

Rnd 2: (1 sc, 1 hdc, 2 dc, 1 hdc, 1 sc) in each ch-3 sp around, join with a sl st to 1st sc.

Rnd 3: Working in back of petals, sl st into back of 1st sc from rnd 1, ch 4, [sl st into back of next sc from rnd 1, ch 4] 4 times, join with a sl st to same sc as 1st sl st with A.

Rnd 4: With A, work (1 sc, 1 hdc, 3 dc, 1 hdc, 1 sc) in each ch-4 sp around, join with a sl st to 1st sc.

Fasten off.

Center Flower

With B, ch 5, join with a sl st to 1st ch to form ring.

Rnd 1: [Ch 2, 1 dc in ring, ch 2, 1 sl st in ring] 5 times.

Fasten off, leaving an 8" (20.5 cm) tail.

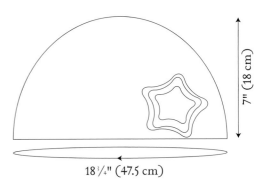

Finishing

Using 8" (20.5cm) tail of center flower, sew center flower to center of larger flower and sew side of hat. Weave in all loose ends. Lightly steam.

Chunky Striped Car Coat

To Fit Bust Size
32–34 (34–36, 37–39, 40–41½)" [81.5–86.5 (86.5–91.5, 94–99, 101.5–105.5) cm]

Finished Bust Size
35 (37½, 40, 42½)" [89 (95, 101.5, 108) cm]
Sizes: X-Small (Small, Medium, Large).
Shown in X-Small.

Materials

A bulky-weight wool and acrylic yarn:
Color A total yardage required: 372 (372, 434, 434) yd [340 (340, 397, 397) m];
Color B total yardage required: 496 (496, 558, 558) yd [453.5 (453.5, 510, 510) m];
Color C total yardage required: 310 (310, 372, 372) yd [283.5 (283.5, 340, 340) m].

Shown:

GGH Aspen (50% Merino Wool, 50% Acrylic; approx 62 yd [57 m] per 1¾ oz [50 g]) ball:
Color A: #5 Dark Red, 6 (6, 7, 7) balls;
Color B: #4 Red, 8 (8, 9, 9) balls;
Color C: #14 Rose, 5 (5, 6, 6) balls.

Size L/11 (8 mm) crochet hook or size to obtain gauge.

Notions

Yarn tapestry needle

STRIPED PATTERN STITCH

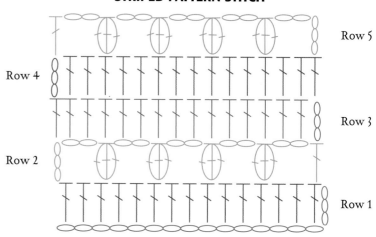

Repeat rows 2 through 4 for striped pattern stitch.
Note: The same pattern row may be worked on both even- and odd-numbered rows, as shown above on rows 2 and 5.

Gauge

12 dc = 5" (12.5 cm) and 8 rows = 7" (18 cm) in pattern st using size L/11 (8 mm) crochet hook. Take time to check gauge.

Stitches and Techniques

(See pages 134–140)
Slip st, single crochet, double crochet, multiple stitches into 1 stitch, cluster st, working into an arch, sewing pieces together.

Notes:
1. Each color is worked for only 1 row, then carried for 2 rows. Do not cut yarn when color is not being used; just carry them along the edges loosely. They can then be hidden in the seams during finishing.
2. To work a "Dc2Cl" (a 2-dc cluster), work 1 dc where specified until 2 lps remain on hk, work 2nd dc where specified until 3 lps remain on hk, yo, draw through 3 lps on hk.
3. To work a "Dc3Cl" (a 3-dc cluster), work 1 dc where specified until 2 lps remain on hk, work 2nd dc where

specified until 3 lps remain on hk, work 3rd dc where specified until 4 lps remain on hk, yo, draw through 4 lps on hk.

4. When counting sts on a row, always count ch-3 as 1 st.

5. Unless otherwise indicated, work to maintain stitch count on row 2 of striped pattern st after any shaping by beginning row 2 as instructed, but ending row depending on how many Dc3Cl's can be completed. If 1 st remains after last Dc3Cl, work 1 dc in t-ch, turn. If 2 sts remain after last Dc3Cl, ch 1, 1 dc in t-ch, turn. If 3 sts remain after last Dc3Cl, work as usual. On next row, work 1 dc in each dc and 1 dc in the ch-1 sp if applicable.

Pattern Stitches

Striped Pattern Stitch

With A, ch a multiple of 3 plus 3 extra.

Row 1: 1 dc in 4th ch from hk and in each ch across, change to B, turn.

Row 2: With B, ch 5, sk 1st 3 sts, *1 Dc3Cl in next st, ch 2, sk 2 sts; rep from * ending with 1 dc in top of t-ch, change to C, turn.

Row 3: With C, ch 3, sk 1st dc, *2 dc in next ch-2 sp, 1 dc in next Dc3Cl; rep from * ending with 2 dc in t-ch sp, 1 dc in 3rd ch of t-ch, change to A, turn.

Row 4: With A, ch 3, sk 1st dc, 1 dc in each st across, 1 dc in top of t-ch, change to B, turn.

Rep rows 2 to 4 for striped patt st.
Note: The same rows are worked both as RS and WS throughout the following instructions.

Back

With A, ch 52 (55, 58, 61).

Row 1 (WS): 1 sc in 2nd ch from hk and in each ch across, change to B, turn: 51 (54, 57, 60) sc.

Row 2 (RS): With B, ch 5, sk 1st 2 sc, *1 Dc3Cl in next sc, ch 2, sk 2 sc; rep from * ending with 1 dc in last sc, change to C, turn: 16 (17, 18, 19) clusters.

Row 3: With C, work row 3 of striped patt st: 52 (55, 58, 61) dc.

For Sizes Medium and Large Only

Rows 4 and 5: Continue in striped patt st.

For All Sizes

Begin decreasing to shape waist:

Row 4 (4, 6, 6) (Dec row): With A, work row 4 of striped patt st, dec 1 st on each side edge by combining 2nd and 3rd dc's from each end as Dc2Cl's: 50 (53, 56, 59) sts.

For Sizes X-Small and Small Only

Work even in striped patt st on rows without dec, and dec 1 st on each side edge as in row 4 on rows 6, 7, 9, 10, 12, and 13: 38 (41, —, —) sts.

Rows 14 and 15: Work even.

For Sizes Medium and Large Only

Work even in striped patt st on rows without dec, and dec 1 st on each side edge as in row 6 on rows 9, 10, 12, 13, 15, and 16: — (—, 44, 47) sts.

Rows 17: Work even.

For All Sizes

Begin increases for back measurement:

Row 16 (16, 18, 18) (Inc row): Inc 1 st on each edge by working 2 dc where 2nd dc and next to last dc are placed: 40 (43, 46, 49) sts.

Rows 17 (17, 19-20, 19-20): Work even in patt. Work even in striped patt st, inc 2 sts as in row 16 (16, 18, 18) on row 18 (18, 21, 21): 42 (45, 48, 51) sts.

Rows 19 (19, 22, 22) to 21 (21, 23, 23): Work even. Fasten off and cut all yarns.

Shape armholes:

For Sizes X-Small and Small Only

Row 22: Sk 1st 2 sts, attach A to next st, ch 3, 1 Dc2Cl over next 2 sts, 1 dc in each st to last 5 sts, 1 Dc2Cl over next 2 sts, 1 dc in next st, sk last st and t-ch, change to B, turn: 36 (39, —, —) sts.

Rows 23 to 29: Work even.

For Sizes Medium and Large Only

Row 24: Sk 1st 3 sts (counting ch's as sts), attach C to next st, ch 3, 1 Dc2Cl over next 2 sts, continue in striped patt st to last 6 sts (counting ch's as sts), 1 Dc2Cl over next 2 sts, 1 dc in next st, sk last 2 sts and t-ch, change to A, turn: — (—, 40, 43) sts.

Rows 25 to — (—, 32, 33): Work even.

For All Sizes

Shape neckline:

Row 30 (30, 33, 34): Work next row of

striped patt st, but work middle 12 (13, 14, 15) sts as sc.
Fasten off.

Right Front

With A, ch 28 (30, 31, 33). Work as for BACK to row 29 (29, 31, 32), shaping waist, bust, and armhole only on one edge: 23 (25, 26, 28) sts.

Shape neckline:

For Size X-Small Only

Row 29: Ch 3, sk 1st st, 1 Dc3Cl in next st, *ch 2, sk 2 sts, 1 Dc3Cl in next st; rep from * to last 6 sts, sk 2 sts, 1 dc in next st, sk last 2 sts and t-ch, change to C, turn: 15 sts.

Row 30: With C, ch 3, sk 1st dc and Dc3Cl, 1 Dc2Cl in next ch-2 sp, 1 dc in next Dc3Cl, 2 dc in next ch-2 sp; rep from * to last Dc3Cl, 1 dc in next Dc3Cl, 1 dc in top of t-ch: 13 sts.
Fasten off.

For Size Small Only

Row 29: Ch 3, sk 1st st, 1 Dc3Cl in next st, *ch 2, sk 2 sts, 1 Dc3Cl in next st; rep from * to last 8 sts, sk 2 sts, 1 dc in next st, sk last 2 sts and t-ch, change to C, turn: 18 sts.

Row 30: With C, ch 3, sk 1st dc and Dc3Cl, 1 Dc3Cl with 1st 2 dc in next ch-2 sp and 3rd dc in next Dc3Cl, 2 dc in next ch-2 sp, 1 dc in next Dc3Cl; rep from * ending with 1 dc in top of t-ch: 14 sts.
Fasten off.

For Size Medium Only

Row 31: With A, work row 4 of striped patt st to last 8 sts, work 1 Dc3Cl over next 3 sts, change to B, sk next 4 sts, sk t-ch, turn: 19 sts.

Row 32: With B, ch 3, sk 1st 4 sts, 1 Dc3Cl in next st, *ch 2, sk 2 sts, 1 Dc3Cl in next st; rep from * ending with ch 1, sk 1 st, 1 dc in top of t-ch, change to C, turn: 16 sts.

Row 33: With A, ch 3, sk 1st dc, 1 dc in next ch-1 sp, 1 dc in next Dc3Cl, * 2 dc in next ch-2 sp, 1 dc in next Dc3Cl; rep from * to last ch-2 sp, 1 dc in next ch-2 sp, 1 Dc2Cl over same ch-2 sp and next Dc3Cl, sk t-ch: 14 sts.
Fasten off.

For Size Large Only

Fasten off and cut all yarn ends.

Row 32: Sk 1st 5 sts, attach B to next st, ch 3, sk 2 sts, 1 Dc3Cl in next st, *ch 2, sk 2 sts, 1 Dc3Cl in next st; rep from * ending with 1 dc in top of t-ch, change to C, turn: 21 sts.

Row 33: With C, work row 3 of striped pattern st to last 2 Dc3Cl's, work 1 Dc3Cl with the 1st dc in the next Dc3Cl, and the 2nd and 3rd dc over the next ch-2 sp, change to A, sk next Dc3Cl, sk t-ch, turn: 17 sts.

Row 34: With A, ch 3, sk 1st Dc3Cl, 1 Dc3Cl over next 3 dc, 1 dc in each st to end, 1 dc in top of t-ch: 15 sts.
Fasten off.

Left Front

Work as for RIGHT FRONT, reversing all shaping.

Sleeves

With A, ch 19 (22, 25, 28).

Row 1: 1 sc in 2nd ch from hk and in each ch across, change to B, turn: 18 (21, 24, 27) sc.

Row 2: With B, ch 5, sk 1st 2 sc, *1 Dc3Cl in next sc, ch 2, sk 2 sc; rep from * ending with 1 dc in last sc, turn.

Row 3: Ch 3, sk 1st dc, 1 Dc3Cl in next ch-2 sp, *ch 2, sk next Dc3Cl, 1 Dc3Cl in next ch-2 sp; rep from * ending with ch 2, sk next Dc3Cl, 1 Dc3Cl in t-ch sp, 1 dc in 3rd ch of t-ch, turn.

Row 4: Ch 5, sk 1st 2 sts, 1 Dc3Cl in next ch-2 sp, *ch 2, sk next Dc3Cl, 1 Dc3cl in next ch-2 sp; rep from * to last Dc3Cl, ch 2, sk last Dc3Cl, 1 dc in top of t-ch, turn.

Row 5: Rep row 3, change to C at end, turn.

Begin inc to shape sleeve:

Row 6 (Inc row): With C, ch 3, sk 1st dc, 2 dc in next Dc3Cl, 2 dc in next ch-2 sp, *1 dc in next Dc3Cl, 2 dc in next ch-2 sp; rep from * ending with 2 dc in last Dc3Cl, 1 dc in top of t-ch, change to A, turn: 20 (23, 26, 29) sts.

For Size X-Small Only

Cont striped patt st, working even on rows without inc, and inc as in row 6 on rows 9, 12, 15, and 18: 28 sts.

For Size Small Only

Cont striped patt st, working even on rows without inc, and inc as in row 6 on rows 9, 12, and 15: 29 sts.

For Sizes X-Small and Small Only

Rows 19 to 22: Work even. Fasten off and cut yarn ends.

Shape cap:

Row 23 (Dec row): Sk 1st 2 sts, attach yarn to next st, ch 3, sk 1 st, 1 Dc3Cl in next st, *ch 2, sk next 2 sts, 1 Dc3Cl in next st; rep from * to last 5 (6, —, —) sts, ch 1 (2, —, —), sk 1 (2, —, —) sts, 1 Dc2Cl over next 2 sts, sk next st, sk t-ch, change to C, turn: 22 (23, —, —) sts.

Row 24 (Dec row): With C, work row 3 of striped patt st, combining 2nd and 3rd dc's from each end as Dc2Cl's, change to A, turn: 20 (21, —, —) sts.

Row 25 (Dec row): With A, work row 4 of striped patt st, combining 2nd and 3rd dc's from each end as Dc2Cl's, change to B, turn: 18 (19, —, —) sts.

Row 26 (Dec row): With B, ch 3, sk 1st 2 sts, 1 Dc3Cl in next st, *ch 2, sk next 2 sts, 1 Dc3Cl in next st; rep from * to last 3 (4, —, —) sts, ch 1 (2, —, —), sk 1 (2, —, —) sts, 1 Dc2Cl over next st and top of t-ch, change to C, turn: 16 (17, —, —) sts.

Row 27 (Dec row): Rep row 24: 14 (15, —, —) sts rem.

Row 28 (Dec row): With A, work row 4 of striped patt st, dec 2 sts on each edge by combining 2nd, 3rd, and 4th dc's from each end as Dc3Cl's, change to B, turn: 10 (11, —, —) sts.

Row 29 (Dec row): With B, ch 3, sk 1st 3 sts, 1 Dc3Cl in next st, ch 2, sk 2 sts, 1 Dc3Cl in next st, sk 2 sts, 0 (1, —, —) dc in next st, 1 dc in top of t-ch: 6 (7, —, —) sts.
Fasten off.

For Sizes Medium and Large Only

Continue in striped patt st, working even on rows without inc, and inc as in row 6 on rows 9, 12, 15, and 18: — (—, 34, 37) sts rem.

Rows 19 to 24: Work even. Fasten off and cut yarn ends.

Shape cap:

Row 25 (Dec row): Sk 1st 3 sts, attach A to next st, ch 3, 1 Dc2Cl over next 2 sts, 1 dc in each st to last 6 sts, 1 Dc2Cl over next 2 sts, 1 dc in next st, sk next 2 sts, sk t-ch, change to B, turn: — (—, 26, 29) sts.

Row 26 (Dec row): With B, ch 3, sk 1st 2 sts, 1 Dc3Cl in next st, *ch 2, sk 2 sts, 1 Dc3Cl in next st; rep from * to last 2 sts, sk 1 st, 1 dc in top of t-ch, change to C, turn: — (—, 24, 27) sts.

Row 27 (Dec row): With C, work row 3 of striped patt st, combining 2nd and 3rd dc's from each end as Dc2Cl's, change to A, turn: — (—, 22, 25) sts.

Row 28 (Dec row): With A, work row 4 of striped pattern st, combining 2nd and 3rd dc's from each end as Dc2Cl's, change to B, turn: — (—, 20, 23) sts.

Rows 29 and 30 (Dec rows): Rep rows 26 and 27: — (—, 16, 19) sts rem.

Row 31 (Dec row): With A, work row 4 of striped patt st, dec 2 sts on either edge by combining 2nd, 3rd, and 4th dc's from each end as Dc3Cl's, change to B, turn: — (—, 12, 15) sts.

Row 32 (Dec row): With B, sk 1st 2 sts, 1 Dc3Cl in next st, [ch 2, sk 2 sts, 1 Dc3Cl in next st] 2 times, ch — (—, 0, 1), sk 2 sts, 1 dc in top of t-ch, change to C, turn: — (—, 9, 12) sts.

For Size Medium Only

Fasten off.

For Size Large Only

Row 33 (Dec row): With C, work row 3 of striped patt st, combining 2nd, 3rd, and 4th dc's from each end as Dc3Cl's: 9 sts.
Fasten off.

For All Sizes

Make second sleeve same as the first.

Finishing

Sew side and shoulder seams. Sew sleeve seams. Set-in sleeves.

Right Front Band

Starting at bottom corner of right front, with RS facing, attach B.

Row 1: Ch 1, work 55 (55, 59, 61) sc evenly along right front edge (approx 2 sc along the edge of 1 row), turn.

Row 2: Ch 1, 1 sc in each sc across, turn.

Rows 3 and 4: Rep row 2.
Fasten off.

Work left front band same as right, but starting at top corner of left front with RS facing. Do not fasten off, but continue around neckline for collar.

Collar

With WS facing, starting at top of left front band, ch 3, work 29 (31, 35, 39) dc evenly along neckline to top corner of right button band.

Row 2: Ch 5, sk 1st 2 sts, *1 Dc3Cl bet next 2nd and 3rd dc, ch 2; rep from * ending with 1 dc in top of t-ch, turn: 14 (15, 17, 19) Dc3Cl's.

Row 3: Ch 3, sk 1st dc, 1 Dc3Cl in next ch-2 sp, *ch 2, sk next Dc3Cl, 1 Dc3Cl in next ch-2 sp; rep from * to last Dc3Cl, ch 2, sk next Dc3Cl, 1 Dc3Cl in t-ch sp, 1 dc in 3rd ch of t-ch, turn: 15 (16, 18, 20) Dc3Cl's.

Row 4 (Inc row): Ch 3, 1 Dc2Cl in 1st dc, *ch 2, sk next Dc3Cl, 1 Dc3cl in next ch-2 sp; rep from * to last Dc3Cl, ch 2, 1 Dc2Cl in next Dc3Cl, 1 dc in top of t-ch, turn: 16 (17, 19, 21) Dc3Cl's.

Row 5: Rep row 2, treating Dc2Cl's from row 4 as Dc3Cl's.

Row 6: Rep row 3.

Fasten off.

With RS facing, attach A to where top corner of right button band and collar meet. Ch 1, work 1 row of sc evenly around collar, working 2 sc at each corner, sl st to where top corner of left button band and collar meet. Fasten off.

Belt

With B, ch 151 (157, 163, 169).

Row 1: 1 sc in 2nd ch from hk and in each ch across, turn: 150 (156, 162, 168) sc.

Rows 2 and 3: Ch 1, 1 sc in each sc across.

Fasten off.

Weave in all loose ends. Lightly steam. Weave belt through holes on row 14 of body as shown in photo.

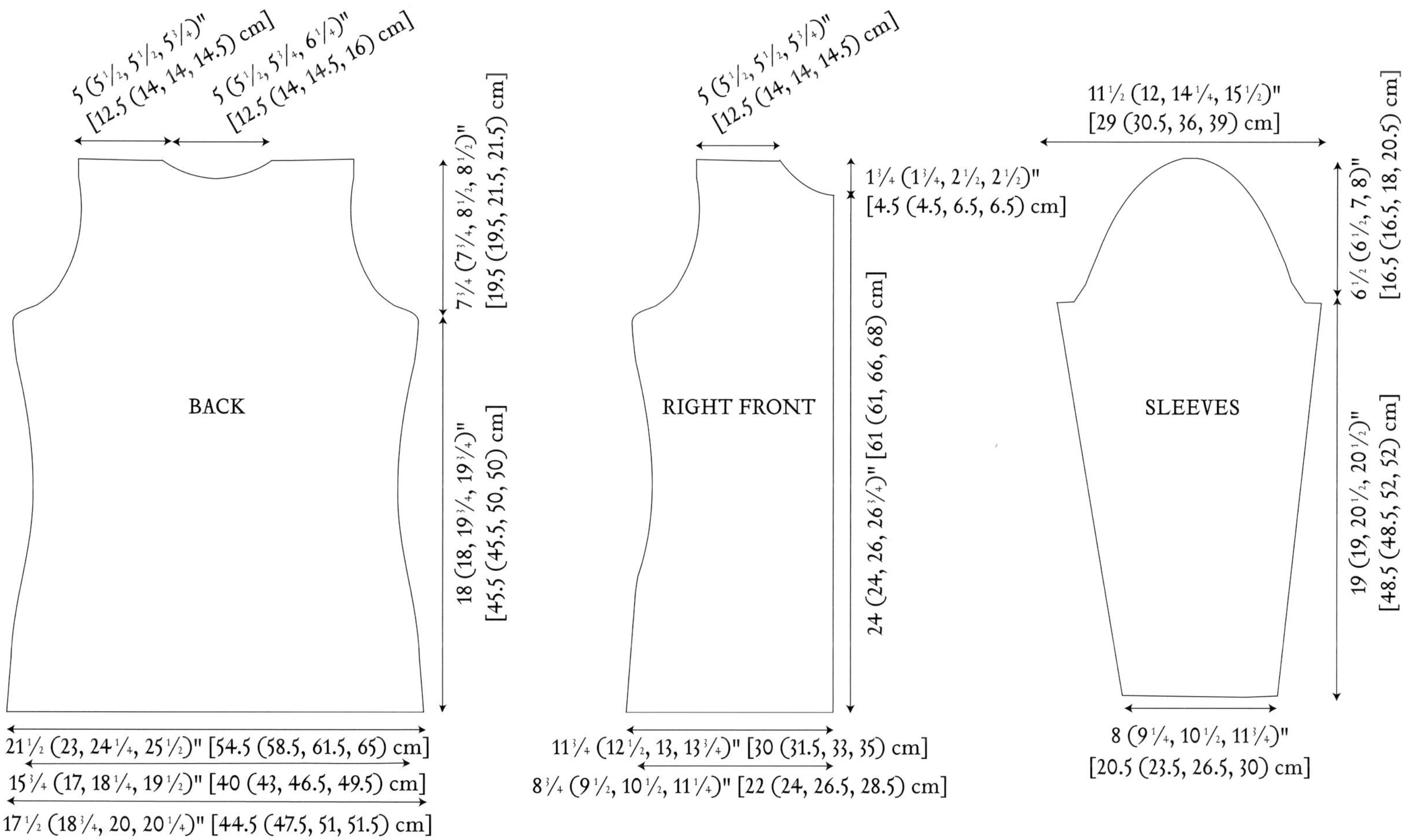
5 (5½, 5½, 5¾)" [12.5 (14, 14, 14.5) cm]
5 (5½, 5¾, 6¼)" [12.5 (14, 14.5, 16) cm]
7¾ (7¾, 8½, 8½)" [19.5 (19.5, 21.5, 21.5) cm]
BACK
18 (18, 19¾, 19¾)" [45.5 (45.5, 50, 50) cm]
21½ (23, 24¼, 25½)" [54.5 (58.5, 61.5, 65) cm]
15¾ (17, 18¼, 19½)" [40 (43, 46.5, 49.5) cm]
17½ (18¾, 20, 20¼)" [44.5 (47.5, 51, 51.5) cm]
5 (5½, 5½, 5¾)" [12.5 (14, 14, 14.5) cm]
1¾ (1¾, 2½, 2½)" [4.5 (4.5, 6.5, 6.5) cm]
RIGHT FRONT
24 (24, 26, 26¾)" [61 (61, 66, 68) cm]
11¾ (12½, 13, 13¾)" [30 (31.5, 33, 35) cm]
8¾ (9½, 10½, 11¼)" [22 (24, 26.5, 28.5) cm]
11½ (12, 14¼, 15½)" [29 (30.5, 36, 39) cm]
6½ (6½, 7, 8)" [16.5 (16.5, 18, 20.5) cm]
SLEEVES
19 (19, 20½, 20½)" [48.5 (48.5, 52, 52) cm]
8 (9¼, 10½, 11¾)" [20.5 (23.5, 26.5, 30) cm]

Macramé Belt

Finished Size

Approx 4" (10 cm) wide x 30¼ (33¼)" [77 (84.5) cm] long. Belt shown is 30¼" (77 cm). Sizes S/M and M/L. Size S/M shown.

Materials

A sport-weight cabled cotton yarn (the tight cabled construction makes the bullion stitch easier to work): total yardage required: 246 yd (225 m).

Shown:

Reynolds Saucy Sport (100% Mercerized Cotton; approx 123 yd [112 m] per 1¾ oz [50 g] ball): #558 Sage, 2 balls.

Size F/5 (4 mm) crochet hook or size to obtain gauge.

Notions

Yarn tapestry needle

Gauge

Measuring from base of 1 bullion st to next bullion st = 3⅛" (8 cm) and approx 5 rows = 2¼" (5.5 cm) in pattern st using size F/5 (4 mm) crochet hook. Take time to check gauge.

BULLION PATTERN STITCH

Row 6 · Row 5 · Row 4 · Row 3 · Row 2 · Row 1

Repeat rows 2 through 5 for bullion pattern stitch.

Stitches and Techniques Used

(See pages 134–140)

Single crochet, treble, multiple stitches into 1 stitch, bullion st, working into an arch, working in the round, joining in the round, fringe.

Pattern Stitches

Bullion Pattern Stitch

Notes:

1. To work a "Bullion st," wrap yarn over hk 10 times, yo, insert hk into st, and draw a lp through, yo and draw through all 12 lps on hk, picking them off one at a time, if needed, ch 1 to close.

2. Not all skipped sts are listed in the bullion pattern instructions below, but are shown in the diagram.

Tip: To help get the last yo through the 12 lps, it is helpful to make sure the 12 lps are sitting on the fatter part of your hook, then use your left hand (assuming you are right-handed) to hold the 12 lps tightly together like a "tunnel" as you do the final yo and pull through all 12 lps in one quick movement.

Ch a multiple of 16 plus 10 extra.

Row 1 (WS): Sk 1 ch, 1 sc in next ch, *ch 5, sk 3 ch, 1 sc in next ch; rep from * to end, turn.

Row 2 (RS): Ch 5, 1 sc in 3rd ch of 1st ch-5 arch, ch 1, sk next ch-5 arch, *(1 Bullion st, [ch 1, 1 Bullion st] 3 times) in next sc, ch 1, sk next ch-5 arch, 1 sc in 3rd ch of next ch-5 arch, ch 5, 1 sc in 3rd ch of next ch-5 arch, ch 1, sk next ch-5 arch; rep from * ending with (1 Bullion st, ch 1, 1 Bullion st, 1 tr) in last sc, turn.

Row 3: Ch 1, 1 sc in 1st tr, ch 5, sk next Bullion st, 1 sc in next ch-1 sp, ch 5, sk next ch-1 sp, 1 sc in 3rd ch of next ch-5 arch, *ch 5, [1 sc in next ch-1 sp, ch 5] 3 times, sk next ch-1 sp, 1 sc in 3rd ch of next ch-5 arch; rep from * ending last rep with 1 sc in 3rd ch of t-ch, turn.

Row 4: Ch 4, (1 Bullion st, ch 1, 1 Bullion st) in 1st sc, ch 1, *sk next ch-5 arch, 1 sc in 3rd ch of next ch-5 arch, ch 5, 1 sc in 3rd ch of next ch-5 arch, ch 1, sk next ch-5 arch, (1 Bullion st, [ch 1, 1 Bullion st] 3 times) in next sc, ch 1; rep from * ending with sk next ch-5 arch, 1 sc in 3rd ch of next ch-5 arch, ch 1, 1 dc in last sc, turn.

Row 5: Ch 1, 1 sc in 1st dc, ch 5, sk next 2 ch-1 sps, *[1 sc in next ch-1 sp, ch 5] 3 times, sk next ch-1 sp, 1 sc in 3rd ch of next ch-5 arch, ch 5, sk next ch-1 sp; rep from * ending with 1 sc in next ch-1 sp, ch 5, 1 sc in top of t-ch, turn. Rep rows 2 through 5 for pattern.

Belt

Ch 154 (170).

Rows 1 to 5: Work rows 1 to 5 of Bullion pattern st.

Fasten off.

Reattach yarn to opposite side of base ch (with RS facing) to work other half of belt.

Row 1: Ch 4, 1 sc in 1st ch-3 sp, ch 1, sk next sc (upside down sc), sk next ch-3 sp, (1 Bullion st, [ch 1, 1 Bullion st] 3 times) in base of next sc, *ch 1, sk next ch-3 sp, sk next sc, 1 sc in next ch-3 sp, ch 5, sk next sc, 1 sc in next ch-3 sp, ch 1, sk next sc, sk next ch-3 sp, (1 Bullion st, [ch 1, 1 Bullion st] 3 times) in next sc; rep from * ending last rep with (1 Bullion st, ch 1, 1 Bullion st, 1 tr) in last sc, turn.

Rows 2 to 4: Rep rows 3 to 5 of Bullion pattern st. Do not fasten off.

With RS facing, work border counterclockwise around edges of belt as follows:

Border Rnd: Work 5 sc in each ch-5 arch along longer edges, work a row of sc evenly along shorter edges, join with a sl st to 1st sc to close round.

Fasten off.

Finishing

Ties: Ch 126 (140). Fasten off. Make 3 more ties. Knot each end tightly and cut yarn close to knot. Fold each tie in half and attach 2 to each end like fringe. Weave in all loose ends.

Flutter-Sleeve Top

To Fit Bust Size

33-35 (36-38, 39-41, 42-44)" [84-89 (91.5-96.5, 99-104, 106.5-112) cm]

Finished Bust Size

33 (36, 39, 42)" [84 (91.5, 99, 106.5) cm]
Sizes: Small, Medium, Large, and X-Large.
Shown in size Small.

Materials

A light weight blend of cotton/viscose yarn: total yardage required: 600 (720, 720, 840) yd [549 (658, 658, 768) m].

Shown:

GGH Mystik (54% Cotton, 46% Viscose; approx 120 yd [110 m] per 1¾ oz [50 g] ball):
#63 Mauve, 5 (6, 6, 7) balls.

Size I/9 (5.5 mm) crochet hook or size to obtain gauge.

Notions

Yarn tapestry needle

Gauge

Four (1 sc, 2 dc) groups = 3" (7.5 cm) and 14 rows = 6" (15 cm) in silt pattern st using size I/9 (5.5 mm) crochet hook. Take time to check gauge.

SILT PATTERN STITCH

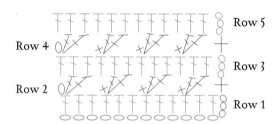

Repeat rows 2 and 3 for silt pattern stitch.

OPEN LACE PATTERN STITCH

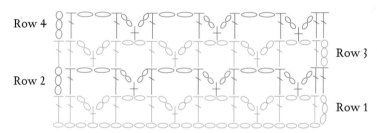

Repeat row 2 for open lace pattern stitch.

Stitches and Techniques Used

(See pages 134–140)

Slip st, single crochet, half double crochet, double crochet, treble, multiple stitches into 1 stitch, cluster st, working into an arch, forming ring, working in the round, joining in the round, sewing pieces together.

Notes:

1. Dc2Cl-work 2 dc into sts/sps as indicated until 1 lp of each dc remains on hk, yo and pull thru all 3 lps on hk.

2. Dc3Cl-work 3 dc into sts/sps as indicated until 1 lp of each dc remains on hk, yo and pull thru all 4 lps on hk.

3. Dc5Cl-work 5 dc into sts/sps as indicated until 1 lp of each dc remains on hk, yo and pull thru all 6 lps on hk.

4. When changing balls of yarn, it is a good idea to knot the 2 ends together when using a slippery viscose blend yarn.

Pattern Stitches

Silt Pattern Stitch

Ch a multiple of 3 plus 3 extra.

Row 1 (RS): Sk 1st 3 chs (counts as 1 dc), 1 dc in next and each ch to end, turn.

Row 2 (WS): Ch 1 (counts as 1 sc), 2 dc in 1st st, *sk 2 sts, (1 sc, 2 dc) in next st; rep from * to last 3 sts, sk 2 sts, 1 sc in top of t-ch, turn.

Row 3: Ch 3 (counts as 1 dc), sk 1st st, 1 dc in next and each st to end, ending with last dc in top of t-ch, turn.

Rep rows 2 and 3 for silt pattern st.

Open Lace Pattern Stitch

Ch a multiple of 7 plus 5 extra.

Row 1: Sk 1st 3 chs (counts as 1 dc), 1 dc in next ch, *ch 2, sk 2 ch, 1 dc in next st, ch 2, sk 1 ch, 1 sc in next ch, ch 2, sk next ch, 1 dc in next ch; rep from * ending with 1 dc in last ch, turn.

Row 2: Ch 3 (counts as 1 dc), sk 1st dc, 1 dc in next dc, *ch 2, sk next ch-2 sp, sk next sc, sk next ch-2 sp, 1 dc in next dc, ch 2, 1 sc in next ch-2 sp, ch 2, 1 dc in next dc; rep from * ending with 1 dc in top of t-ch, turn.

Rep row 2 for open pattern st.

Back

With A, ch 69 (75, 81, 87).

Rows 1 to 3: Work in silt pattern st for 3 rows: 67 (73, 79, 85) dc (counting ch-3 as 1 dc).

Work open stitch row:

Row 4: Ch 3, sk 1st dc, 1 dc in next dc, *ch 1, sk next dc, 1 dc in next dc; rep from * ending with 1 dc in top of t-ch, turn.

Row 5: Ch 3, sk 1st dc, *1 dc in next dc, 1 dc in next ch-1 sp; rep from * to last 2 sts, 1 dc in next dc, 1 dc in top of t-ch, turn: 67 (73, 79, 85) dc (counting ch-3 as 1 dc).

Row 6: Rep row 2 of silt pattern st.

Rows 7 to 22: Rep rows 3 and 2 of silt pattern st 8 times.

Shape bodice:

Row 23 (Dec row): Ch 3, sk 1st st, 1 dc in each of next 19 (21, 23, 25) sts, work 1 Dc5Cl over next 5 sts, 1 dc in each of next 8 (9, 10, 11) sts, 1 Dc2Cl over next 2 sts, 1 dc in each of next 8 (9, 10, 11) sts, 1 Dc5Cl over next 5 sts, 1 dc in each of next 18 (20, 22, 24) sts, 1 dc in top of t-ch, turn: 58 (64, 70, 76) sts (counting ch-3 as 1 st).

Work single crochet band:

Row 24: Ch 1, 1 sc in each st across, 1 sc in top of t-ch, turn: 58 (64, 70, 76) sc.

Rows 25 to 28: Ch 1, 1 sc in each st across, sk t-ch, turn.

Increase for bust width:

Row 29 (Inc row): Ch 3, sk 1st sc, 1 dc in each of next 19 (21, 23, 25) sc, 5 dc in next sc, 1 dc in each of next 8 (9, 10, 11) sc, 2 dc in next sc, 1 dc in each of next 8 (9, 10, 11) sc, 5 dc in next sc, 1 dc in each of next 19 (21, 23, 25) sc, turn: 67 (73, 79, 85) dc (counting ch-3 as 1 dc).

Row 30: Rep row 2 of silt pattern st.

Rows 31 to 34 (34, 36, 36): Rep rows 3 and 2 of silt pattern st 2 (2, 3, 3) times.

Shape armholes:

For Sizes Small, Medium, and Large Only

Row 35 (35, 37, —): Ch 1, sk 1st st, 1 sl st in each of next 3 sts, ch 3, 1 Dc2Cl over next 2 sts, 1 dc in each st across to last 5 sts, 1 Dc2Cl over next 2 sts, sk 2 sts, sk t-ch, turn: 59 (65, 71, —) sts (counting ch-3 as 1 st).

For Size X-Large Only

Row 37: Ch 1, sk 1st st, 1 sl st in each of next 5 sts, ch 3, 1 Dc3Cl over next 3 sts, 1 dc in each st across to last 9 sts, 1 Dc3Cl over next 3 sts, sk 5 sts, sk t-ch, turn: 71 sts (counting ch-3 as 1 st).

For All Sizes

Row 36 (36, 38, 38): Ch 1, 2 dc in 1st st, *sk 2 sts, (1 sc, 2 dc) in next st; rep from * to last 4 sts, sk 2 sts, 1 sc in next st, sk t-ch, turn.

Row 37 (37, 39, 39): Rep row 3 of silt pattern st: 58 (64, 70, 70) dc (counting ch-3 as 1 dc).

Row 38 (38, 40, 40): Rep row 2 of silt pattern st.

Change to open lace pattern st:

For Size Small Only

Row 39: Ch 3, 1 dc in 1st st, *ch 2, sk 2 sts, 1 dc in next st, ch 2, sk 1 st, 1 sc in next st, ch 2, sk next st, 1 dc in next st; rep from * ending with 1 dc in top of t-ch, turn.

For Sizes Medium, Large, and X-Large Only

Row —(39, 41, 41): Ch 3, 1 dc in 1st st, *ch 2, sk 2 sts, 1 dc in next st, ch 2, sk 1 st, 1 sc in next st, ch 2, sk next st, 1 dc in next st; rep from *, ending last rep with last dc in t-ch, 1 dc in same t-ch, turn.

For All Sizes

Row 40 (40, 42, 42): Work row 2 of open lace pattern st.

Rows 41 (41, 43, 43) to 50 (50, 54, 54): Rep row 2 of open lace pattern st.
Fasten off.

Front

Work same as for BACK through Row 32 (32, 34, 34): 67 (73, 79, 85) dc (counting ch-3 as 1 dc).

Begin neck shaping, left side (as worn):
Row 33 (33, 35, 35): Ch 3, sk 1st st, 1 dc in each of next 29 (32, 35, 38) sts, 1 Dc3Cl over next 3 sts, sk rem half of row, turn: 31 (34, 37, 40) sts (counting ch-3 as 1 st).

Row 34 (34, 36, 36): Rep row 2 of silt pattern st.

Continue shaping neckline and AT THE SAME TIME, begin armhole shaping:

For Sizes Small, Medium, and Large Only

Row 35 (35, 37, —): Ch 1, sk 1st st, 1 sl st in each of next 3 sts, ch 3, 1 Dc2Cl over next 2 sts, 1 dc in each st across to last 4 sts, 1 Dc3Cl over next 3 sts, sk t-ch, turn: 24 (27, 30, —) sts (counting ch-3 as 1 st).

For Size X-Large Only

Row 37: Ch 1, sk 1st st, 1 sl st in each of next 5 sts, ch 3, 1 Dc3Cl over next 3 sts, 1 dc in each st across to last 4 sts, 1 Dc3Cl over next 3 sts, sk t-ch, turn: 30 sts (counting ch-3 as 1 st).

For All Sizes

Row 36 (36, 38, 38): Ch 1, 2 dc in 1st st, *sk 2 sts, (1 sc, 2 dc) in next st; rep from * to last 2 sts, sk 1 st, 1 sc in top of t-ch, turn.

Row 37 (37, 39, 39): Ch 3, sk 1st st, 1 dc in each st across to last 4 sts, 1 Dc3Cl over next 3 sts, sk t-ch, turn: 22 (25, 28, 28) sts (counting ch-3 as 1 dc).

Row 38 (38, 40, 40): Rep row 2 of silt pattern st.

Begin open lace pattern st:

For Sizes Small, Large, and X-Large Only

Row 39 (—, 41, 41): Ch 3, 1 dc in 1st st, [ch 2, sk 2 sts, 1 dc in next st, ch 2, sk next st, 1 sc in next st, ch 2, sk next st, 1 dc in next st] 2 (—, 3, 3) times, ch 2, sk 2 sts, 1 dc in next st, sk next st, 1 dc in next st, sk 1 (—, 0, 0) st, sk t-ch, turn.

Row 40 (—, 42, 42): Ch 4, sk 1st 2 dc, sk next ch-2 sp, 1 dc in next dc, [ch 2, sk next ch-2 sp, sk next sc, sk next ch-2 sp, 1 dc in next dc, ch 2, 1 sc in next ch-2 sp, ch 2, 1 dc in next dc] 2 (—, 3, 3) times, 1 dc in top of t-ch, turn.

Row 41 (—, 43, 43): Ch 3, sk 1st dc, 1 dc in next dc, [ch 2, sk next ch-2 sp, sk next sc, sk next ch-2 sp, 1 dc in next dc, ch 2, 1 sc in next ch-2 sp, ch 2, 1 dc in next dc] 2 (—, 3, 3) times, sk t-ch, turn.

Row 42 (—, 44, 44): Ch 3, sk 1st dc, sk next ch-2 sp, sk next sc, sk next ch-2 sp, 1 dc in next dc, ch 2, 1 sc in next ch-2 sp, ch 2, 1 dc in next dc, [ch 2, sk next ch-2 sp, sk next sc, sk next ch-2 sp, 1 dc in next dc, ch 2, 1 sc in next ch-2 sp, ch 2, 1 dc in next dc] 1 (—, 2, 2) times, 1 dc in top of t-ch, turn.

Row 43 (—, 45, 45): Ch 3, sk 1st dc, 1 dc in next dc, ch 2, sk next ch-2 sp, sk next sc, sk next ch-2 sp, 1 dc in next dc, [ch 2, 1 sc in next ch-2 sp, ch 2, 1 dc in next dc, ch 2, sk next ch-2 sp, sk next sc, sk next ch-2 sp, 1 dc in next dc] 1 (—, 2, 2) times, sk t-ch, turn.

Row 44 (—, 46, 46): Ch 5, sk 1st dc, 1 sc in next ch-2 sp, ch 2, 1 dc in next dc, [ch 2, sk next ch-2 sp, sk next sc, sk next ch-2 sp, 1 dc in next dc, ch 2, 1 sc in next ch-2 sp, ch 2, 1 dc in next dc] 1 (—, 2, 2) times, 1 dc in top of t-ch, turn.

Row 45 (—, 47, 47): Ch 3, sk 1st dc, 1 dc in next dc, [ch 2, sk next ch-2 sp, sk next sc, sk next ch-2 sp, 1 dc in next dc, ch 2, 1 sc in next ch-2 sp, ch 2, 1 dc in next dc] 1 (—, 2, 2) times, ch 2, sk next ch-2 sp, sk next sc, sk next 2 ch, 1 dc in next ch of t-ch, turn.

Row 46 (—, 48, 48): Rep row 44 (—, 46, 46).

Rows 47 (—, 49, 49) to 50 (—, 54, 54): Rep rows 45 (—, 47, 47) and 44 (—, 46, 46) above 2 (—, 3, 3) times. Fasten off.

For Size Medium Only

Row 39: Ch 3, 1 dc in 1st st, [ch 2, sk 2 sts, 1 dc in next st, ch 2, sk next st, 1 sc in next st, ch 2, sk next st, 1 dc in next st] 3 times, sk next st, 1 dc in next st, sk t-ch, turn.

Row 40: Ch 4, sk 1st 2 dc, sk next ch-2 sp, sk next sc, sk next ch-2 sp, 1 dc in next dc, ch 2, 1 sc in next ch-2 sp, ch 2, 1 dc in next dc, [ch 2, sk next ch-2 sp, sk next sc, sk next ch-2 sp, 1 dc in next dc, ch 2, 1 sc in next ch-2 sp, ch 2, 1 dc in next dc] 2 times, 1 dc in top of t-ch, turn.

Row 41: Ch 3, sk 1st dc, 1 dc in next dc, [*ch 2, sk next ch-2 sp, sk next sc, sk next ch-2 sp, 1 dc in next dc*, ch 2, 1 sc in next ch-2 sp, ch 2, 1 dc in next dc] 2 times, rep from * to * 1 time, sk t-ch, turn.

Row 42: Ch 3, sk 1st dc, sk next ch-2 sp, 1 dc in next dc, [ch 2, sk next ch-2 sp, sk next sc, sk next ch-2 sp, 1 dc in next dc, ch 2, 1 sc in next ch-2 sp, ch 2, 1 dc in next dc] 2 times, 1 dc in top of t-ch, turn.

Row 43: Ch 3, sk 1st dc, 1 dc in next dc, ch 2, sk next ch-2 sp, sk next sc, sk next ch-2 sp, 1 dc in next dc, ch 2, 1 sc in next ch-2 sp, ch 2, 1 dc in next dc, ch 2, sk next ch-2 sp, sk next sc, sk next ch-2 sp, 1 dc in next dc, ch 2, 1 sc in next ch-2 sp, ch 2, 1 dc in next dc, sk t-ch, turn.

Row 44: Ch 5, sk 1st dc, sk next ch-2 sp, sk next sc, sk next ch-2 sp, 1 dc in next dc, ch 2, 1 sc in next ch-2 sp, ch 2, 1 dc in next dc, ch 2, sk next ch-2 sp, sk next sc, sk next ch-2 sp, 1 dc in next dc, ch 2, 1 sc in next ch-2 sp, ch 2, 1 dc in next dc, 1 dc in top of t-ch, turn.

Row 45: Ch 3, sk 1st dc, 1 dc in next dc, ch 2, sk next ch-2 sp, sk next sc, sk next ch-2 sp, 1 dc in next dc, ch 2, 1 sc in next ch-2 sp, ch 2, 1 dc in next dc, ch 2, sk next ch-2 sp, sk next sc, sk next ch-2 sp, 1 dc in next dc, ch 2, 1 sc in next ch-2 sp, ch 2, 1 dc in 3rd ch of t-ch, turn.

Row 46: Rep row 44.

Rows 47 to 50: Rep rows 45 and 44 two times.
Fasten off.

For All Sizes

Rejoin yarn to row 33 (33, 35, 35) to work right top piece:

Row 33 (33, 35, 35): With RS of work facing, beg at neckline and attach yarn to next st, ch 3, 1 Dc2Cl over next 2 sts, 1 dc in each st to t-ch, sk t-ch, turn: 32 (35, 38, 41) sts (counting ch-3 as 1 st).

Row 34 (34, 36, 36): Ch 1, 2 dc in 1st st, *sk 2 sts, (1 sc, 2 dc) in next st; rep from * to last dc, 1 dc in next dc, sk t-ch, turn.

Continue to shape neckline and AT THE SAME TIME, begin armhole shaping:

For Sizes Small, Medium, and Large Only

Row 35 (35, 37, —): Ch 3, sk 1st st, 1 Dc3Cl over next 3 sts, 1 dc in each st to last 5 sts, 1 Dc2Cl over next 2 sts, sk next 2 sts, sk t-ch, turn: 25 (28, 31, —) sts (counting ch-3 as 1 st).

For Size X-Large Only

Row 37: Ch 3, sk 1st st, 1 Dc3Cl over next 3 sts, 1 dc in each st across to last 9 sts, 1 Dc3Cl over next 3 sts, sk 5 sts, sk t-ch, turn: 30 sts (counting ch-3 as 1 st).

For All Sizes

Row 36 (36, 38, 38): Ch 1, 2 dc in 1st st, sk 2 (2, 1, 1) sts, (1 sc, 2 dc) in next st, *sk 2 sts (1 sc, 2 dc) in next st; rep from * to last 3 sts, sk 1 st, 1 sc in next st, sk t-ch, turn.

Row 37 (37, 39, 39): Ch 3, sk 1st st, 1 Dc3Cl over next 3 sts, 1 dc in each st to t-ch, 1 dc in t-ch: 23 (26, 29, 29) sts (counting ch-3 as 1 st).

Row 38 (38, 40, 40): Ch 1, 2 dc in 1st st, *sk 2 sts, (1 sc, 2 dc) in next st; rep from * to last 4 sts, sk 2 sts, 1 sc in next st, sk t-ch, turn.

Begin open lace pattern st:

For Sizes Small, Large, and X-Large Only

Row 39 (—, 41, 41): Ch 1, sk 1 (—, 0, 0) st, 1 sl st in next st, ch 3, sk 1 st, 1 dc in next st, [ch 2, sk 2 sts, 1 dc in next st, ch 2, sk 1 st, 1 sc in next st, ch 2, sk 1 st, 1 dc in next st] 2 (—, 3, 3) times, ch

2, sk 2 sts, 1 dc in next st, 1 dc in top of t-ch, turn.

Row 40 (—, 42, 42): Ch 3, sk 1st dc, 1 dc in next dc, [ch 2, 1 sc in next ch-2 sp, ch 2, 1 dc in next dc, ch 2, sk next ch-2 sp, sk next sc, sk next ch-2 sp, 1 dc in next dc] 2 (—, 3, 3) times, sk next ch-2 sp, sk next dc, 1 tr in top of t-ch, turn.

Row 41 (—, 43, 43): Ch 5, sk tr and dc, 1 sc in next ch-2 sp, ch 2, 1 dc in next dc, ch 2, sk next ch-2 sp, sk next sc, sk next ch-2 sp, 1 dc in next dc, [ch 2, 1 sc in next ch-2 sp, ch 2, 1 dc in next dc, ch 2, sk next ch-2 sp, sk next sc, sk next ch-2 sp, 1 dc in next dc] 1 (—, 2, 2) times, 1 dc in top of t-ch, turn.

Row 42 (—, 44, 44): Ch 3, sk 1st dc, 1 dc in next dc, ch 2, 1 sc in next ch-2 sp, ch 2, 1 dc in next dc, [ch 2, sk next ch-2 sp, sk next sc, sk next ch-2 sp, 1 dc in next dc, ch 2, 1 sc in next ch-2 sp, ch 2, 1 dc in next dc] 1 (—, 2, 2) times, sk next ch-2 sp, sk next sc, sk 2 ch of t-ch, 1 dc in next ch of t-ch, turn.

Row 43 (—, 45, 45): Ch 5, sk 1st 2 dc, sk next ch-2 sp, sk next sc, sk next ch-2 sp, 1 dc in next dc, [ch 2, 1 sc in next ch-2 sp, ch 2, 1 dc in next dc, ch 2, sk next ch-2 sp, sk next sc, sk next ch-2 sp, 1 dc in next dc] 1 (—, 2, 2) times, 1 dc in top of t-ch, turn.

Row 44 (—, 46, 46): Ch 3, sk 1st dc, 1 dc in next dc, [ch 2, 1 sc in next ch-2 sp, ch 2, 1 dc in next dc, ch 2, sk next ch-2 sp, sk next sc, sk next ch-2 sp, 1 dc in next dc] 1 (—, 2, 2) times, ch 2, 1 sc in t-ch sp, ch 2, 1 dc in 3rd ch of t-ch, turn.

Row 45 (—, 47, 47): Ch 5, sk 1st dc, sk next ch-2 sp, sk next sc, sk next ch-2 sp, 1 dc in next dc, [ch 2, 1 sc in next ch-2 sp, ch 2, 1 dc in next dc, ch 2, sk next ch-2 sp, sk next sc, sk next ch-2 sp, 1 dc in next dc] 1 (—, 2, 2) times, 1 dc in top of t-ch, turn.

Row 46 (—, 48, 48): Rep row 44 (—, 46, 46).

Rows 47 (—, 49, 49) to 50 (—, 54, 54): Rep rows 45 (—, 47, 47) and 44 (—, 46, 46) above 2 (—, 3, 3) times.

Fasten off.

For Size Medium Only

Row 39: Ch 3, sk 1st 2 sts, 1 dc in next st, [ch 2, sk 1 st, 1 sc in next st, ch 2, sk 1 st, 1 dc in next st, ch 2, sk 2 sts, 1 dc in next st] 3 times, 1 dc in top of t-ch, turn.

Row 40: Ch 3, sk 1st dc, 1 dc in next dc, [ch 2, 1 sc in next ch-2 sp, ch 2, 1 dc in next dc, ch 2, sk next ch-2 sp, sk next sc, sk next ch-2 sp, 1 dc in next dc] 2 times, ch 2, 1 sc in next ch-2 sp, ch 2, 1 dc in next dc, sk next ch-2 sp, sk next sc, sk next ch-2 sp, sk next dc, 1 tr in top of t-ch, turn.

Row 41: Ch 5, sk tr and dc, sk next ch-2 sp, sk next sc, sk next ch-2 sp, 1 dc in next dc, ch 2, 1 sc in next ch-2 sp, ch 2, 1 dc in next dc, ch 2, sk next ch-2 sp, sk next sc, sk next ch-2 sp, 1 dc in next dc, ch 2, 1 sc in next ch-2 sp, ch 2, 1 dc in next dc, ch 2, sk next ch-2 sp, sk next sc, sk next ch-2 sp, 1 dc in next dc, 1 dc in top of t-ch, turn.

Row 42: Ch 3, sk 1st dc, 1 dc in next dc, ch 2, 1 sc in next ch-2 sp, ch 2, 1 dc in next dc, ch 2, sk next ch-2 sp, sk next sc, sk next ch-2 sp, 1 dc in next dc, ch 2, 1 sc in next ch-2 sp, ch 2, 1 dc in next dc, ch 2, 1 sc in next ch-2 sp, ch 2, 1 dc in next dc, sk 2 ch of t-ch, 1 dc in next ch of t-ch, turn.

Row 43: Ch 5, sk 1st 2 dc, 1 sc in next ch-2 sp, ch 2, 1 dc in next dc, ch 2, sk next ch-2 sp, sk next sc, sk next ch-2 sp, 1 dc in next dc, ch 2, 1 sc in next ch-2 sp, ch 2, 1 dc in next dc, ch 2, sk next ch-2 sp, sk next sc, sk next ch-2 sp, 1 dc in next dc, 1 dc in top of t-ch, turn.

Row 44: Ch 3, sk 1st dc, 1 dc in next dc, ch 2, 1 sc in next ch-2 sp, ch 2, 1 dc in next dc, ch 2, sk next ch-2 sp, sk next sc, sk next ch-2 sp, 1 dc in next dc, ch 2, 1 sc in next ch-2 sp, ch 2, 1 dc in next dc, ch 2, sk next ch-2 sp, sk next sc, 1 dc in 3rd ch of t-ch, turn.

Row 45: Ch 5, sk 1st dc, 1 sc in next ch-2 sp, ch 2, 1 dc in next dc, ch 2, sk next ch-2 sp, sk next sc, sk next ch-2 sp, 1 dc in next dc, ch 2, 1 sc in next ch-2 sp, ch 2, 1 dc in next dc, ch 2, sk next ch-2 sp, sk next sc, sk next ch-2 sp, 1 dc in next dc, 1 dc in top of t-ch, turn:

Row 46: Rep row 44.

Rows 47 to 50: Rep rows 45 and 44 two times.

Fasten off.

Sleeves

Ch 37 (37, 44, 44).

Row 1: Sk 1st 8 ch, 1 dc in next ch, *ch 2, sk 1 ch, 1 sc in next ch, ch 2, sk 1 ch,

1 dc in next ch, ch 2, sk 2 ch, 1 dc in next ch; rep from * to end, turn.

Row 2: Ch 5, sk 1st dc, 1 sc in next ch-2 sp, ch 2, 1 dc in next dc, *ch 2, sk next ch-2 sp, sk next sc, sk next ch-2 sp, 1 dc in next dc, ch 2, 1 sc in next ch-2 sp, ch 2, 1 dc in next dc; rep from * 2 (2, 3, 3) times, ch 2, sk next ch-2 sp, sk next sc, sk next ch-2 sp, 1 dc in next dc, sk next 2 ch of t-ch, 1 dc in 3rd ch of t-ch, turn.

Row 3: Ch 3, sk 1st 2 dc, sk next ch-2 sp, 1 dc in next dc, *ch 2, sk next ch-2 sp, sk next sc, sk next ch-2 sp, 1 dc in next dc, ch 2, 1 sc in next ch-2 sp, ch 2, 1 dc in next dc; rep from * 2 (2, 3, 3) times, ch 2, sk next ch-2 sp, sk next sc, sk 2 ch of t-ch, 1 dc in 3rd ch of t-ch, turn.

Row 4: Ch 5, sk 1st dc, 1 sc in next ch-2 sp, ch 2, 1 dc in next dc, *ch 2, sk next ch-2 sp, sk next sc, sk next ch-2 sp, 1 dc in next dc, ch 2, 1 sc in next ch-2 sp, ch 2, 1 dc in next dc; rep from * 1 (1, 2, 2) times, ch 2, sk next ch-2 sp, sk next sc, sk next ch-2 sp, 1 dc in next dc, sk next ch-2 sp, 1 dc in next dc, sk t-ch, turn.

Row 5: Ch 3, sk 1st 2 dc, sk next ch-2 sp, 1 dc in next dc, *ch 2, sk next ch-2 sp, sk next sc, sk next ch-2 sp, 1 dc in next dc, ch 2, 1 sc in next ch-2 sp, ch 2, 1 dc in next dc; rep from * 1 (1, 2, 2) times, ch 2, sk next ch-2 sp, sk next sc, sk 2 ch of t-ch, 1 dc in 3rd ch of t-ch, turn.

Row 6: Ch 5, sk 1st dc, 1 sc in next ch-2 sp, ch 2, 1 dc in next dc, *ch 2, sk next

ch-2 sp, sk next sc, sk next ch-2 sp, 1 dc in next dc, ch 2, 1 sc in next ch-2 sp, ch 2, 1 dc in next dc; rep from * 0 (0, 1, 1) times, ch 2, sk next ch-2 sp, sk next sc, sk next ch-2 sp, 1 dc in next dc, sk next ch-2 sp, 1 dc in next dc, sk t-ch, turn.

Row 7: Ch 3, sk 1st 2 dc, sk next ch-2 sp, 1 dc in next dc, *ch 2, sk next ch-2 sp, sk next sc, sk next ch-2 sp, 1 dc in next dc, ch 2, 1 sc in next ch-2 sp, ch 2, 1 dc in next dc; rep from * 0 (0, 1, 1) times, ch 2, sk next ch-2 sp, sk next sc, sk 2 ch of t-ch, 1 dc in 3rd ch of t-ch, turn.

For Sizes Small and Medium
Fasten off.

For Sizes Large and X-Large
Row 8: Ch 5, sk 1st dc, 1 sc in next ch-2 sp, ch 2, 1 dc in next dc, ch 2, sk next ch-2 sp, sk next sc, sk next ch-2 sp, 1 dc in next dc, ch 2, 1 sc in next ch-2 sp, ch 2, 1 dc in next dc, ch 2, sk next ch-2 sp, sk next sc, sk next ch-2 sp, 1 dc in next dc, sk next ch-2 sp, 1 dc in next dc, sk t-ch, turn.
Fasten off.

For All Sizes
Make 3 more sleeve pieces same as the first.

Flower Motif
Ch 6. Join with a sl st to form ring.
Rnd 1: [Ch 3, 1 sc in ring] 5 times, join with a sl st to 1st ch of 1st ch-3.

Rnd 2: (2 dc, 1 tr, 2 dc) in each ch-3 sp around, join with a sl st to 1st dc.

Rnd 3: Sk 1st dc, 1 sl st in next dc, 1 sl st in next tr, [ch 8, 1 sl st in next tr of next petal] 5 times, join with a sl st to 1st sl st.

Rnd 4: Work 12 hdc in each ch-8 arch around, join with a sl st to 1st hdc. Fasten off.

Finishing
Sew side seams leaving 3" (7.5 cm) open at lower edge for side slits. Sew shoulder seams. Sew base chain edge of each sleeve piece along armhole edges as shown.

Starting at the top of a slit, work 1 row of sc down one side of slit to the lower edge, then along the bottom edges of FRONT and BACK, and along side edges of second slit, working 3 sc at each corner. Join with a sl st to first sc. Fasten off.

Sew flower motif to center of front single crochet band. Tack top petals of flower in place to keep flower flat against top. Lightly steam. Weave in all loose ends.

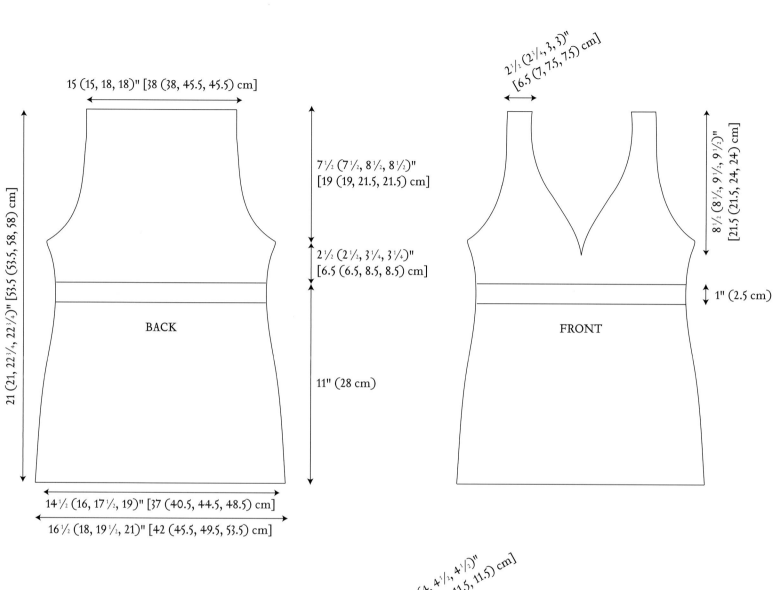

15 (15, 18, 18)" [38 (38, 45.5, 45.5) cm]

7 1/2 (7 1/2, 8 1/2, 8 1/2)" [19 (19, 21.5, 21.5) cm]

2 1/2 (2 1/2, 3 1/4, 3 1/4)" [6.5 (6.5, 8.5, 8.5) cm]

21 (21, 22 3/4, 22 3/4)" [53.5 (53.5, 58, 58) cm]

BACK

11" (28 cm)

14 1/2 (16, 17 1/2, 19)" [37 (40.5, 44.5, 48.5) cm]

16 1/2 (18, 19 1/2, 21)" [42 (45.5, 49.5, 53.5) cm]

2 1/2 (2 3/4, 3, 3)" [6.5 (7, 7.5, 7.5) cm]

8 1/2 (8 1/2, 9 1/4, 9 1/2)" [21.5 (21.5, 24, 24) cm]

FRONT

1" (2.5 cm)

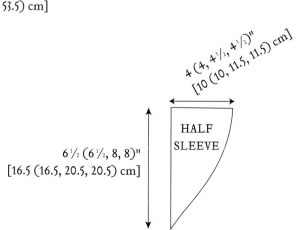

4 (4, 4 1/2, 4 1/2)" [10 (10, 11.5, 11.5) cm]

HALF SLEEVE

6 1/2 (6 1/2, 8, 8)" [16.5 (16.5, 20.5, 20.5) cm]

Slim-Fitting Cardigan

To Fit Bust Size
33-35 (35-37, 37-39)" [84-89 (89-94, 94-99) cm]

Finished Bust Size
34 (36, 38)" [86.5 (91.5, 96.5) cm]

Sizes: Small (Medium, Large)
Note: Instructions are given for smallest size, with larger sizes in parentheses. Where there is only one instruction, it applies to all sizes. Size small shown.

Materials

A light DK-weight merino wool yarn: total yardage required: 1179 (1179, 1310) yd [1080 (1080, 1200) m].

Shown:

Jaeger Matchmaker (100% Pure Wool; approx 131 yd [120 m] per 1¾ oz [50 g] ball):
#663 Eggshell, 9 (9, 10) balls.

Size H/8 (5 mm) crochet hook or size to obtain gauge.

Notions

Yarn tapestry needle; 5 (6, 6) 32 Ligne (1³⁄₁₆" [20 mm]) buttons, or 18 Ligne (⁷⁄₁₆" [11.5 mm]) Full ball pearl buttons; sewing thread; sewing needle.

WAVY PATTERN STITCH

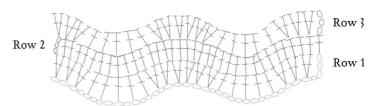

Repeat rows 2 and 3 for wavy pattern stitch.

LACE BORDER PATTERN STITCH

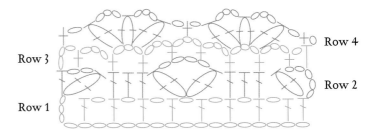

Shown:

Full ball pearl buttons—18 Ligne (⁷⁄₁₆" [11.5 mm]) from The Button Store at www.hushcobuttons.com.

Gauge

17 sts (1 wavy pattern repeat) = 4" (10 cm) and 8 rows = 4" (10 cm) in wavy lace pattern st using size H/8 (5 mm) crochet hook. 16 dc = 4" (10 cm) and 8 rows = 4" (10 cm) in plain dc stitch. Take time to check gauge.

Stitches and Techniques Used

(See page 134–140)

Slip st, single crochet, double crochet, multiple stitches into 1 stitch, cluster st, working into an arch, sewing pieces together.

Notes:
1. To work a "Dc2Cl"—(a 2-dc cluster)—work 1 dc in st/sp as instructed until 2 lps remain on hk, work 2nd dc

in same st/sp until 3 lps remain on hk, yo, draw through 3 lps on hk.

2. To work a "Dc3Cl"—(a 3-dc cluster)—work 1 dc in st/sp as instructed until 2 lps remain on hk, work 2nd dc in same st/sp until 3 lps remain on hk, work 3rd dc in same st/sp until 4 lps remain on hk, yo, draw through 4 lps on hk.

Pattern Stitches

Wavy Pattern Stitch

Ch a multiple of 17 plus 4 extra.

Row 1 (RS): Sk 1st 4 ch, *2 dc in each of next 3 ch, [sk 1 ch, 1 dc in next ch] 5 times, sk 1 ch, 2 dc in each of next 3 ch; rep from * to end, turn.

Row 2 (WS): Ch 3 (counts as 1 dc), sk 1st dc, 1 dc in each dc across, 1 dc in top of t-ch, turn.

Row 3: Ch 3 (counts as 1 dc), sk 1st dc, *2 dc in each of next 3 dc, [sk 1 dc, 1 dc in next dc] 5 times, sk 1 dc, 2 dc in each of next 3 dc; rep from * ending last rep with last 2 dc in top of t-ch, turn.

Rep rows 2 and 3 for wavy pattern st.

Lace Border Pattern Stitch

Ch a multiple of 8 plus 4 extra.

Row 1 (WS): Sk 1st 4 ch, 1 dc in next ch, *ch 1, sk 1 ch, 1 dc in next ch; rep from * to last ch, 1 dc in last ch, turn.

Row 2 (RS): Ch 5, 1 Dc2Cl in 1st dc, sk next dc, sk next ch-1 sp, 1 dc in next dc, 1 dc in next ch-1 sp, 1 dc in next dc, *sk next ch-1 sp, sk next dc, (1 Dc2Cl, ch 4, 1 Dc2Cl) in next ch-1 sp, sk next dc, sk next ch-1 sp, 1 dc in next dc, 1 dc in next ch-1 sp, 1 dc in next dc; rep from * to last dc, sk next ch-1 sp, sk next dc, (1 Dc2Cl, ch 2, 1 dc) in top of t-ch, turn.

Row 3: Ch 3, 1 sc in next ch-2 sp, ch 3, sk next Dc2Cl, 1 sc in next dc, ch 3, sk 1 dc, 1 sc in next dc, *ch 3, (1 sc, ch 3, 1 sc) in next ch-4 sp, ch 3, sk next Dc2Cl, 1 sc in next dc, ch 3, sk 1 dc, 1 sc in next dc; rep from * to last Dc2Cl, ch 3, (1 sc, ch 1, 1 hdc) in t-ch sp, turn.

Row 4: Ch 1, 1 sc in 1st hdc, *ch 1, sk next ch-3 sp, (1 Dc2Cl, ch 3, 1 Dc2Cl, ch 3, 1 Dc2Cl) in next ch-3 sp, ch 1, sk next ch-3 sp, 1 sc in next ch-3 sp; rep from * to end.

Back

Ch 67 (71, 75).

Row 1 (RS): Sk 1st 3 ch, 1 dc in each of next 6 (8, 10) ch, begin wavy pattern st as follows: *2 dc in each of next 3 ch, [sk 1 ch, 1 dc in next ch] 5 times, sk 1 ch, 2 dc in each of next 3 ch; rep from * to last 7 (9, 11) ch, 1 dc in each of next 7 (9, 11) ch, turn: 65 (69, 73) sts (counting ch-3 as 1 dc).

Row 2 (WS): Ch 3, sk 1st dc, 1 dc in each dc across, 1 dc in top of t-ch, turn.

Row 3: Ch 3, sk 1st dc, 1 dc in each of next 6 (8, 10) dc, *2 dc in each of next 3 dc, [sk 1 dc, 1 dc in next dc] 5 times, sk 1 dc, 2 dc in each of next 3 dc; rep from * to last 7 (9, 11) sts, 1 dc in each of next 6 (8, 10) dc, 1 dc in top of t-ch, turn.

Continue in pattern as established, working 3 reps of wavy pattern st in the center, with plain dc stitches at each edge.

AT THE SAME TIME, begin shaping chest by inc 1 dc at each edge on rows 5, 10 and 15: 71 (75, 79) sts (counting ch-3 as 1 dc).
Work even until row 25.

Shape armholes:

Row 25: Sl st in 1st 4 (5, 6) sts, ch 3, dec 1 by working Dc2Cl over next 2 dc, 1 dc in each of next 4 (5, 6) dc, work in wavy pattern st to last 10 (12, 14) sts, 1 dc in each of next 4 (5, 6) sts, 1 Dc2Cl over next 2 dc, 1 dc in next dc, sk last 3 (4, 5) sts, turn: 63 (65, 67) sts.

Continue in pattern as established, dec 1 dc each edge on next row and every other row once: 59 (61, 63) sts. Work even until 39 (40, 41) rows completed. Fasten off.

Left Front

Ch 30 (32, 34).

Row 1 (RS): Sk 1st 3 ch, 1 dc in each of next 6 (8, 10) ch, begin wavy pattern st: 2 dc in each of next 3 ch, [sk 1 ch, 1 dc in next dc] 5 times, sk 1 dc, 2 dc in each of next 3 ch, 1 dc in each of next 4 ch, turn: 28 (30, 32) sts.

Row 2 (WS): Ch 3, sk 1st dc, 1 dc in each dc across, 1 dc in top of t-ch, turn.

Row 3: Ch 3, sk 1st dc, 1 dc in each of next 6 (8, 10) dc, begin wavy pattern st: 2 dc in each of next 3 dc, [sk 1 dc, 1 dc in next dc] 5 times, sk 1 dc, 2 dc in each of next 3 dc, 1 dc in each of next 3 dc, 1 dc in top of t-ch, turn.

Continue in pattern as established, working 1 rep of wavy pattern st in the center, with plain dc sts at each edge.

AT THE SAME TIME, begin shaping by inc 1 dc at armhole edge on rows 5, 10 and 15: 31 (33, 35) sts (counting ch-3 as 1 dc).
Work even until row 25.

Shape armholes:

Row 25: Sl st in 1st 4 (5, 6) dc, ch 3, dec 1 by working Dc2Cl over next 2 dc, 1 dc in each of next 4 (5, 6) dc, work in wavy pattern st to last 4 sts, 1 dc in each of next 3 sts, 1 dc in top of t-ch, turn: 27 (28, 29) sts.

Continue in pattern as established, dec 1 dc at armhole edge on next row and every other row once: 25 (26, 27) sts.
Work even to row 37 (38, 38).

For Size Small Only

Shape neck:

Row 37: Ch 3, sk 1st dc, 1 dc in each of next 3 dc, 2 dc in each of next 3 dc, [sk 1 dc, 1 dc in next dc] 5 times, sk 1 dc, dec 1 by working 1 Dc2Cl over next 2 dc, sk 5 sts, turn: 16 sts.

Row 38: Ch 3, sk 1st st, 1 Dc3Cl over next 3 sts, 1 dc in each st to t-ch, 1 dc in top of t-ch, turn: 14 sts.

Row 39: Ch 3, sk 1st st, 1 dc in each of next 3 sts, 2 dc in each of next 3 sts,

[sk next st, 1 dc in next st] 2 times, sk next st, 1 Dc2Cl over next st and top of t-ch: 13 sts.
Fasten off.

For Size Medium Only

Row 38: Sl st in 1st 6 sts, ch 3, 1 Dc2Cl over next 2 sts, [sk next st, 1 dc in next st] 4 times, sk next st, 2 dc in each of next 3 sts, 1 dc in each of next 5 sts, 1 dc in top of t-ch, turn: 18 sts.

Row 39: Ch 3, sk 1st st, 1 dc in each dc to last 3 sts, 1 Dc3Cl over next 2 sts and top of t-ch, turn: 16 sts.

Row 40: Ch 3, sk 1st st, 1 Dc3Cl over next 3 sts, sk next st, 1 dc in next st, 2 dc in each of next 3 sts, 1 dc in each of next 5 sts, 1 dc in top of t-ch: 15 sts.
Fasten off.

For Size Large Only

Row 38: Sl st in 1st 6 sts, ch 3, 1 Dc2Cl over next 2 sts, 1 dc in next st, [sk next st, 1 dc in next st] 4 times, sk next st, 2 dc in each of next 3 sts, 1 dc in each of next 5 sts, 1 dc in top of t-ch, turn: 19 sts.

Row 39: Ch 3, sk 1st st, 1 dc in each st to last 3 sts, 1 Dc3Cl over next 2 sts and top of t-ch, turn: 17 sts.

Row 40: Ch 3, sk 1st st, 1 Dc2Cl over next 2 sts, [sk next st, 1 dc in next st] 2 times, sk next st, 2 dc in each of next 3 sts, 1 dc in each of next 5 sts, 1 dc in top of t-ch: 16 sts.

Row 41: Ch 3, sk 1st st, 1 dc in each st to last 2 sts, 1 Dc2Cl over next st and top of t-ch: 15 sts.
Fasten off.

Right Front

Ch 30 (32, 34).

Row 1 (RS): Sk 1st 3 ch, 1 dc in next ch, 1 dc in each of next 3 dc, 2 dc in each of next 3 ch, [sk 1 ch, 1 dc in next dc] 5 times, sk 1 dc, 2 dc in each of next 3 ch, 1 dc in each of next 7 (9, 11) dc, turn: 28 (30, 32) sts.

Row 2 (WS): Ch 3, sk 1st dc, 1 dc in each dc across, 1 dc in top of t-ch, turn.

Row 3: Ch 3, sk 1st dc, 1 dc in each of next 3 dc, 2 dc in each of next 3 dc, [sk 1 dc, 1 dc in next dc] 5 times, sk 1 dc, 2 dc in each of next 3 dc, 1 dc in each of next 6 (8, 10) dc, 1 dc in top of t-ch, turn.

Continue in pattern as established, working 1 rep of wavy pattern st in the center, with plain dc sts at each edge.

AT THE SAME TIME, begin shaping by inc 1 dc at armhole edge on rows 5, 10 and 15: 31 (33, 35) sts (counting ch-3 as 1 dc).
Work even until row 25.

Shape armholes:

Row 25: Ch 3, sk 1st dc, 1 dc in each of next 3 dc, work in wavy pattern st to last 10 (12, 14) sts, 1 dc in each of next 4 (5, 6) dc, dec 1 by working Dc2Cl over next 2 dc, 1 dc in next dc, sk 3 (4, 5) sts, turn: 27 (28, 29) sts.

Continue in pattern as established, dec 1 dc at armhole edge on next row and every other row once: 25 (26, 27) sts.
Work even to row 37 (38, 38).

For Size Small Only

Fasten off.

Shape neck:

Row 37: Reattach yarn to 6th st, ch 3, 1 dc in next st, [sk next st, 1 dc in next st] 5 times, sk next st, 2 dc in each of next 3 sts, 1 dc in each of next 3 sts, 1 dc in top of t-ch, turn: 17 sts.

Row 38: Ch 3, sk 1st st, 1 dc in each st to last 5 sts, 1 Dc3Cl over next 3 sts, 1 dc in next st, sk t-ch, turn: 14 sts.

Row 39: Ch 3, sk 1st st, 1 Dc2Cl over next 2 sts, 1 dc in next st, sk next st, 1 dc in next st, sk next st, 2 dc in each of next 3 sts, 1 dc in each of next 3 sts, 1 dc in top of t-ch: 14 sts.
Fasten off.

For Size Medium Only

Row 38: Ch 3, sk 1st st, 1 dc in each of next 5 sts, 2 dc in each of next 3 sts, [sk next st, 1 dc in next st] 4 times, sk next st, 1 Dc2Cl over next 2 sts, 1 dc in next st, sk 5 sts, turn: 18 sts.

Row 39: Ch 3, sk 1st st, 1 Dc3Cl over next 3 sts, 1 dc in each dc to t-ch, 1 dc in top of t-ch, turn: 16 sts.

Row 40: Ch 3, sk 1st st, 1 dc in each of next 5 sts, 2 dc in each of next 3 sts, [sk next st, 1 dc in next st] 2 times, 1 Dc3Cl over next 2 sts and top of t-ch: 15 sts.
Fasten off.

For Size Large Only

Row 38: Ch 3, sk 1st st, 1 dc in each of next 5 sts, 2 dc in each of next 3 sts, [sk next st, 1 dc in next st] 5 times, 1

Dc2Cl over next 2 sts, 1 dc in next st, sk 5 sts, turn: 19 sts.

Row 39: Ch 3, sk 1st st, 1 Dc3Cl over next 3 sts, 1 dc in each dc to t-ch, 1 dc in top of t-ch, turn: 17 sts.

Row 40: Ch 3, sk 1st st, 1 dc in each of next 5 sts, 2 dc in each of next 3 sts, [sk next st, 1 dc in next st] 2 times, 1 dc in next st, 1 Dc3Cl over next 2 sts and top of t-ch: 16 sts.

Row 41: Ch 3, sk 1st st, 1 Dc2Cl over next 2 sts, 1 dc in each dc to t-ch, 1 dc in top of t-ch: 15 sts.
Fasten off.

Sleeves

Ch 38 (40, 42).

Row 1 (RS): Sk 1st 4 ch, 1 dc in each of next 0 (1, 2) ch, begin wavy pattern st: *2 dc in each of next 3 ch, [sk next ch, 1 dc in next ch] 5 times, sk next ch, 2 dc in each of next 3 ch; rep from * to last 0 (1, 2) ch, 1 dc in each of next 0 (1, 2) ch: 35 (37, 39).

For Sizes Small and Medium Only

Continue in wavy pattern st with plain dc sts at either edge. AT THE SAME TIME, inc 1 dc each edge every 4th row 7 (6, —) times, then every other row 0 (2, —) times: 49 (53, —) sts. Keep new dc's at each edge in plain dc stitch.
Work even to row 30.

Shape sleeve cap:

Row 30: Sl st in 1st 4 (5, —) sts, ch 3, dec 1 by working 1 Dc2Cl over next 2 dc, 1

dc in each dc across to last 6 (7, —) sts, 1 Dc2Cl over next 2 dc, 1 dc in next dc, sk last 3 (4, —) sts, turn: 41 (43, —) sts.

For Size Large Only

Continue in wavy pattern st with plain dc sts at either edge. AT THE SAME TIME, inc 1 dc each edge every alternating 4th and 2nd row 5 times, then every 4th row once more: 57 sts. Keep new dc's at each edge in plain dc stitch. Work even to row 31.

Shape sleeve cap:

Row 31: Sl st in 1st 6 sts, ch 3, dec 1 by working 1 Dc2Cl over next 2 dc, 1 dc in each of next 3 dc, 2 dc in each of next 3 dc, [sk 1 dc, 1 dc in next dc] 5 times, sk 1 dc, 2 dc in each of next 6 dc, [sk 1 dc, 1 dc in next dc] 5 times, sk 1 dc, 2 dc in each of next 3 dc, 1 dc in each of next 4 dc, 1 Dc2Cl over next 2 dc, 1 dc in next dc, sk last 5 sts, turn: 45 sts.

For All Sizes

Continue in pattern as established, dec 1 dc at each edge on next 2 (2, 3) rows: 37 (39, 39) sts.

Continue shaping cap as follows:

For Size Small Only

Row 33: Ch 3, sk 1st st, 1 Dc2Cl over next 2 dc, 2 dc in each of next 2 dc, [sk next dc, 1 dc in next dc] 5 times, sk next dc, 2 dc in each of next 6 dc, [sk next dc, 1 dc in next dc] 5 times, sk next dc, 2 dc in each of next 2 dc, 1 Dc2Cl over next dc and top of t-ch, turn: 33 sts.

Row 34: Ch 3, sk 1st st, 1 Dc2Cl over next 2 sts, 1 dc in each st across to last 3 sts, 1 Dc2Cl over next 2 sts, 1 dc in top of t-ch, turn: 31 sts.

Row 35: Ch 3, sk 1st st, 1 Dc2Cl over next 2 sts, 1 dc in next st, [sk next st, 1 dc in next st] 4 times, sk next st, 2 dc in each of next 6 sts, [sk next dc, 1 dc in next st] 5 times, 1 Dc2Cl over next st and top of t-ch, turn: 25 sts.

Row 36: Rep row 34: 23 sts.

Row 37: Ch 3, sk 1st st, 1 Dc2Cl over next 2 sts, 1 dc in next st, [sk next st, 1 dc in next st] 2 times, sk next st, 2 dc in each of next 6 sts, [sk next st, 1 dc in next st] 3 times, 1 Dc2Cl over next st and top of t-ch, turn: 21 sts.

Row 38: Ch 3, sk 1st st, 1 Dc3Cl over next 3 sts, 1 dc in each st across to last 4 sts, 1 Dc3Cl over next 3 sts, 1 dc in top of t-ch, turn: 17 sts.

Row 39: Ch 3, sk 1st st, 1 Dc3Cl over next 3 sts, 1 dc in next st, sk next st, 2 dc in each of next 6 sts, sk next st, 1 dc in next st, 1 Dc3Cl over next 2 sts and top of t-ch: 17 sts.

Fasten off.

For Size Medium Only

Row 33: Ch 3, sk 1st st, 1 Dc2Cl over next 2 dc, 2 dc in each of next 3 dc, [sk next dc, 1 dc in next dc] 5 times, sk next dc, 2 dc in each of next 6 dc, [sk next dc, 1 dc in next dc] 5 times, sk next dc, 2 dc in each of next 3 dc, 1 Dc2Cl over next dc and top of t-ch, turn: 37 sts.

Row 34: Ch 3, sk 1st st, 1 Dc2Cl over next 2 sts, 1 dc in each st across to last 3 sts, 1 Dc2Cl over next 2 sts, 1 dc in top of t-ch, turn: 35 sts.

Row 35: Ch 3, sk 1st st, 1 Dc2Cl over next 2 sts, 2 dc in next st, [sk next st, 1 dc in next st] 5 times, sk next st, 2 dc in each of next 6 sts, [sk next st, 1 dc in next st] 5 times, sk next st, 2 dc in next st, 1 Dc2Cl over next st and top of t-ch, turn: 29 sts.

Row 36: Rep row 34: 27 sts.

Row 37: Ch 3, sk 1st st, 1 dc in each of next 3 sts, [sk next st, 1 dc in next st] 3 times, sk next st, 2 dc in each of next 6 sts, [sk next st, 1 dc in next st] 4 times, 1 dc in next st, 1 dc in top of t-ch, turn: 25 sts.

Row 38: Ch 3, sk 1st st, 1 Dc3Cl over next 3 sts, 1 dc in each st across to last 4 sts, 1 Dc3Cl over next 3 sts, 1 dc in top of t-ch, turn: 21 sts.

Row 39: Ch 3, sk 1st st, 1 Dc3Cl over next 3 sts, 1 dc in next st, sk next st, 1 dc in next st, sk next st, 2 dc in each of next 6 sts, [sk next st, 1 dc in next st] 2 times, 1 Dc3Cl over next 2 sts and top of t-ch, turn: 19 sts.

Row 40: Ch 3, sk 1st st, 1 dc in each st across, 1 dc in top of t-ch: 17 sts.

Fasten off.

For Size Large Only

Row 35: Ch 3, sk 1st st, 1 Dc2Cl over next 2 sts, 2 dc in each of next 3 sts, [sk next st, 1 dc in next st] 5 times, sk next st, 2 dc in each of next 6 sts, [sk next st, 1 dc in next st] 5 times, sk

next st, 2 dc in each of next 3 sts, 1 Dc2Cl over next st and top of t-ch, turn: 37 sts.

Row 36: Ch 3, sk 1st st, 1 Dc2Cl over next 2 sts, 1 dc in each st across to last 3 sts, 1 Dc2Cl over next 2 sts, 1 dc in top of t-ch, turn: 35 sts.

Row 37: Ch 3, sk 1st st, 1 dc in each of next 2 sts, 2 dc in next st, [sk next st, 1 dc in next st] 5 times, sk next st, 2 dc in each of next 6 sts, [sk next st, 1 dc in next st] 5 times, sk next st, 2 dc in next st, 1 dc in next st, 1 dc in top of t-ch, turn: 31 sts.

Row 38: Rep row 36: 29 sts.

Row 39: Ch 3, sk 1st st, 1 dc in each of next 4 sts, [sk next st, 1 dc in next st] 3 times, sk next st, 2 dc in each of next 6 sts, [sk next st, 1 dc in next st] 4 times, 1 dc in each of next 2 sts, 1 dc in top of t-ch: 27 sts.

Row 40: Ch 3, sk 1st st, 1 Dc3Cl over next 3 sts, 1 dc in each dc across to last 4 sts, 1 Dc3Cl over next 3 sts, 1 dc in top of t-ch, turn: 23 sts.

Row 41: Ch 3, sk 1st st, 1 Dc2Cl over next 2 sts, 1 dc in next st, [sk next st, 1 dc in next st] 2 times, sk next st, 2 dc in each of next 6 sts, [sk next st, 1 dc in next st] 3 times, 1 Dc2CL over next st and top of t-ch, turn: 21 sts.

Row 42: Ch 3, sk 1st st, 1 dc in each st across, 1 dc in top of t-ch: 21 sts.

Fasten off.

For All Sizes

Make second sleeve same as the first.

Finishing

Cuffs

With WS facing, attach yarn to cuff edge. Working on opposite side of base chain, work row 1.

Row 1 (WS): Ch 3, 1 dc in next ch, [ch 1, 1 dc in base ch] 15 (15, 19) times evenly across cuff edge, 1 dc in corner, turn.

Rows 2 to 4: Work rows 2 to 4 of lace border st.
Fasten off.

Work 2nd lace border cuff same as the first.

Sew side and shoulder seams. Sew sleeve and cuff seams, then fit-in sleeves.

Bottom Edging

With WS facing, attach yarn to bottom left edge corner. Working on opposite side of base chain, work row 1.

Row 1 (WS): Ch 3, 1 dc in next st, [ch 1, 1 dc in base ch] 59 (63, 67) times evenly across bottom edge to bottom right edge corner, 1 dc in same corner, turn.

Rows 2 to 4: Work rows 2 to 4 of lace border st.
Fasten off.

Left Front Edging

With WS facing, attach yarn to bottom left edge (of bottom edging just worked). Working along short edge of bottom edging, then along the side of the left front, work row 1.

Row 1 (WS): Ch 3, 1 dc in next st, [ch 1, 1 dc in next st] 39 (39, 43) times evenly to top left front corner, 1 dc in same corner, turn.

Rows 2 to 4: Work rows 2 to 4 of lace border st.
Fasten off.

Right Front Edging

Work same as for Left Front Edging, but beg Row 1 at top Right Front Edge corner.

Collar

With WS facing, attach yarn to same corner as the last dc of Row 1 of Left Front Edging (do not pick up sts along left front edging for collar). Working along the left front neckline, then back neckline, then right front neckline, work row 1.

Row 1 (RS of Collar): Ch 3, 1 dc in next st, [ch 1, 1 dc in next st] 27 (31, 35) times evenly along neckline to right front top corner (do not pick up sts along right front edging for collar), 1 dc in same corner, turn.

Row 2 (Inc row): Ch 3, 1 dc in 1st st, ch 1, 1 dc in next st, ch 1, 1 dc in next ch-1 sp, *ch 1, 1 dc in next st; rep from * to last 2 ch-1 sps, ch 1, 1 dc in next ch-1 sp, ch 1, 1 dc in next st, ch 1, 2 dc in top of t-ch, turn: 31 (35, 39) ch-1 sps.

Row 3: Ch 3, sk 1st st, 1 dc in next st, *ch 1, 1 dc in next st; rep from * ending with 1 dc in top of t-ch, turn.

Row 4 (Inc row): Rep row 2: 35 (39, 43) ch-1 sps.

Row 5: Work row 2 of lace border st.

Row 6: Ch 3, sk 1st st, 1 dc in next ch-2 sp, ch 1, sk next Dc2Cl, 1 dc in next dc, ch 1, sk 1 dc, 1 dc in next dc, *ch 1, (1 dc, ch 1, 1 dc) in next ch-4 sp, ch 1, sk next Dc2Cl, 1 dc in next dc, ch 1, sk 1 dc, 1 dc in next dc; rep from * to last 2 sts, ch 1, 2 dc in t-ch sp, turn.

Rows 7 to 9: Work rows 2 to 4 of lace border st.
Fasten off.

Sew buttons along left front lace border edging to match every other ch-4 sp from row 2 of right front lace border edging. If using full ball pearl buttons as shown, reinforce and tighten buttonholes to fit using sewing thread.

Lightly steam. Weave in all loose ends.

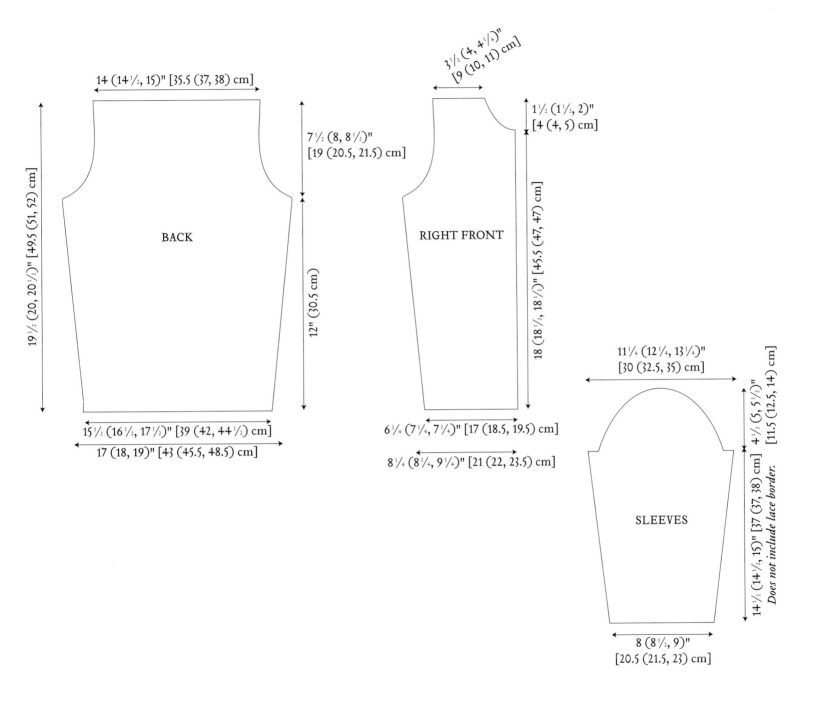

14 (14 1/2, 15)" [35.5 (37, 38) cm]

7 1/2 (8, 8 1/2)"
[19 (20.5, 21.5) cm]

BACK

19 1/2 (20, 20 1/2)" [49.5 (51, 52) cm]

12" (30.5 cm)

15 1/2 (16 1/2, 17 1/2)" [39 (42, 44 1/2) cm]

17 (18, 19)" [43 (45.5, 48.5) cm]

3 1/2 (4, 4 1/4)"
[9 (10, 11) cm]

1 1/2 (1 1/2, 2)"
[4 (4, 5) cm]

RIGHT FRONT

18 (18 1/2, 18 1/2)" [45.5 (47, 47) cm]

6 3/4 (7 1/4, 7 3/4)" [17 (18.5, 19.5) cm]

8 1/4 (8 3/4, 9 1/4)" [21 (22, 23.5) cm]

11 1/4 (12 3/4, 13 3/4)"
[30 (32.5, 35) cm]

4 1/2 (5, 5 1/2)"
[11.5 (12.5, 14) cm]

SLEEVES

14 1/2 (14 1/2, 15)" [37 (37, 38) cm]
Does not include lace border.

8 (8 1/2, 9)"
[20.5 (21.5, 23) cm]

Romantic Summer Shawl

Finished Size

Width: 56" (142 cm), measured across top
Length: 18½" (47 cm), measured down the
center; excluding fringe. One size.

Materials

A medium worsted-weight tape yarn:
total yardage required: 672 yd (614.5 m).

Shown:

Crystal Palace Yarns Mikado Ribbon
(50% Cotton, 50% Viscose; approx 112
yd [102 m] per 1¾ oz [50 g] ball);
#2681 Vintage Rose, 6 balls.

Size K/10½ (7 mm) crochet hook or
size to obtain gauge.

Notions

Yarn tapestry needle

Gauge

Base of 1 triple puff st to base of next
triple puff stitch = 2¾" (7 cm) and 6
rows = 3½" (9 cm) in lace pattern st
using size K/10½ (7 mm) crochet hook.
Take time to check gauge.
NOTE: To work a Puff st: [yo, insert
hook, yo and draw a lp through] 3
times (7 lps on hook); yo, draw thru
all 7 lps on hook, ch 1 to close puff st.

LACE PATTERN STITCH

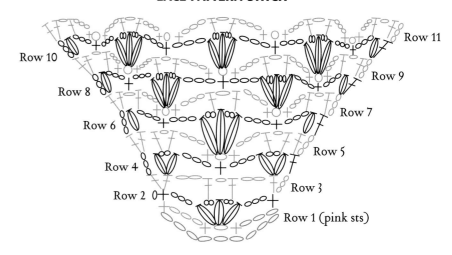

Repeat rows 8 and 9 for lace pattern stitch.

Stitches and Techniques Used

(See page 134–140)

Single crochet, double crochet, multiple stitches into 1 stitch, puff st, working into an arch, fringe.

Lace Pattern Stitch

Starting at lower point, ch 12.

Row 1: Sk 1st 6 ch, 1 sc in next ch, ch 1, sk 1 ch, 1 sc in next ch, ch 3, sk 2 ch, 1 sc in last ch, turn.

Row 2: Ch 1, 1 sc in 1st sc, ch 3, sk next ch-3 sp, sk next sc, (1 Puff st, ch 2, 1 Puff st, ch 2, 1 Puff st) in next ch-1 sp, ch 3, sk next sc, sk next 2 ch, 1 sc in next ch of t-ch, turn.

Row 3: Ch 3, 1 dc in 1st sc, ch 2, sk next ch-3 sp, sk next Puff st, 1 dc in next ch-2 sp, ch 1, sk next Puff st, 1 dc in next ch-2 sp, ch 2, sk next Puff st, sk next ch-3 sp, 2 dc in last sc, turn.

Row 4: Ch 3, sk 1st dc, (1 Puff st, ch 2, 1 Puff st) in next dc, ch 3, sk next ch-2 sp, sk next dc, 1 sc in next ch-1 sp, ch 3, sk next dc, sk next ch-2 sp, (1 Puff st, ch 2, 1 Puff st) in next dc, 1 dc in top of t-ch, turn.

Row 5: Ch 3, 1 dc in 1st dc, sk next Puff

st, (1 dc, ch 1, 1 dc) in next ch-2 sp, ch 3, sk next Puff st, 1 sc in next ch-3 sp, ch 1, sk next sc, 1 sc in next ch-3 sp, ch 3, sk next Puff st, (1 dc, ch 1, 1 dc) in next ch-2 sp, sk next Puff st, 2 dc in top of t-ch, turn.

Row 6: Ch 3, sk 1st dc, 1 Puff st in next dc, ch 3, sk next dc, 1 sc in next ch-1 sp, ch 3, sk next dc, sk next ch-3 sp, sk next sc, (1 Puff st, ch 2, 1 Puff st, ch 2, 1 Puff st) in next ch-1 sp, ch 3, sk next sc, sk next ch-3 sp, sk next dc, 1 sc in next ch-1 sp, ch 3, sk next dc, 1 Puff st in next dc, 1 dc in top of t-ch, turn.

Row 7: Ch 3, 1 dc in 1st dc, ch 1, sk next Puff st, (1 dc, ch 3, 1 sc) in next ch-3 sp, ch 1, sk next sc, 1 sc in next ch-3 sp, ch 3, sk next Puff st, 1 dc in next ch-2 sp, ch 1, sk next Puff st, 1 dc in next ch-2 sp, ch 3, sk next Puff st, 1 sc in next ch-3 sp, ch 1, sk next sc, (1 sc, ch 3, 1 dc) in next ch-3 sp, ch 1, sk next Puff st, 2 dc in top of t-ch, turn.

Row 8: Ch 3, 1 Puff st in 1st dc, ch 3, sk next dc, 1 sc in next ch-1 sp, ch 3, *sk next dc, sk next ch-3 sp, sk next sc, (1 Puff st, ch 2, 1 Puff st, ch 2, 1 Puff st) in next ch-1 sp, ch 3, sk next sc, sk next ch-3 sp, sk next dc, 1 sc in next ch-1 sp, ch 3; rep from * ending with sk last dc, (1 Puff st, 1 dc) in top of t-ch, turn.

Row 9: Ch 3, 1 dc in 1st dc, ch 1, sk next Puff st, (1 dc, ch 3, 1 sc) in next ch-3 sp, *ch 1, sk next sc, 1 sc in next ch-3 sp, ch 3, sk next Puff st, 1 dc in next ch-2 sp, ch 1, sk next Puff st, 1 dc in next ch-2 sp, ch 3, sk next Puff

st, 1 sc in next ch-3 sp; rep from * ending with ch 1, sk next sc, (1 sc, ch 3, 1 dc) in next ch-3 sp, ch 1, sk last Puff st, 2 dc in top of t-ch, turn. Rep rows 8 and 9 for lace pattern st.

Shawl

Ch 12 and follow lace pattern st until 43 rows completed, or until shawl is desired width at the top, ending with an odd-numbered row.
Fasten off.

Finishing

Cut 14" (35.5 cm) lengths of yarn for fringe. Using 3 strands for each fringe, attach fringe to each end of each odd-numbered row (e.g. Row 1, 3, 5, etc.), attach to the ch-3 sp at one side edge of shawl and the sp created by the final dc on the other side edge. Attach one fringe to the ch-1 sp at the bottom tip of shawl.

Weave in all loose ends.

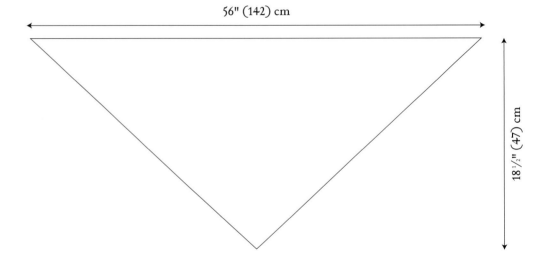

56" (142) cm

18½" (47) cm

Bold Lace Cardigan

To Fit Bust Size
35-37" (89-94 cm)

Finished Bust Size
36" (91.5 cm)

Materials

A thick and thin bulky-weight yarn in wool and acrylic blend: total yardage required 552 yd (504 m).

Shown:

Katia Dulce Plus (50% Wool, 50% Acrylic; approx 46 yd [42 m] per 1¾ oz [50 g] ball):
#55 Stone, 12 balls.

Size N/15 (10 mm) crochet hook or size to obtain gauge.

Notions

Tapestry needle; four 55 Ligne (1⅜" [3.5 cm]) buttons; sewing thread; sewing needle.

Shown:

Four resin leaf buttons #1351 from The Button Store at www.hushcobuttons.com.

Gauge

1 pattern repeat = 3½" (9 cm) measured from 1 sc to next sc in open pattern st using size N/15 (10 mm) crochet hook. 4 rows = 4" (10 cm) in open pattern st. Take time to check gauge.

Stitches And Techniques Used

(See pages 134–140)
Slip st, single crochet, double crochet, treble, multiple stitches into 1 stitch, working into an arch, working around the front and back stem of a stitch, sewing pieces together.

Special Abbreviations

1dc/rf (or FPdc) = work 1 dc around the front of the stem (post) of the dc in the previous row, which will cause the dc to lie in the front of the work.

OPEN PATTERN STITCH

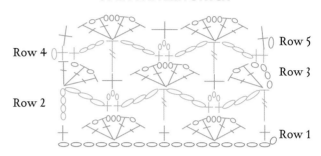

Repeat rows 2-5 for open pattern stitch.

SINGLE RIB PATTERN STITCH

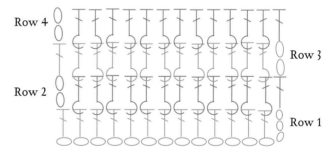

Repeat row 2 for single rib pattern stitch.

1dc/rb (or BPdc) = work 1 dc around the back of the stem (post) of the dc in the previous row, which will cause the dc to lie in the back of the work.

Pattern Stitches

Open Pattern Stitch

Ch a multiple of 8 plus 2 extra.

Row 1 (RS): Sk 1st ch, 1 sc in next ch, *sk 3 ch, (1 dc, ch 1, 1 dc, ch 3, 1 dc, ch 1, 1 dc) in next ch, sk 3 ch, 1 sc in next ch; rep from * to end, turn.

Row 2 (WS): Ch 7 (counts as 1 tr, ch 3), sk 1 st sc, *sk [1 dc, ch-1 sp, 1 dc], (1 sc, ch 3, 1 sc) in next ch-3 sp, ch 3, sk [1 dc, ch-1 sp, 1 dc], 1 tr in next sc, ch 3; rep from * ending by omitting ch 3 at end of last rep, turn.

Row 3: Ch 4 (counts as 1 dc, ch 1), (1 dc, ch 1, 1 dc) in 1st tr, sk next ch-3 sp, sk next sc, 1 sc in next ch-3 sp, *sk next sc, sk ch-3, (1 dc, ch 1, 1 dc, ch 3, 1 dc, ch 1, 1 dc) in next tr, sk next ch-3 sp, sk next sc, 1 sc in next ch-3 sp; rep from * to last sc and t-ch, sk next sc, sk 3 ch, (1 dc, ch 1, 1 dc, ch 1, 1 dc) in next ch of t-ch, turn.

Row 4: Ch 1, 1 sc in 1st dc, 1 sc in next ch-1 sp, ch 3, sk [1 dc, ch 1, 1 dc], 1 tr in next sc, *ch 3, sk [1 dc, ch 1, 1 dc], (1 sc, ch 3, 1 sc) in next ch-3 sp, ch 3, sk [1 dc, ch 1, 1 dc], 1 tr in next sc; rep from * to last 3 dc, ch 3, sk [1 dc, ch 1, 1 dc], 2 sc in t-ch sp, turn.

Row 5: Ch 1, 1 sc in 1st sc, *sk next sc, sk ch-3 sp, (1 dc, ch 1, 1 dc, ch 3, 1 dc, ch 1, 1 dc) in next tr, sk next ch-3 sp, sk next sc, 1 sc in next ch-3 sp; rep from * to end placing last sc in last sc, turn. Rep rows 2 through 5 for open pattern st.

Single Rib Pattern Stitch

Ch a multiple of 2 plus 2 extra.

Row 1: Sk 1st 3 ch, 1 dc in next and each ch to end, turn.

Row 2: Ch 2 (count as 1 dc), sk 1st dc, *1dc/rf around next st, 1dc/rb around next st; rep from * ending with 1 dc in top of t-ch, turn. Rep row 2 for single rib pattern st.

Back

Note: Open fan = 1 (1 dc, ch 1, 1 dc, ch 3, 1 dc, ch 1, 1 dc) stitch grouping. The basic open patt stitch is modified slightly to accommodate number of stitches required for size. Follow Open Pattern Stitch rows only when instructions specify to do so.
Ch 45.

Row 1 (RS): Sk 1st 4 ch, (1 dc, ch 1, 1 dc) in next ch, *sk 3 ch, 1 sc in next ch, sk 3 ch, (1 dc, ch 1, 1 dc, ch 3, 1 dc, ch 1, 1 dc) in next ch; rep from * ending with sk 3 ch, 1 sc in next ch, sk 3 ch, (1 dc, ch 1, 1 dc) in next ch, turn.

Row 2 (WS): Work row 4 of open pattern st.

Row 3: Work row 5 of open pattern st: 5 open fans.

Row 4: Work row 2 of open pattern st.

Shape waist:

Row 5 (Dec begins): Ch 4 (counts as 1 dc, ch 1), 1 dc in 1st tr, sk next ch-3 sp, 1 sc in next ch-3 sp, *(1 dc, ch 1, 1 dc, ch 3, 1 dc, ch 1, 1 dc) in next tr, sk next ch-3 sp, 1 sc in next ch-3 sp; rep from * to t-ch sp, sk 3 ch, (1 dc, ch 1, 1 dc) in next ch of t-ch, turn.

Row 6: Ch 1, 1 sc in 1st dc, ch 1, *1 tr in next sc, ch 3, (1 sc, ch 3, 1 sc) in next ch-3 sp, ch 3; rep from * ending with ch 1, 1 sc in 3rd ch of t-ch, turn.

Row 7: Sl st in 1st sc, sl st in next ch-1 sp, sl st in next tr, ch 4, (1 dc, ch 1, 1 dc) in same tr, *sk next ch-3 sp, 1 sc in next ch-3 sp, sk next ch-3 sp, (1 dc, ch 1, 1 dc, ch 3, 1 dc, ch 1, 1 dc) in next tr; rep from * ending last rep with (1 dc, ch 1, 1 dc, ch 1, 1 dc) in last tr, turn. Dec completed: 4 open fans.

Row 8: Work row 2 of open pattern st.

Row 9: Work row 5 of open pattern st.

Shape bust:

Row 10 (Inc begins): Ch 4, 1 tr in 1st sc, *ch 3, (1 sc, ch 3, 1 sc) in next ch-3 sp, ch 3, 1 tr in next sc; rep from * ending with 1 tr in same sc as last tr, turn.

Row 11: Ch 4, sk 1st tr, (1 dc, ch 3, 1 dc, ch 1, 1 dc) in next tr, *sk next ch-3 sp, 1 sc in next ch-3 sp, (1 dc, ch 1, 1 dc, ch 3, 1 dc, ch 1, 1 dc) in next tr; rep from * ending last rep with last dc placed in 4th ch of t-ch, turn.

Row 12: Ch 7 (counts as 1 tr, ch 3), *(1 sc, ch 3, 1 sc) in next ch-3 sp, ch 3, 1 tr in next sc, ch 3; rep from * to last fan, (1 sc, ch 3, 1 sc) in next ch-3 sp, ch 3, 1 tr

in 3rd ch of t-ch, turn; inc completed;
5 open fans (count on next row).

Row 13: Work row 3 of open pattern st.

Row 14: Work row 4 of open pattern st.

Row 15: Work row 5 of open pattern st.

Shape armholes:

Row 16: Sl st in 1st 2 sts, sl sl in next ch-1 sp, sl st in next st, sl st in next ch-3 sp, ch 1, 2 sc in same ch-3 sp, ch 3, 1 tr in next sc, *ch 3, (1 sc, ch 3, 1 sc) in next ch-3 sp, ch 3, 1 tr in next sc; rep from * to last open fan, ch 3, 2 sc in next ch-3 sp, sk last 2 sts and last ch-1 sp, turn.

Row 17: Work row 5 of open pattern st; shaping completed: 4 open fans.

Row 18: Work row 2 of open pattern st.

Row 19: Work row 3 of open pattern st.

Row 20: Work row 4 of open pattern st.

Row 21: Work row 5 of open pattern st.

Row 22: Work row 2 of open pattern st.

Left Front

Ch 21.

Row 1 (RS): Sk 1st 4 ch, (1 dc, ch 1, 1 dc) in next ch, sk 3 ch, 1 sc in next ch, sk 3 ch, (1 dc, ch 1, 1 dc, ch 3, 1 dc, ch 1, 1 dc) in next ch, sk 3 ch, 1 sc in next ch, sk 3 ch, (1 dc, ch 1, 1 dc) in next ch, turn.

Row 2 (WS): Work row 4 of open pattern st.

Row 3: Work row 5 of open pattern st: 2 open fans.

Row 4: Work row 2 of open pattern st.

Shape waist:

Row 5 (Dec begins): Ch 4 (counts as 1 dc, ch 1), 1 dc in 1st tr, sk next ch-3 sp, 1 sc in next ch-3 sp, (1 dc, ch 1, 1 dc, ch 3, 1 dc, ch 1, 1 dc) in next tr, sk next ch-3 sp, 1 sc in next ch-3 sp, sk 3 ch, (1 dc, ch 1, 1 dc) in next ch of t-ch, turn.

Row 6: Ch 1, 1 sc in 1st dc, 1 sc in next ch-1 sp, 1 tr in next sc, ch 3, (1 sc, ch 3, 1 sc) in next ch-3 sp, ch 3, 1 tr in next sc, ch 1, 1 sc in 3rd ch of t-ch, turn.

Row 7: Sl st in 1st sc, sl st in next ch-1 sp, sl st in next tr, ch 4, (1 dc, ch 1, 1 dc) in same tr, sk next ch-3 sp, 1 sc in next ch-3 sp, sk next ch-3 sp, (1 dc, ch 1, 1 dc, ch 3, 1 dc, ch 1, 1 dc) in next tr, sk next ch-3 sp, sk next sc, 1 sc in next sc, turn; dec completed: 1½ open fans.

Row 8: Ch 7 (counts as 1 tr, ch 3), sk next ch-1 sp, (1 sc, ch 3, 1 sc) in next ch-3 sp, ch 3, 1 tr in next sc, ch 3, 2 sc in t-ch sp, turn.

Row 9: Ch 1, 1 sc in 1st sc, sk next ch-3 sp, (1 dc, ch 1, 1 dc, ch 3, 1 dc, ch 1, 1 dc) in next tr, sk next ch-3 sp, 1 sc in next ch-3 sp, (1 dc, ch 1, 1 dc, ch 1, 1 dc) in 4th ch of t-ch, turn.

Shape bust:

Row 10 (Inc begins): Ch 1, 1 sc in 1st dc, 1 sc in next ch-1 sp, ch 3, 1 tr in next sc, ch 3, (1 sc, ch 3, 1 sc) in next ch-3 sp, ch 3, 2 tr in next sc, turn.

Row 11: Ch 4, sk 1st tr, (1 dc, ch 3, 1 dc, ch 1, 1 dc) in next tr, sk next ch-3 sp, 1 sc in next ch-3 sp, (1 dc, ch 1, 1 dc, ch 3, 1 dc, ch 1, 1 dc) in next tr, sk next ch-3 sp, sk next sc, 1 sc in next sc, turn.

Row 12: Ch 7 (counts as 1 tr, ch 3), (1 sc, ch 3, 1 sc) in next ch-3 sp, ch 3, 1 tr in next sc, ch 3, (1 sc, ch 3, 1 sc) in next ch-3 sp, ch 3, 1 tr in 3rd ch of t-ch, turn; inc completed: 2 open fans (count on next row).

Row 13: Ch 4 (counts as 1 dc, ch 1), (1 dc, ch 1, 1 dc) in 1st tr, sk next ch-3 sp, 1 sc in next ch-3 sp, (1 dc, ch 1, 1 dc, ch 3, 1 dc, ch 1, 1 dc) in next tr, sk next ch-3 sp, 1 sc in next ch-3 sp, (1 dc, ch 1, 1 dc, ch 1, 1 dc) in 4th ch of t-ch, turn.

Row 14: Ch 1, 1 sc in 1st dc, 1 sc in next ch-1 sp, ch 3, 1 tr in next sc, ch 3, sk next ch-1 sp, (1 sc, ch 3, 1 sc) in next ch-1 sp, ch 3, 1 tr in next sc, ch 3, sk next ch-1 sp, 2 sc in t-ch sp, turn.

Row 15: Ch 1, 1 sc in 1st sc, sk next ch-3 sp, (1 dc, ch 1, 1 dc, ch 3, 1 dc, ch 1, 1 dc) in next tr, sk next ch-3 sp, 1 sc in next ch-3 sp, sk next ch-3 sp, (1 dc, ch 1, 1 dc, ch 3, 1 dc, ch 1, 1 dc) in next tr, sk next ch-3 sp, sk next sc, 1 sc in next sc, turn.

Shape armholes:

Row 16: Ch 7, (1 sc, ch 3, 1 sc) in next ch-3 sp, ch 3, 1 tr in next sc, ch 3, 2 sc in next ch-3 sp, sk last 2 sts, sk next ch-1 sp, turn.

Row 17: Ch 1, 1 sc in 1st sc, sk next ch-3 sp, (1 dc, ch 1, 1 dc, ch 3, 1 dc, ch 1, 1 dc) in next tr, sk next ch-3 sp, 1 sc in next ch-3 sp, (1 dc, ch 1, 1 dc, ch 1, 1 dc) in 4th ch of t-ch, turn; shaping completed: 1½ open fans.

Row 18: Ch 1, 1 sc in 1st dc, 1 sc in next ch-1 sp, ch 3, 1 tr in next sc, ch 3, sk next ch-1 sp, (1 sc, ch 3, 1 sc) in next ch-1 sp, ch 3, 1 tr in next sc, turn.

Row 19: Ch 4 (counts as 1 dc, ch 1), (1 dc, ch 1, 1 dc) in 1st tr, sk next ch-3 sp, 1 sc in next ch-3 sp, (1 dc, ch 1, 1 dc, ch 3, 1 dc, ch 1, 1 dc) in next tr, sk next ch-3 sp, sk next sc, 1 sc in next sc, turn.

Row 20: Ch 7 (counts as 1 tr, ch 3), sk next ch-1 sp, (1 sc, ch 3, 1 sc) in next ch-3 sp, ch 3, 1 tr in next sc, ch 3, 2 sc in t-ch sp, turn.

Begin neck shaping:

Row 21: Ch 1, 1 sc in 1st sc, sk next ch-3 sp, (1 dc, ch 1, 1 dc, ch 3, 1 dc, ch 1, 1 dc) in next tr, sk next ch-3 sp, 1 sc in next ch-3 sp, sk next sc and t-ch, turn.

Row 22: Ch 5, (1 sc, ch 3, 1 sc) in next ch-3 sp, ch 3, 1 tr in next sc.
Fasten off.

Right Front
Ch 21.

Row 1 (RS): Sk 1st 4 ch, (1 dc, ch 1, 1 dc) in next ch, *sk 3 ch, 1 sc in next ch, sk 3 ch, (1 dc, ch 1, 1 dc, ch 3, 1 dc, ch 1, 1 dc) in next ch; rep from * ending with sk 3 ch, 1 sc in next ch, sk 3 ch, (1 dc, ch 1, 1 dc) in next ch, turn.

Row 2 (WS): Work row 4 of open pattern st.

Row 3: Work row 5 of open pattern st: 2 open fans.

Row 4: Work row 2 of open pattern st.

Shape waist:

Row 5 (Dec begins): Ch 4 (counts as 1 dc, ch 1), (1 dc, ch 1, 1 dc) in 1st tr, sk next ch-3 sp, 1 sc in next ch-3 sp, (1 dc, ch 1, 1 dc, ch 3, 1 dc, ch 1, 1 dc) in next tr, sk next ch-3 sp, 1 sc in next ch-3 sp, sk 3 ch, (1 dc, ch 1, 1 dc) in next ch of t-ch, turn.

Row 6: Ch 1, 1 sc in 1st dc, ch 1, 1 tr in next sc, ch 3, (1 sc, ch 3, 1 sc) in next ch-3 sp, ch 3, 1 tr in next sc, ch 3, 2 sc in t-ch sp, turn.

Row 7: Ch 1, 1 sc in 1st sc, sk next ch-3 sp, (1 dc, ch 1, 1 dc, ch 3, 1 dc, ch 1, 1 dc) in next tr, sk next ch-3 sp, 1 sc in next ch-3 sp, (1 dc, ch 1, 1 dc, ch 1, 1 dc) in last tr, turn; dec completed: 1½ open fans.

Row 8: Ch 1, 1 sc in 1st dc, 1 sc in next ch-1 sp, ch 3, 1 tr in next sc, ch 3, sk next ch-1 sp, (1 sc, ch 3, 1 sc) in next ch-1 sp, ch 3, 1 tr in next sc, turn.

Row 9: Ch 4 (counts as 1 dc, ch 1), (1 dc, ch 1, 1 dc) in 1st tr, sk next ch-3 sp, 1 sc in next ch-3 sp, (1 dc, ch 1, 1 dc, ch 3, 1 dc, ch 1, 1 dc) in next tr, sk next ch-3 sp, sk next sc, 1 sc in next sc, turn.

Row 10: Ch 7, (1 sc, ch 3, 1 sc) in next ch-3 sp, ch 3, 1 tr in next sc, ch 3, 2 sc in t-ch sp, turn.

Shape bust:

Row 11 (Inc begins): Ch 1, 1 sc in 1st sc, (1 dc, ch 3, 1 dc, ch 1, 1 dc) in next tr, sk next ch-3 sp, 1 sc in next ch-3 sp, (1 dc, ch 1, 1 dc, ch 3, 1 dc, ch 1, 1 dc) in 4th ch of t-ch, turn.

Row 12: Ch 7 (counts as 1 tr, ch 3), (1 sc, ch 3, 1 sc) in next ch-3 sp, ch 3, 1 tr in next sc, ch 3, (1 sc, ch 3, 1 sc) in next ch-3 sp, ch 3, 1 tr in next sc, turn; inc completed: 2 open fans (count on next row).

Row 13: Ch 4 (counts as 1 dc, ch 1), (1 dc, ch 1, 1 dc) in 1st tr, sk next ch-3 sp, 1 sc in next ch-3 sp, (1 dc, ch 1, 1 dc, ch 3, 1 dc, ch 1, 1 dc) in next tr, sk next ch-3 sp, 1 sc in next ch-3 sp, (1 dc, ch 1, 1 dc, ch 1, 1 dc) in 4th ch of t-ch, turn.

Row 14: Ch 1, 1 sc in 1st dc, 1 sc in next ch-1 sp, ch 3, 1 tr in next sc, ch 3, sk next ch-1 sp, (1 sc, ch 3, 1 sc) in next ch-1 sp, ch 3, 1 tr in next sc, ch 3, sk next ch-1 sp, 2 sc in t-ch sp, turn.

Row 15: Ch 1, 1 sc in 1st sc, sk next ch-3 sp, (1 dc, ch 1, 1 dc, ch 3, 1 dc, ch 1, 1 dc) in next tr, sk next ch-3 sp, 1 sc in next ch-3 sp, sk next ch-3 sp, (1 dc, ch 1, 1 dc, ch 3, 1 dc, ch 1, 1 dc) in next tr, sk next ch-3 sp, sk next sc, 1 sc in next sc, turn.

Shape armholes:

Row 16: Sl st in 1st 2 sts, sl sl in next ch-1 sp, sl st in next st, sl st in next ch-3 sp, ch 1, 2 sc in same ch-3 sp, ch 3, 1 tr in next sc, ch 3, (1 sc, ch 3, 1 sc) in next ch-3 sp, ch 3, 1 tr in next sc, turn.

Row 17: Ch 4 (counts as 1 dc, ch 1), (1 dc, ch 1, 1 dc) in 1st tr, sk next ch-3 sp, 1 sc in next ch-3 sp, (1 dc, ch 1, 1 dc, ch 3, 1 dc, ch 1, 1 dc) in next tr, sk next ch-3 sp, sk next sc, 1 sc in next sc, turn; shaping completed: 1½ open fans.

Row 18: Ch 7 (counts as 1 tr, ch 3), sk next ch-1 sp, (1 sc, ch 3, 1 sc) in next ch-3 sp, ch 3, 1 tr in next sc, ch 3, 2 sc in t-ch sp, turn.

Row 19: Ch 1, 1 sc in 1st sc, sk next ch-3 sp, (1 dc, ch 1, 1 dc, ch 3, 1 dc, ch 1, 1 dc) in next tr, sk next ch-3 sp, 1 sc in next ch-3 sp, (1 dc, ch 1, 1 dc, ch 1, 1 dc) in 4th ch of t-ch, turn.

Row 20: Ch 1, 1 sc in 1st dc, 1 sc in next ch-1 sp, ch 3, 1 tr in next sc, ch 3, sk next ch-1 sp, (1 sc, ch 3, 1 sc) in next ch-1 sp, ch 3, 1 tr in next sc, turn.

Row 21: Sl st in 1st tr, sk sl in next 3 ch, sl st in next sc, sl st in next ch-3 sp, ch 1, 1 sc in same ch-3 sp, (1 dc, ch 1, 1 dc, ch 3, 1 dc, ch 1, 1 dc) in next tr, sk next ch-3 sp, sk next sc, 1 sc in next sc, turn.

Row 22: Ch 7, (1 sc, ch 1, 1 dc) in next ch-3 sp, ch 1, 1 tr in next sc.
Fasten off.

Sleeves

Ch 20.

Work in single rib pattern st for 3 rows.

Begin open pattern st.

Row 1: Ch 1, 1 sc in 1st dc, [sk 2 dc, (1 dc, ch 1, 1 dc, ch 3, 1 dc, ch 1, 1 dc) in next dc, sk 2 dc, 1 sc in next dc] 2 times, sk 1 dc, (1 dc, ch 1, 1 dc, ch 3, 1 dc, ch 1, 1 dc) in next dc, sk 2 dc, 1 sc in next dc, turn.

Row 2: Work row 2 of open pattern st.

Rows 3 to 9: Continue in open pattern st.

Row 10 (Inc begins): Ch 4, 1 tr in 1st sc, *ch 3, (1 sc, ch 3, 1 sc) in next ch-3 sp, ch 3, 1 tr in next sc; rep from * ending with 1 tr in same sc as last tr, turn.

Row 11: Ch 4, sk 1st tr, (1 dc, ch 3, 1 dc, ch 1, 1 dc) in next tr, *sk next ch-3 sp, 1 sc in next ch-3 sp, (1 dc, ch 1, 1 dc, ch 3, 1 dc, ch 1, 1 dc) in next tr; rep from * ending last rep with last dc placed in 4th ch of t-ch, turn.

Shape sleeve cap:

Row 12: Sl st in 1st dc, sl st in next ch-1 sp, sl st in next dc, sl st in next ch-3 sp, ch 1, 2 sc in same ch-3 sp, ch 3, 1 tr in next sc, *ch 3, (1 sc, ch 3, 1 sc) in next ch-3 sp, ch 3, 1 tr in next sc; rep from * to last open fan, ch 3, 2 sc in next ch-3 sp, sk next dc and t-ch, turn.

Row 13: Work row 5 of open pattern st: 3 open fans.

Row 14: Ch 5, [(1 sc, ch 3, 1 sc) in next ch-3 sp, ch 3, 1 tr in next sc, ch 3] 2 times, (1 sc, ch 3, 1 sc) in next ch-3 sp, ch 1, 1 tr in next sc, turn.

Row 15: Ch 3, 1 sc in next ch-3 sp, [(1 dc, ch 1, 1 dc, ch 3, 1 dc, ch 1, 1 dc) in next tr, sk next ch-3 sp, 1 sc in next ch-3 sp] 2 times, 1 dc in 4th ch of t-ch, turn.

Row 16: Ch 5, (1 sc, ch 3, 1 sc) in next ch-3 sp, ch 3, 1 tr in next sc, ch 3, (1 sc, ch 3, 1 sc) in next ch-3 sp, ch 1, 1 tr in top of t-ch, turn.

Row 17: Ch 3, 1 sc in next ch-3 sp, (1 dc, ch 1, 1 dc, ch 3, 1 dc, ch 1, 1 dc) in next tr, sk next ch-3 sp, 1 sc in next ch-3 sp, 1 dc in 4th ch of t-ch, turn. Fasten off.

Make second sleeve same as the first.

Finishing

Sew side and shoulder seams. Sew sleeve seams and fit-in sleeves.

Edging

With RS facing, work 36 dc along right front edge. Work in single rib pattern st for 3 rows. Fasten off.

With RS facing, work 36 dc along left front edge. Work in single rib pattern st for 3 rows. Do not fasten off. Turn corner counter-clockwise (RS facing) and work 1 row of sc evenly along bottom edge. Fasten off.

Collar

With WS facing, work 13 dc evenly along left front neck edge, beginning at outer corner of left front edging. Continue, working 22 dc evenly along back neck edge, then 13 dc evenly along right front neck edge to outer corner of right front edging.

Work 7 rows of single rib pattern st.

Fasten off.

Button bars

Ch 11.

Row 1: Sk 1st 4 ch, 1 sc in each of next 4 ch, sk 3 ch, sl st in next ch. Fasten off. Make 2nd button bar same as the first.

Sew button bars securely to right front edge, the first one 4¾" (12 cm) from the base of the collar, the second one 10" (25.5 cm) from the base of the collar. Sew the buttons on using sewing thread and sewing needle.

Lightly steam. Weave in all loose ends.

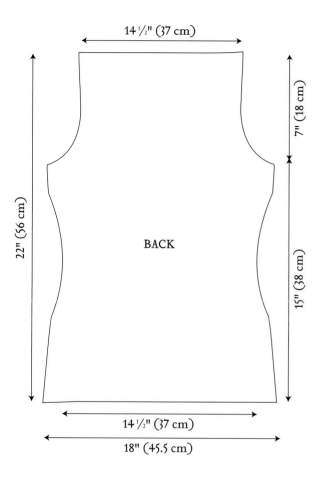

14 1/2" (37 cm)

7" (18 cm)

22" (56 cm)

BACK

15" (38 cm)

14 1/2" (37 cm)

18" (45.5 cm)

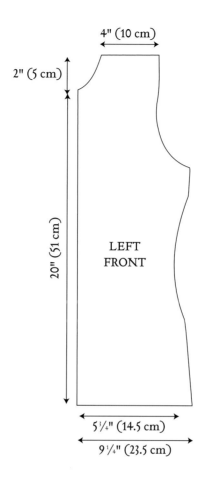

4" (10 cm)

2" (5 cm)

20" (51 cm)

LEFT
FRONT

5 3/4" (14.5 cm)

9 1/4" (23.5 cm)

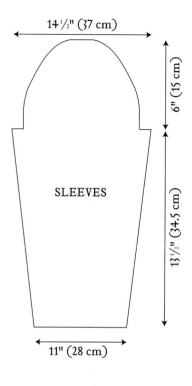

14 1/2" (37 cm)

6" (15 cm)

SLEEVES

13 1/2" (34.5 cm)

11" (28 cm)

Ruffled-Strap Tank

To Fit Bust Size

33-34½ (36½-38, 40-41½)" [84-87.5 (92.5-96.5, 101.5-105.5) cm]

Finished Bust Size

32½ (36, 39½)" [82.5 (91.5, 100.5) cm]
Sizes: Small, Medium, and Large
Size Small shown.

Materials

A light-weight alpaca blend yarn:
Color A total yardage required: 432 (432, 540) yd [395 (395, 494) m];
Color B total yardage required: 216 (216, 324) yd [198 (198, 296.5) m].

Shown:

Classic Elite Miracle (50% Alpaca, 50% Tencel; approx 108 yd [99 m] per 1¾ oz [50 g] per ball):
Color A: #3329 Fundy Bay Blue, 4 (4, 5) balls;
Color B: #3392 Geneva Blue, 2 (2, 3) balls.

Size H/8 (5 mm) crochet hook or size to obtain gauge.

Notions

Yarn tapestry needle

Gauge

Five pinwheels [i.e., each ([1 dc, ch 1] 4 times, 1 dc) group as counted on the odd rows of pinwheel lace pattern st] = 9" (23 cm) and approx 7 rows = 3" (7.5 cm) in pinwheel lace pattern st using size H/8 (5 mm) crochet hook. Take time to check gauge.

Stitches and Techniques Used

(See pages 134-140)

Slip st, single crochet, double crochet, multiple stitches into 1 stitch, cluster st, working into an arch, sewing pieces together.

Pattern Stitches

Pinwheel Lace Pattern Stitch

Notes:

1. To work a "Dc2Cl" (a 2-dc cluster), work 1 dc where specified until 2 lps remain on hk, work 2nd dc where specified until 3 lps remain on hk, yo, draw through 3 lps on hk. The 2 partial dc's

PINWHEEL LACE PATTERN STITCH

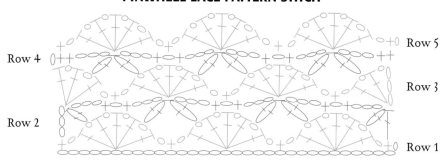

Repeat rows 2 through 5 for pinwheel lace pattern stitch.

may be worked in different sts/sps or in the same st/sp.

2. When working on top of a Dc3Cl or Dc4Cl, work into the closing ch. When working on top of a Dc2Cl, work into the top of the Dc2Cl as if it were a dc.

3. To count a pinwheel after shaping, each pinwheel is a ([1 dc, ch 1] 4 times, 1 dc) group.

Ch a multiple of 10 plus 2 extra.

Row 1 (RS): Work 1 sc in 2nd ch from hk, *ch 1, sk 4 ch, ([1 dc, ch 1] 5 times) in next ch, sk 4 ch, 1 sc in next ch; rep from * to end, turn.

Row 2 (WS): Ch 3, sk 1st sc, sk next ch-1 sp, sk next dc, 1 Dc2Cl in next ch-1 sp, ch 3, sk next dc, 1 sc in next ch-1 sp, ch 1, sk next dc, 1 sc in next ch-1 sp, ch 3, *sk next dc, 1 Dc4Cl as follows— 1 Dc2Cl in next ch-1 sp until 3 lps remain on hk, sk next dc, sk next ch-1 sp, sk next sc, sk next ch-1 sp, sk next

dc, 1 Dc2Cl in next ch-1 sp until 5 lps total on hk, yo, pull through all 5 lps, ch 1 to close the "Dc4Cl," ch 3, sk next dc, 1 sc in next ch-1 sp, ch 1, sk next dc, 1 sc in next ch-1 sp, ch 3; rep from * ending with sk next dc, 1 Dc3Cl as follows—1 Dc2Cl in next ch-1 sp until 3 lps remain on hk, sk next dc, sk next ch-1 sp, 1 dc in next sc until 4 lps total on hk, yo, pull through all 4 lps, ch 1 to close the "Dc3Cl," turn.

Row 3: Ch 4, (1 dc, ch 1, 1 dc) in 1st Dc3Cl, ch 1, *sk next ch-3 sp, sk next sc, 1 sc in next ch-1 sp, ch 1, sk next sc, sk next ch-3 sp, ([1 dc, ch 1] 5 times) in next Dc4Cl; rep from * ending with sk next ch-3 sp, sk next sc, 1 sc in next ch-1 sp, ch 1, sk next sc, sk next ch-3 sp, (1 dc, ch 1, 1 dc, ch 1, 1 dc) in last Dc2Cl, turn.

Row 4: Ch 1, 1 sc in 1st dc, 1 sc in next ch-1 sp, ch 3, *sk next dc, 1 Dc4Cl as in Row 2 over next 1st and 4th ch-1 sps, ch 3, sk next dc, 1 sc in next ch-1 sp, ch 1, sk next dc, 1 sc in next ch-1 sp, ch 3; rep from * ending last rep with 2 sc in t-ch sp, turn.

Row 5: Ch 1, 1 sc in 1st sc, ch 1, *sk next sc, sk next ch-3 sp, ([1 dc, ch 1] 5 times) in next Dc4Cl, sk next ch-3 sp, sk next sc, 1 sc in next ch-1 sp, ch 1; rep from * ending last rep with 1 sc in last sc, turn.

Rep rows 2 through 5 for pinwheel lace pattern stitch.

Back

With A, ch 92 (102, 112).

Work in pinwheel patt st for 10 rows: 9 (10, 11) pinwheels (count on row 9). Begin dec to shape waist as follows:

Row 11: Ch 4, 1 dc in 1st Dc3Cl, ch 1, *sk next ch-3 sp, sk next sc, 1 sc in next ch-1 sp, ch 1, sk next sc, sk next ch-3 sp, ([1 dc, ch 1] 5 times) in next Dc4Cl; rep from * ending with sk next ch-3 sp, sk next sc, 1 sc in next ch-1 sp, ch 1, sk next sc, sk next ch-3 sp, (1 dc, ch 1, 1 dc) in last Dc2Cl, turn.

Row 12: Ch 3, *sk next dc, 1 Dc4Cl over next 1st and 4th ch-1 sps, ch 3, sk next dc, 1 sc in next ch-1 sp, ch 1, sk next dc, 1 sc in next ch-1 sp, ch 3; rep from * ending with sk next dc, 1 Dc4Cl over next 1st ch-1 sp and t-ch sp, 1 dc in same t-ch sp, turn.

Row 13: Ch 4, sk 1st dc, (1 dc, ch 1, 1 dc) in 1st Dc4Cl, ch 1, *sk next ch-3 sp, sk next sc, 1 sc in next ch-1 sp, ch 1, sk next sc, sk next ch-3 sp, ([1 dc, ch 1] 5 times) in next Dc4Cl; rep from * ending last rep with ([1 dc, ch 1] 2 times) in last Dc4Cl, 1 dc in t-ch sp, turn. Decrease complete: 8 (9, 10) pinwheels (counting 2 half-pinwheels at ends as 1 pinwheel).

Row 14: Work row 4 of pinwheel pattern st.

Row 15: Work row 5 of pinwheel patt.

Rows 16 to 19: Work rows 2 to 5 of pinwheel patt st.

Rows 20: Work row 2 of pinwheel patt st.

Begin increases for chest shaping as follows:

Row 21: Ch 4, ([1 dc, ch 1] 3 times) in 1st Dc3Cl, *sk next ch-3 sp, sk next sc, 1 sc in next ch-1 sp, ch 1, sk next sc, sk next ch-3 sp, ([1 dc, ch 1] 5 times) in next Dc4Cl; rep from * ending last rep with ([1 dc, ch 1] 3 times, 1 dc) in last Dc2Cl, change to B, turn. Work in B for remaining rows of back.

Row 22: Ch 4, *sk next dc, 1 sc in next ch-1 sp, ch 1, sk next dc, 1 sc in next ch-1 sp, ch 3, sk next dc, 1 Dc4Cl over next 1st and 4th ch-1 sps, ch 3; rep from * ending with sk next dc, 1 sc in next ch-1 sp, sk next dc, (1 sc, ch 1, 1 dc) in t-ch sp, turn.

Row 23: Ch 4, 1 dc in 1st dc, ch 1, sk next ch-1 sp, *sk next sc, 1 sc in next ch-1 sp, ch 1, sk next sc, sk next ch-3 sp, ([1 dc, ch 1] 5 times) in next Dc4Cl, sk next ch-3 sp; rep from * ending with sk next sc, 1 sc in next ch-1 sp, ch 1, sk next sc, sk next ch-3 sp, (1 dc, ch 1, 1 dc) in t-ch sp, turn.

Row 24: Ch 1, 1 sc in 1st dc, ch 3, *1 Dc4Cl over next 1st and 4th ch-1 sps, ch 3, sk next dc, 1 sc in next ch-1 sp, ch 1, sk next dc, 1 sc in next ch-1 sp, ch 3, sk next dc; rep from * ending last rep with 1 Dc4Cl over next 1st ch-1 sp and t-ch sp, (ch 3, 1 sc) in same t-ch sp, turn.

Row 25: Ch 1, 1 sc in 1st sc, ch 1, *sk next ch-3 sp, ([1 dc, ch 1] 5 times) in next Dc4Cl, sk next ch-3 sp, sk next sc, 1 sc in next ch-1 sp, ch 1, sk next sc; rep from * ending last rep with 1 sc in last sc, turn.

Row 26 to 28: Rep rows 2 through 4 of pinwheel patt st.

Row 29: Ch 1, sk 1st sc, 1 sc in next sc, 2 sc in next ch-3 sp, 1 sc in next Dc4Cl, *2 sc in next ch-3 sp, 1 sc in next sc, sk next ch-1 sp, 1 sc in next sc, 2 sc in next ch-3 sp, 1 sc in next Dc4Cl; rep from * ending with 2 dc in next ch-3 sp, 1 sc in each of last 2 sc. Fasten off.

Front

Work same as for BACK through row 28. Fasten off.

Work all remaining rows of front in B.

For Size Small Only

Left Side of Bodice

Shape armholes and neckline as follows:

Row 29: With RS facing, attach B to 1st Dc4Cl, ch 4, 1 dc in same Dc4Cl, ch 1, sk next ch-3 sp, sk next sc, 1 sc in next sc, *ch 1, sk next sc, sk next ch-3 sp, ([1 dc, ch 1] 5 times) in next Dc4Cl, sk next ch-3 sp, sk next sc, 1 sc in next ch-1 sp; rep from * 2 times, turn: 3⅓ pinwheels.

Row 30: Ch 1, sk 1st sc, [sl st in next ch-1 sp, sl st in next dc] 2 times, ch 1, *1 sc in next ch-1 sp, ch 1, sk next dc, 1 sc in next ch-1 sp, ch 3, sk next dc, 1 Dc4Cl over next 1st and 4th ch-1 sps, ch 3, sk next dc; rep from * 1 time, 1 sc in next ch-1 sp, ch 1, sk next dc, 1 sc in next ch-1 sp, ch 3, sk next dc, 1 Dc4Cl over next ch-1 sp and t-ch sp, ch 3, 1 sc in same t-ch sp, turn.

Row 31: Ch 1, 1 sc in 1st sc, ch 1, sk next ch-3 sp, ([1 dc, ch 1] 4 times) in next Dc4Cl, sk next ch-3 sp, sk next sc, 1 sc in next ch-1 sp, *ch 1, sk next sc, sk next ch-3 sp, ([1 dc, ch 1] 5 times) in next Dc4Cl, sk next ch-3 sp, sk next sc, 1 sc in next ch-1 sp; rep from * 1 time, turn: 2⅔ pinwheels.

Row 32: Ch 1, sk 1st sc, [sl st in next ch-1 sp, sl st in next dc] 2 times, ch 1, *1 sc in next ch-1 sp, ch 1, sk next dc, 1 sc in next ch-1 sp, ch 3, sk next dc, 1 Dc4Cl over next 1st and 4th ch-1 sps, ch 3, sk next dc; rep from * 1 time, 1 sc in next ch-1 sp, ch 1, sk next dc, 1 sc in next ch-1 sp, turn.

Row 33: Ch 1, sk next sc, 1 sc in next ch-1 sp, *ch 1, sk next sc, sk next ch-3 sp, ([1 dc, ch 1] 5 times) in next Dc4Cl, sk next ch-3 sp, sk next sc, 1 sc in next ch-1 sp; rep from * 1 time, turn: 2 pinwheels.

Row 34: Ch 1, sk 1st sc, [sl st in next ch-1 sp, sl st in next dc] 2 times, ch 1, 1 sc in next ch-1 sp, ch 1, sk next dc, 1 sc in next ch-1 sp, ch 3, sk next dc, 1 Dc4Cl over next 1st and 4th ch-1 sps, ch 3, sk next dc, 1 sc in next ch-1 sp, ch 1, sk next dc, 1 sc in next ch-1 sp, ch 1, sk next dc, 1 Dc3Cl over next ch-1 sp and last sc, turn.

Row 35: Ch 4, 1 dc in 1st Dc3Cl, ch 1, sk next ch-1 sp, sk next sc, 1 sc in next ch-1 sp, ch 1, sk next sc, sk next ch-3 sp, ([1 dc, ch 1] 5 times) in next Dc4Cl, sk next ch-3 sp, sk next sc, 1 sc in next ch-1 sp, turn: 1⅓ pinwheels.

Row 36: Ch 1, sk 1st sc, [sl st in next ch-1 sp, sl st in next dc] 2 times, ch 1, 1 sc in next ch-1 sp, ch 1, sk next dc, 1 sc in next ch-1 sp, ch 3, sk next dc, 1 Dc4CL over next ch-1 sp and t-ch sp, turn.

Row 37: Ch 4, 1 Dc2Cl over 1st Dc4Cl and last ch-1 sp.

Do not fasten off. Continue to crochet left strap as follows:
Ch 46, turn.

Row 1: 1 sc in 2nd ch from hk and in each ch across, sl st to top of Row 37 to make strap more secure, turn: 45 sc. (Ch fewer or more sts to adjust strap length for personal fit.)

Row 2: Ch 1, 1 sc in each sc across. Fasten off.

Right Side of Bodice

Shape armholes and neckline as follows:

Row 29: With RS facing, return to where row 29 of the left bodice ended, sk next sc, sk next ch-3 sp, sk next Dc4Cl, sk next ch-3 sp, attach B to next sc, ch 1, 1 sc in next ch-1 sp, ch 1, *sk next sc, sk next ch-3 sp, ([1 dc, ch 1] 5 times) in next Dc4Cl, sk next ch-3 sp, sk next sc, 1 sc in next ch-1 sp, ch 1; rep from * 2 times, sk next sc, sk next ch-3 sp, (1 dc, ch 1, 1 dc) in next Dc4Cl, turn: 3⅓ pinwheels.

Row 30: Ch 1, 1 sc in 1st dc, ch 3, 1 Dc4Cl over next 1st and 4th ch-1 sps, ch 3, sk next dc, 1 sc in next ch-1 sp, ch 1, sk next dc, 1 sc in next ch-1 sp, *ch 3, sk next dc, 1 Dc4Cl over next 1st and 4th ch-1 sps, ch 3, sk next dc, 1 sc in next ch-1 sp, ch 1, sk next dc, 1 sc in next ch-1 sp; rep from * 1 time, turn.

Row 31: Ch 1, sk 1st sc, *1 sc in next ch-1 sp, ch 1, sk next sc, sk next ch-3 sp, ([1 dc, ch 1] 5 times) in next Dc4Cl, sk next ch-3 sp, sk next sc; rep from * 1 time, 1 sc in next ch-1 sp, ch 1, sk next sc, sk next ch-3 sp, ([1 dc, ch 1] 4 times) in next Dc4Cl, sk next ch-3 sp, 1 sc in next sc, turn: 2⅔ pinwheels.

Row 32: Ch 1, sk 1st sc, sl st in next ch-1 sp, sl st in next dc, ch 1, *1 sc in next ch-1 sp, ch 1, sk next dc, 1 sc in next ch-1 sp, ch 3, sk next dc, 1 Dc4Cl over next 1st and 4th ch-1 sps, ch 3, sk next dc; rep from * 1 time, 1 sc in next ch-1 sp, ch 1, sk next dc, 1 sc in next ch-1 sp, turn.

Row 33: Ch 1, sk 1st sc, *1 sc in next ch-1 sp, ch 1, sk next sc, sk next ch-3 sp, ([1 dc, ch 1] 5 times) in next Dc4Cl, sk next ch-3 sp, sk next sc; rep from * 1 time, 1 sc in next ch-1 sp, turn: 2⅛ pinwheels.

Row 34: Ch 3, sk 1st sc, sk next ch-1 sp, sk next dc, 1 Dc2Cl in next ch-1 sp, ch 1, sk next dc, 1 sc in next ch-1 sp, ch 1, sk next dc, 1 sc in next ch-1 sp, ch 3, sk next dc, 1 Dc4Cl over next 1st and 4th ch-1 sps, ch 3, sk next dc, 1 sc in next ch-1 sp, ch 1, sk next dc, 1 sc in next ch-1 sp, turn.

Row 35: Ch 1, sk 1st sc, 1 sc in next ch-1 sp, ch 1, sk next sc, sk next ch-3 sp, ([1 dc, ch 1] 5 times) in next Dc4Cl, sk next ch-3 sp, sk next sc, 1 sc in next ch-1 sp, ch 1, sk next sc, sk next ch-1 sp, (1 dc, ch 1, 1 dc) in next Dc2Cl, turn: 1⅛ pinwheels.

Row 36: Ch 3, 1 Dc3Cl over next 1st and 4th ch-1 sps, ch 3, sk next dc, 1 sc in next ch-1 sp, ch 1, sk next dc, 1 sc in

next ch-1 sp, turn.

Row 37: Ch 3, sk 1st sc, 1 Dc2Cl over next next ch-1 sp and next Dc3Cl.

Do not fasten off. Continue to crochet right strap as follows:
Ch 46, turn.

Row 1: 1 sc in 2nd ch from hk and in each ch across, sl st to top of Row 37 to make strap more secure, turn: 45 sc. (Ch fewer or more sts to adjust strap length for personal fit.)

Row 2: Ch 1, 1 sc in each sc across. Fasten off.

For Size Medium Only

Left Side of Bodice
Shape armholes and neckline as follows:

Row 29: With RS facing, attach B to 1st Dc4Cl, ch 4, 1 dc in same Dc4Cl, ch 1, sk next ch-3 sp, sk next sc, 1 sc in next sc, *ch 1, sk next sc, sk next ch-3 sp, ([1 dc, ch 1] 5 times) in next Dc4Cl, sk next ch-3 sp, sk next sc, 1 sc in next ch-1 sp; rep from * 2 times, ch 1, sk next sc, sk next ch-3 sp, (1 dc, ch 1, 1 dc) in next Dc4Cl, turn: 3⅔ pinwheels (⅓ at each end).

Row 30: Ch 3, sk 1st dc, 1 Dc4Cl over next 1st and 4th ch-1 sps, ch 3, sk next dc, *1 sc in next ch-1 sp, ch 1, sk next dc, 1 sc in next ch-1 sp, ch 3, sk next dc, 1 Dc4Cl over next 1st and 4th ch-1 sps, ch 3, sk next dc; rep from * 1 time, 1 sc in next ch-1 sp, ch 1, sk next sc, 1 sc in next ch-1 sp, ch 1, sk next dc, 1 Dc4Cl over next ch-1 sp and next t-ch, ch 3, 1 sc in same t-ch sp, turn.

Row 31: Ch 1, 1 sc in 1st sc, ch 1, sk next ch-3 sp, ([1 dc, ch 1] 4 times) in next Dc4Cl, sk next ch-3 sp, sk next sc, 1 sc in next ch-1 sp, *ch 1, sk next sc, sk next ch-3 sp, ([1 dc, ch 1] 5 times) in next Dc4Cl, sk next ch-3 sp, sk next sc, 1 sc in next ch-1 sp; rep from * 1 time, ch 1, sk next sc, sk next ch-3 sp, (1 dc, ch 1, 1 dc) in top of t-ch, turn: 3 pinwheels total.

Row 32: Ch 3, sk 1st dc, 1 Dc4Cl over next 1st and 4th ch-1 sps, ch 3, sk next dc, *1 sc in next ch-1 sp, ch 1, sk next dc, 1 sc in next ch-1 sp, ch 3, sk next dc, 1 Dc4Cl over next 1st and 4th ch-1 sps, ch 3, sk next dc; rep from * 1 time, 1 sc in next ch-1 sp, ch 1, sk next dc, 1 sc in next ch-1 sp, turn.

Row 33: Ch 1, sk 1st sc, 1 sc in next ch-1 sp, *ch 1, sk next sc, sk next ch-3 sp, ([1 dc, ch 1] 5 times) in next Dc4Cl, sk next ch-3 sp, sk next sc, 1 sc in next ch-1 sp; rep from * 1 time, ch 1, sk next sc, sk next ch-3 sp, (1 dc, ch 1, 1 dc) in top of t-ch, turn: 2⅛ pinwheels.

Row 34: Ch 3, sk 1st dc, 1 Dc4Cl over next 1st and 4th ch-1 sps, ch 3, sk next dc, 1 sc in next ch-1 sp, ch 1, sk next dc, 1 sc in next ch-1 sp, ch 3, sk next dc, 1 Dc4Cl over next 1st and 4th ch-1 sps, ch 3, sk next dc, 1 sc in next ch-1 sp, ch 1, sk next dc, 1 sc in next ch-1 sp, ch 1, sk next dc, 1 Dc3Cl over next ch-1 sp and last sc, turn.

Row 35: Ch 4, 1 dc in 1st Dc3Cl, ch 1, sk next ch-1 sp, sk next sc, 1 sc in next ch-1 sp, ch 1, sk next sc, sk next ch-3 sp, ([1 dc, ch 1] 5 times) in next Dc4Cl, sk next ch-3 sp, sk next sc, 1 sc in next ch-1 sp, ch 1, sk next sc, sk next ch-3 sp, (1 dc, ch 1, 1 dc) in top of t-ch, turn: 1⅔ pinwheels.

Row 36: Ch 3, sk 1st dc, 1 Dc4Cl over next 1st and 4th ch-1 sps, ch 3, sk next dc, 1 sc in next ch-1 sp, ch 1, sk next dc, 1 sc in next ch-1 sp, ch 3, sk next dc, 1 Dc4Cl over next ch-1 sp and t-ch sp, turn.

Row 37: Ch 4, (1 dc, ch 1, 1 dc) in 1st Dc4Cl, ch 1, sk next ch-3 sp, sk next sc, 1 sc in next ch-1 sp, ch 1, sk next sc, sk next ch-3 sp, (1 dc, ch 1, 1 dc) in top of t-ch, turn: ⅔ pinwheel total.

Row 38: Ch 3, sk 1st dc, 1 Dc4Cl over next 1st and 4th ch-1 sps, ch 1, sk next dc, 1 dc in t-ch sp, turn.

Row 39: Ch 3, sk 1st dc, 1 Dc2Cl over next ch-1 sp and top of t-ch.

Do not fasten off. Continue to crochet left strap as follows:
Ch 51, turn.

Row 1: 1 sc in 2nd ch from hk and in each ch across, sl st to top of Row 39 to make strap more secure, turn: 50 sc. (Ch fewer or more sts to adjust strap length for personal fit.)

Row 2: Ch 1, 1 sc in each sc across. Fasten off.

Right Side of Bodice
Shape armholes and neckline as follows:
Row 29: With RS facing, return to where row 29 of the left bodice ended, sk next ch-3 sp, sk next sc, sk next ch-1 sp, sk next sc, sk next ch-3 sp, attach B to next Dc4Cl, ch 4, 1 dc in same Dc4Cl,

ch 1, sk next ch-3 sp, sk next sc, 1 sc in next ch-1 sp, ch 1, *sk next sc, sk next ch-3 sp, ([1 dc, ch 1] 5 times) in next Dc4Cl, sk next ch-3 sp, sk next sc, 1 sc in next ch-1 sp, ch 1; rep from * 2 times, sk next sc, sk next ch-3 sp, (1 dc, ch 1, 1 dc) in next Dc4Cl, turn: 3⅔ pinwheels (⅓ at each end).

Row 30: Ch 1, 1 sc in 1st dc, ch 3, 1 Dc4Cl over next 1st and 4th ch-1 sps, ch 3, sk next dc, 1 sc in next ch-1 sp, ch 1, sk next dc, 1 sc in next ch-1 sp, *ch 3, sk next dc, 1 Dc4Cl over next 1st and 4th ch-1 sps, ch 3, sk next dc, 1 sc in next ch-1 sp, ch 1, sk next dc, 1 sc in next ch-1 sp; rep from * 1 time, ch 3, sk next dc, 1 Dc4Cl over next ch-1 sp and t-ch sp, 1 dc in same t-ch sp, turn.

Row 31: Ch 4, sk 1st dc, 1 dc in next Dc4Cl, ch 1, sk next ch-3 sp, sk next sc, *1 sc in next ch-1 sp, ch 1, sk next sc, sk next ch-3 sp, ([1 dc, ch 1] 5 times) in next Dc4Cl, sk next ch-3 sp, sk next sc; rep from * 1 time, 1 sc in next ch-1 sp, ch 1, sk next sc, sk next ch-3 sp, ([1 dc, ch 1] 4 times) in next Dc4Cl, sk next ch-3 sp, 1 sc in last sc, turn: 3 pinwheels total.

Row 32: Ch 1, sk 1st sc, sl st in next ch-1 sp, sl st in next dc, ch 1, *1 sc in next ch-1 sp, ch 1, sk next dc,1 sc in next ch-1 sp, ch 3, sk next dc, 1 Dc4Cl over next 1st and 4th ch-1 sps, ch 3, sk next dc; rep from * 1 time, 1 sc in next ch-1 sp, ch 1, sk next dc, 1 sc in next ch-1 sp, ch 3, sk next dc, 1 Dc4Cl over next ch-1 sp and t-ch sp, 1 dc in same t-ch sp, turn.

Row 33: Ch 4, sk 1st dc, 1 dc in next Dc4Cl, ch 1, sk next ch-3 sp, sk next sc, *1 sc in next ch-1 sp, ch 1, sk next sc, sk next ch-3 sp, ([1 dc, ch 1] 5 times) in next Dc4Cl, sk next ch-3 sp, sk next sc; rep from * 1 time, 1 sc in next ch-1 sp, turn: 2⅓ pinwheels.

Row 34: Ch 3, sk 1st sc, sk next ch-1 sp, sk next dc, 1 Dc2Cl in next ch-1 sp, ch 1, sk next dc, 1 sc in next ch-1 sp, ch 1, sk next dc, 1 sc in next ch-1 sp, ch 3, sk next dc, 1 Dc4Cl over next 1st and 4th ch-1 sps, ch 3, sk next dc, 1 sc in next ch-1 sp, ch 1, sk next dc, 1 sc in next ch-1 sp, ch 3, sk next dc, 1 Dc4Cl over next ch-1 sp and t-ch sp, 1 dc in same t-ch sp, turn.

Row 35: Ch 4, sk 1st dc, 1 dc in next Dc4Cl, ch 1, sk next ch-3 sp, sk next sc, 1 sc in next ch-1 sp, ch 1, sk next sc, sk next ch-3 sp, ([1 dc, ch 1] 5 times) in next Dc4Cl, sk next ch-3 sp, sk next sc, 1 sc in next ch-1 sp, ch 1, sk next sc, sk next ch-1 sp, (1 dc, ch 1, 1 dc) in last Dc2Cl, turn: 1⅔ pinwheels.

Row 36: Ch 3, sk 1st dc, 1 Dc3Cl over next 1st and 4th ch-1 sps, ch 3, sk next dc, 1 sc in next ch-1 sp, ch 1, sk next dc, 1 sc in next ch-1 sp, ch 3, sk next dc, 1 Dc4Cl over next ch-1 sp and t-ch sp, 1 dc in same t-ch sp, turn.

Row 37: Ch 4, sk 1st dc, 1 dc in next Dc4Cl, ch 1, sk next ch-3 sp, sk next sc, 1 sc in next ch-1 sp, ch 1, sk next sc, sk next ch-3 sp, (1 dc, ch 1, 1 dc) in next Dc3Cl, ch 1, 1 dc in top of t-ch, turn: ⅔ pinwheel total.

Row 38: Ch 3, sk 1st dc, sk next ch-1 sp,

sk next dc, 1 Dc4Cl over next ch-1 sp and t-ch sp, 1 dc in same t-ch sp, turn.

Row 39: Ch 3, sk 1st dc, 1 Dc2Cl over next Dc4Cl and top of t-ch.

Do not fasten off. Continue to crochet right strap as follows:
Ch 51, turn.

Row 1: 1 sc in 2nd ch from hk and in each ch across, sl st to top of Row 36 to make strap more secure, turn: 50 sc. (Ch fewer or more sts to adjust strap length for personal fit.)

Row 2: Ch 1, 1 sc in each sc across. Fasten off.

For Size Large Only

Left Side of Bodice
Shape armholes and neckline as follows:

Row 29: With RS facing, attach B to 1st Dc4Cl, ch 4, 1 dc in same Dc4Cl, ch 1, sk next ch-3 sp, sk next sc, 1 sc in next ch-1 sp, *ch 1, sk next sc, sk next ch-3 sp, ([1 dc, ch 1] 5 times) in next Dc4Cl, ch 1, sk next ch-3 sp, sk next sc, 1 sc in next ch-1 sp; rep from * 3 more times, turn: 4⅓ pinwheels.

Row 30: Ch 1, sk 1st sc, [sl st in next ch-1 sp, sl st in next dc] 2 times, ch 1, *1 sc in next ch-1 sp, ch 1, sk next dc, 1 sc in next ch-1 sp, ch 3, sk next dc, 1 Dc4Cl over next 1st and 4th ch-1 sps, ch 3, sk next dc; rep from * 2 times, 1 sc in next ch-1 sp, ch 1, sk next dc, 1 sc in next ch-1 sp, ch 3, sk next dc, 1 Dc4Cl over next ch-1 sp and t-ch sp, ch 3, 1 sc in same t-ch sp, turn.

Row 31: Ch 1, 1 sc in 1st sc, ch 1, sk next ch-3 sp, ([1 dc, ch 1] 4 times) in next Dc4Cl, sk next ch-3 sp, sk next sc, 1 sc in next ch-1 sp, *ch 1, sk next sc, sk next ch-3 sp, ([1 dc, ch 1] 5 times) in next Dc4Cl, ch 3, sk next dc, 1 sc in next ch-1 sp, ch 1, sk next dc, 1 sc in next ch-1 sp; rep from * 2 times, turn: 3⅔ pinwheels.

Row 32: Ch 1, sk 1st sc, [sl st in next ch-1 sp, sl st in next dc] 2 times, ch 1, *1 sc in next ch-1 sp, ch 1, sk next dc, 1 sc in next ch-1 sp, ch 3, sk next dc, 1 Dc4Cl over next 1st and 4th ch-1 sps, ch 3, sk next dc; rep from * 2 times, 1 sc in next ch-1 sp, ch 1, sk next dc, 1 sc in next ch-1 sp, turn.

Row 33: *Ch 1, sk next sc, 1 sc in next ch-1 sp, ch 1, sk next sc, sk next ch-3 sp, ([1 dc, ch 1] 5 times) in next Dc4Cl, sk next ch-3 sp, sk next sc, 1 sc in next ch-1 sp; rep from * 2 times, turn: 3 pinwheels.

Row 34: Ch 1, sk 1st sc, [sl st in next ch-1 sp, sl st in next dc] 2 times, ch 1, 1 sc in next ch-1 sp, ch 1, sk next dc, 1 sc in next ch-1 sp, *ch 3, sk next dc, 1 Dc4Cl over next 1st and 4th ch-1 sps, ch 3, sk next dc, 1 sc in next ch-1 sp, ch 1, sk next dc, 1 sc in next ch-1 sp; rep from * 1 time, ch 1, sk next dc, 1 Dc3Cl over next ch-1 sp and last sc, turn.

Row 35: Ch 4, 1 dc in 1st Dc3Cl, ch 1, sk next ch-1 sp, sk next sc, 1 sc in next ch-1 sp, *ch 1, sk next sc, sk next ch-3 sp, ([1 dc, ch 1] 5 times) in next Dc4Cl, sk next ch-3 sp, sk next sc, 1 sc in next ch-1 sp; rep from * 1 time, turn: 2⅓ pinwheels.

Row 36: Ch 1, sk 1st sc, [sl st in next ch-1 sp, sl st in next dc] 2 times, ch 1, *sc in next ch-1 sp, ch 1, sk next dc, 1 sc in next ch-1 sp, ch 3, sk next dc*, 1 Dc4Cl over next 1st and 4th ch-1 sps, ch 3, sk next dc; rep from * to * once, 1 Dc4Cl over next ch-1 sp and t-ch sp, ch 3, 1 dc in same t-ch sp, turn.

Row 37: Ch 1, 1 sc in 1st sc, ch 1, sk next ch-3 sp, ([1 dc, ch 1] 4 times) in next Dc4Cl, sk next ch-3 sp, sk next sc, 1 sc in next ch-1 sp, ch 1, ([1 dc, ch 1] 5 times) in next Dc4Cl, sk next ch-3 sp, sk next sc, 1 sc in next ch-1 sp, turn: 1⅔ pinwheels.

Row 38: Ch 1, sk 1st sc, [sl st in next ch-1 sp, sl st in next dc] 2 times, ch 1, 1 sc in next ch-1 sp, ch 1, sk next dc, 1 sc in next ch-1 sp, ch 3, sk next dc, 1 Dc4Cl over next 1st and 4th ch-1 sps, ch 3, sk next dc, 1 sc in next ch-1 sp, ch 1, sk next dc, 1 sc in next ch-1 sp, turn.

Row 39: Ch 1, sk 1st sc, 1 sc in next ch-1 sp, ch 1, sk next sc, sk next ch-3 sp, ([1 dc, ch 1] 5 times) in next Dc4Cl, sk next ch-3 sp, sk next sc, 1 sc in next ch-1 sp, turn: 1 pinwheel.

Row 40: Ch 1, sk 1st sc, [sl st in next ch-1 sp, sl st in next dc] 2 times, ch 1, 1 sc in next ch-1 sp, ch 1, sk next dc, 1 sc in next ch-1 sp, ch 3, sk next dc, 1 Dc3Cl over next ch-1 sp and last sc, turn.

Row 41: Ch 3, 1 Dc2Cl over next Dc3Cl and last ch-1 sp.

Do not fasten off. Continue to crochet left strap as follows:
Ch 51, turn.

Row 1: 1 sc in 2nd ch from hk and in each ch across, sl st to top of Row 37 to make strap more secure, turn: 50 sc. (Ch fewer or more sts to adjust strap length for personal fit.)

Row 2: Ch 1, 1 sc in each sc across. Fasten off.

Right Side of Bodice
Shape armholes and neckline as follows:

Row 29: With RS facing, return to where row 29 of the left side of bodice ended, sk next sc, sk next ch-3 sp, sk next Dc4Cl, sk next ch-3 sp, attach B to next sc, ch 1, 1 sc in next ch-1 sp, ch 1, *sk next sc, sk next ch-3 sp, ([1 dc, ch 1] 5 times) in next Dc4Cl, sk next ch-3 sp, sk next sc, 1 sc in next ch-1 sp, ch 1; rep from * 3 times, sk next sc, sk next ch-3 sp, (1 dc, ch 1, 1 dc) in next Dc4Cl, turn: 4⅓ pinwheels.

Row 30: Ch 1, 1 sc in 1st dc, *ch 3, 1 Dc4Cl over next 1st and 4th ch-1 sps, ch 3, sk next dc, 1 sc in next ch-1 sp, ch 1, sk next dc, 1 sc in next ch-1 sp; rep from * 3 times, turn.

Row 31: Ch 1, sk 1st sc, *1 sc in next ch-1 sp, ch 1, sk next sc, sk next ch-3 sp, ([1 dc, ch 1] 5 times) in next Dc4Cl, sk next ch-3 sp, sk next sc; rep from * 2 times, 1 sc in next ch-1 sp, ch 1, sk next sc, sk next ch-3 sp, ([1 dc, ch 1] 4 times) in next Dc4Cl, sk next ch-3 sp, 1 sc in next sc, turn: 3⅔ pinwheels.

Row 32: Ch 1, sk 1st sc, sl st in next ch-1 sp, sl st in next dc, ch 1, *1 sc in next ch-1 sp, ch 1, sk next dc,1 sc in next ch-

1 sp, ch 3, sk next dc, 1 Dc4Cl over next 1st and 4th ch-1 sps, ch 3, sk next dc; rep from * 2 times, 1 sc in next ch-1 sp, sk next dc, 1 sc in next ch-1 sp, turn.

Row 33: Ch 1, sk 1st sc, *1 sc in next ch-1 sp, ch 1, sk next sc, sk next ch-3 sp, ([1 dc, ch 1] 5 times) in next Dc4Cl, sk next ch-3 sp, sk next sc; rep from * 2 times, 1 sc in next sc, turn: 3 pinwheels.

Row 34: Ch 3, sk 1st sc, sk next ch-1 sp, sk next dc, 1 Dc2Cl in next ch-1 sp, ch 1, sk next dc, 1 sc in next ch-1 sp, ch 1, sk next dc, 1 sc in next ch-1 sp, *ch 3, sk next dc, 1 Dc4Cl over next 1st and 4th ch-1 sps, ch 3, sk next dc, 1 sc in next ch-1 sp, ch 1, sk next dc, 1 sc in next ch-1 sp; rep from * 1 time, turn.

Row 35: Ch 1, sk 1st sc, 1 sc in next ch-1 sp, *ch 1, sk next sc, sk next ch-3 sp, ([1 dc, ch 1] 5 times) in next Dc4Cl, sk next ch-3 sp, sk next sc, 1 sc in next ch-1 sp; rep from * 1 time, ch 1, sk next sc, sk next ch-1 sp, (1 dc, ch 1 1 dc) in Dc2Cl, turn: 2⅓ pinwheels.

Row 36: Ch 1, 1 sc in 1st dc, *ch 3, 1 Dc4Cl over next 1st and 4th ch-1 sps, ch 3, sk 1 dc, 1 sc in next ch-1 sp, ch 1, sk next dc, 1 sc in next ch-1 sp, sk next dc; rep from * 1 time, turn.

Row 37: Ch 1, sk 1st sc, 1 sc in next ch-1 sp, ch 1, sk next sc, sk next ch-3 sp, ([1 dc, ch 1] 5 times) in next Dc4Cl, sk next ch-3 sp, sk next sc, 1 sc in next ch-1 sp, ch 1, sk next sc, sk next ch-3 sp, ([1 dc, ch 1] 4 times) in next Dc4Cl, sk next ch-3 sp, 1 sc in last sc, turn: 1⅔ pinwheels.

Row 38: Ch 1, sk 1st sc, sl st in next ch-1

sp, sl st in next dc, ch 1, 1 sc in next ch-1 sp, ch 1, sk next dc, 1 sc in next ch-1 sp, ch 3, sk next dc, 1 Dc4Cl over next 1st and 4th ch-1 sps, ch 3, sk next dc, 1 sc in next ch-1 sp, ch 1, sk next dc, 1 sc in next ch-1 sp, turn.

Row 39: Ch 1, sk 1st sc, 1 sc in next ch-1 sp, ch 1, sk next sc, ([1 dc, ch 1] 5 times) in next Dc4Cl, sk next ch-3 sp, sk next sc, 1 sc in next ch-1 sp, turn: 1 pinwheel.

Row 40: Ch 3, sk 1st sc, sk next ch-1 sp, sk next dc, 1 Dc2Cl in next ch-1 sp, ch 3, sk next dc, 1 sc in next ch-1 sp, ch 1, sk next dc, 1 sc in next ch-1 sp, turn.

Row 41: Ch 3, sk 1st sc, 1 Dc2Cl over next ch-1 sp and last Dc2Cl.

Do not fasten off. Continue to crochet right strap as follows:
Ch 51, turn.

Row 1: 1 sc in 2nd ch from hk and in each ch across, sl st to top of Row 36 to make strap more secure, turn: 50 sc. (Ch fewer or more sts to adjust strap length for personal fit.)

Row 2: Ch 1, 1 sc in each sc across. Fasten off.

Finishing

Sew side seams. Sew straps to back.

Left Armhole and Ruffled Strap Edging

Attach A to top of left side seam with RS facing.

Begin working along armhole edge of left side of bodice as follows:

Ch 1, work 20 (25, 30) sc evenly along left edge of left side of bodice to where strap begins.

Continue row, working ruffled edge along outer edge of strap as follows: 1 sc in 1st st of strap, ch 1, sk next st, *([1 dc, ch 1] 3 times) in next st, sk next 2 sts; rep from * ending last rep with sk 2 (1, 1) st, 1 sc in last st, sl st to back piece where strap is sewn on. Fasten off.

Right Ruffled Strap and Armhole Edging

Work armhole edging similarly for right outer edge, starting at outer edge of back strap and working around to armhole/right edge of right bodice

Neck Edging

Attach A to inner edge of back left strap with RS facing.

Row 1: Ch 1, 1 sc in 1st st of left strap and in each st of strap, 25 (30, 35) sc evenly along neck edge of left bodice, 8 sc along center front neckline, 25 (30, 35) sc along neck edge of right bodice, sl st to back piece where right strap is sewn on. Fasten off.

Bottom Edging

Attach B at bottom right corner (at the seam) of front piece with RS facing.

Rnd 1: Ch 1, 1 sc in base of each pinwheel

and sc and 4 sc in each ch-4 sp around, join with a sl st to 1st sc. Fasten off.

Waist Tie

With A, ch 200 (220, 230). Fasten off. Secure each end with a tight overhand knot and trim yarn end. Weave through row 22, leaving ties out in front as shown in photo.

Weave in all loose ends. Block to shape as necessary.

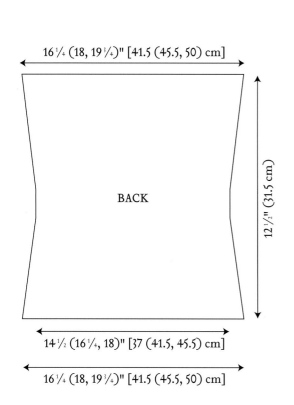

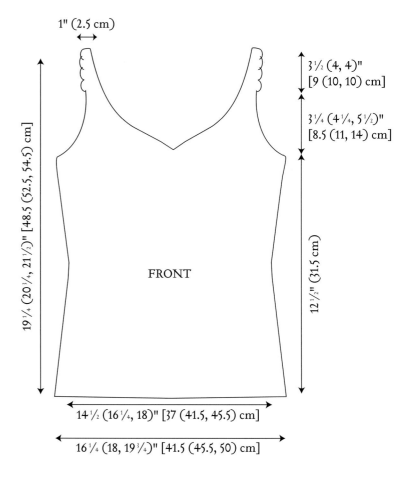

Textured Shaped Purse

Finished Size

Approx. 9" (23 cm) high x 10¼" (26 cm) wide

Materials

A medium worsted-weight wool yarn: total yardage required: 260 yd (238m).

Shown:

Classic Elite Bazic Wool (100% Superwash Wool; approx 65 yd [59.5 m] per 1¾ oz [50 g] ball): #2935 Citrine, 4 balls.

Size I/9 (5.5 mm) crochet hook or size to obtain gauge.

Notions

2 triangular wood purse handles: 6" (15 cm) high x 8½" (21.5 cm) wide; yarn tapestry needle; lining fabric, approx. 20" x 15" (51 x 38 cm); sewing pins; sewing thread to match yarn; sewing needle.

Shown:

Style #27217 Wood Handles in Natural from M&J Trim; satin lining fabric.

Gauge

7 shells = 8" (20.5 cm) and 8 rows = 4 ¼" (11 cm) in diagonal shell pattern st using size I/9 (5.5 mm) crochet hook. Take time to check gauge.

DIAGONAL SHELL PATTERN STITCH

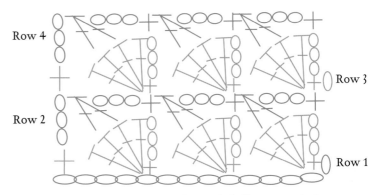

Row 4 / Row 3 / Row 2 / Row 1

Repeat rows 2 and 3 for diagonal shell pattern stitch.

Stitches and Techniques Used

(See pages 134-140)
Single crochet, double crochet, multiple stitches into 1 stitch, cluster st, sewing pieces together.

Special Abbreviations

Shell = (1 sc, ch 3, 4 dc) into same st.
Dc2tog = work 2 dc into sts as indicated until 1 lp of each remains on hk, yo and pull thru all 3 lps on hk.

Pattern Stitches

Diagonal Shell Pattern Stitch

Ch a multiple of 4 plus 2 extra.

Row 1 (RS): 1 shell in 2nd ch from hk, *sk 3 ch, 1 shell in next ch; rep from * to last 4 ch, sk 3 ch, 1 sc in last ch, turn.

Row 2: Ch 3 (counts as 1 dc), sk 1st sc, *sk 1 dc, 1 Dc2tog over next 2 dc, ch 3, sk 1 dc, 1 sc in top of ch-3; rep from * to end, turn.

Row 3: Ch 1, 1 shell in 1st sc, *sk next ch-3 sp, sk next Dc2tog, 1 shell in next sc; rep from * ending with sk ch-3 sp, sk Dc2tog, 1 sc in top of t-ch, turn. Work rows 1 to 3, then rep rows 2 and 3 for diagonal shell pattern st.

Back of Purse

Note: Basic diagonal shell patt is modified on some rows to accommodate shaping. Follow text instructions carefully.

Begin at lower edge with A, ch 22.

Row 1 (RS): 1 shell in 2nd ch from hk, *sk 3 ch, 1 shell in next ch; rep from * to last 4 ch, sk 3 ch, 1 sc in last ch, turn: 5 shells.

Row 2 (WS): Ch 3, sk 1st sc, *sk 1 dc, 1 Dc2tog over next 2 dc, ch 3, sk 1 dc, 1 sc in top of ch-3; rep from * to last shell, sk 1 dc, 1 Dc2tog over next 2 dc, ch 3, sk 1 dc, 1 sc in next dc, 1 sc in top of t-ch, turn.

Row 3: Ch 1, 1 shell in 1st sc, 4 dc in same sc, sk next sc, *sk next ch-3 sp, sk next Dc2tog, 1 shell in next sc; rep from * ending with sk ch-3 sp, sk Dc2tog, 1 shell into top of t-ch, turn: 7 shells (counting 8-dc group as 2 shells).

Row 4: Ch 3, *sk 1 dc, 1 Dc2tog over next 2 dc, ch 3, sk 1 dc, 1 sc in top of ch-3; rep from * to last 9 sts, sk 1 dc, 1 Dc2tog over next 2 dc, ch 3, sk 1 dc, 1 sc in next dc, sk 1 dc, 1 Dc2tog over next 2 dc, ch 3, 1 sc in top of t-ch, turn.

Row 5: Ch 1, 1 shell in 1st sc, 4 dc in same sc, *sk next ch-3 sp, sk next Dc2tog, 1 shell in next sc; rep from * ending with sk ch-3 sp, sk Dc2tog, 1 shell into top of t-ch, turn: 9 shells (counting 8-dc group as 2 shells).

Row 6: Rep row 4.

Row 7: Work row 3 of diagonal shell pattern st: 9 shells.

Row 8: Work row 2 of diagonal shell pattern st.

Rows 9 to 14: Rep rows 3 and 2 of diagonal shell pattern st.

Change to plain dc fabric:

Row 15: Ch 3, sk 1st sc, 2 dc in next ch-3 sp, 1 dc in next Dc2tog, *1 dc in next sc, 2 dc in next ch-3 sp, 1 dc in next Dc2tog; rep from * ending with 1 dc in top of t-ch, turn: 37 dc (counting ch-3 as 1 dc).

Row 16: Ch 3, sk 1st dc, 1 Dc3tog over next 3 dc, 1 dc in each dc to last 4 sts, 1 Dc3tog over next 3 dc, 1 dc in top of t-ch, turn: 33 sts.

Row 17: Rep row 16: 29 sts.

Row 18: Ch 3, sk 1st dc, 1 dc in each dc to end, 1 dc in top of t-ch, turn.

Row 19: Rep row 18.

Fasten off.

Front of Purse

Make same as for BACK.

Finishing

Using one side of purse, trace the purse shape on a piece of paper. Add a ⅜" (1 cm) seam allowance to traced shape along sides and ½" (1.3 cm) at top and cut shape out from paper. Use this paper as a guide to cut lining fabric (see diagram at right) to match shape of purse.

With RS of purse pieces together and WS facing outward, sew bottom and side seams, leaving top 4 rows of back and front unseamed. Turn purse right side out.

Attach one handle by folding one unseamed edge of purse over bottom bar of a handle. Using yarn and yarn needle, stitch in place on WS. Stitch second handle to other edge of purse in the same way.

Weave in all loose ends.

Lining: With RS together, sew lining side seams with sewing thread by hand or machine, leaving top 2" (5 cm) unseamed. Insert lining inside purse with WS of lining facing WS of purse, and fold top edges down so that the top edges align with the crocheted fabric where it is folded over the bottom bar of handle (so lining will cover stitching of crocheted fabric to the handles). Pin in place. Using sewing needle and thread, stitch into place by hand.

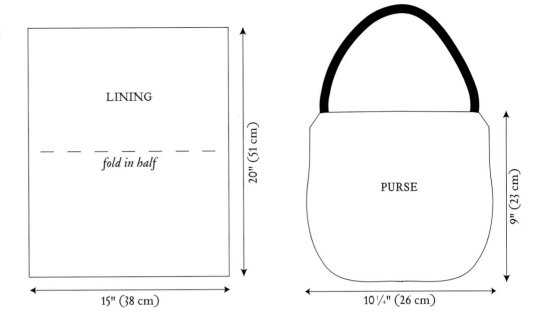

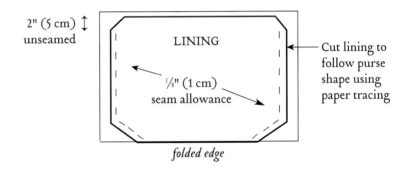

Flirty Skirt

To Fit Hip Size

34-35 (36-37, 38-39, 40-42)" [86.5-89 (91.5-94, 96.5-99, 101.5-106.5) cm]

Finished Hip Size

35 (37, 38½, 42)" [89 (94, 98, 106.5) cm]

Finished Waist Size

28 (30, 31½, 35)" [71 (76, 80, 89) cm]

Sizes: Small, Medium, Large, and X-Large

Note: The wavy scallop hem ruffles slightly for size S. The ruffle is more prominent in sizes M, L, and XL.

Size Small shown.

Materials

A light-weight cotton blend yarn:

Color A total yardage required: 436 (545, 545, 654) yd [400 (500, 500, 600) m];

Color B total yardage required: 327 (327, 436, 436) yd [300 (300, 400, 400) m];

Color C total yardage required: 109 (218, 218, 218) yd [100 (200, 200, 200) m].

Shown:

Cascade Yarns Pima Tencel (50% Pima Cotton, 50% Tencel; approx 109 yd [100 m] per 1¾ oz [50 g] ball):

Color A: #1273 Terra Cotta, 4 (5, 5, 6) balls;

Color B: #3183 Mandarin Orange, 3 (3, 4, 4) balls;

Color C: #0258 Gold (C), 1 (2, 2, 2) balls.

Size H/8 (5 mm) crochet hook or size to obtain gauge.

Notions

Yarn tapestry needle; 3 buttons about ¹¹⁄₁₆" (18 mm) in diameter; sewing needle; sewing thread to match color A.

Gauge

8 (1 sc, 2 dc) groups = 7" (18 cm) and 9 rows = 4" (10 cm) in silt pattern st using size H/8 (5 mm) crochet hook. Take time to check gauge.

Stitches and Techniques Used

(See page 134-140)

Slip st, single crochet, double crochet, treble, double treble, multiple stitches into 1 stitch, sewing pieces together.

WAVY SCALLOP PATTERN STITCH

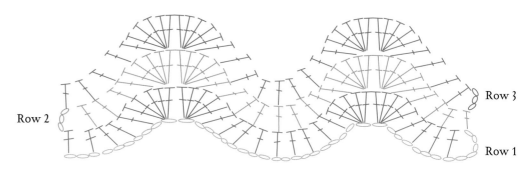

Repeat row 2 for wavy scallop pattern stitch.

SILT PATTERN STITCH

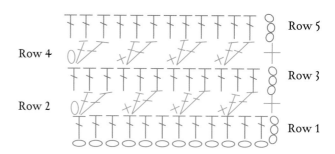

Repeat rows 2 and 3 for silt pattern stitch.

Pattern Stitches

Wavy Scallop Pattern Stitch

Ch a multiple of 19 plus 4 extra.

Row 1: Sk 1st 4 ch, *[sk 1 ch, 1 dc in next ch] 4 times, 5 dc in each of next 2 ch, 1 dc in next ch, [sk 1 ch, 1 dc in next ch] 4 times; rep from * to end, turn.

Row 2: Ch 3, sk 1st dc, *[sk 1 dc, 1 dc in next dc] 4 times, 5 dc in each of next 2 dc, 1 dc in next dc, [sk 1 dc, 1 dc in next dc] 4 times; rep from * ending last rep with last dc in top of t-ch, turn. Rep row 2 for wavy scallop pattern st.

Silt Pattern Stitch

Ch a multiple of 3 plus 3 extra.

Row 1 (RS): Sk 1st 3 ch, 1 dc in next and each ch to end, turn.

Row 2: Ch 1, 2 dc in 1st st, *sk 2 sts, (1 sc, 2 dc) in next st; rep from * to last 3 sts, sk 2 sts, 1 sc in top of t-ch, turn.

Row 3: Ch 3, sk 1st st, 1 dc in next and each st to end, ending with last dc in top of t-ch, turn.

Rep rows 2 and 3 for silt pattern st.

Notes:

1. To change colors, work last st of row until 2 lps remain on hk. Yo using new color and draw through 2 lps on hk.

2. To work a "Dc2Cl" st, work a dc into 2 sts as indicated, leaving last lp of each dc on hk, yo and draw through all 3 lps on hk.

3. To work a "DTr3Cl" st, work a dtr into 3 sts as indicated, leaving last lp of each dtr on hk, yo and draw through all 4 lps on hk.

4. To work a "DTr2Cl" st, work a dtr into 2 sts as indicated, leaving last lp of each dtr on hk, yo and draw through all 3 lps on hk.

Back

With A, ch 118 (137, 137, 156).

Row 1: Work row 1 of wavy scallop pattern st.

Continue in wavy scallop pattern st, changing colors as follows:

Row 2: Cont in A.

Row 3: Cont in A, change to B at end.

Row 4: Cont in B.

Row 5: Cont in B, change to C at end.

Row 6: Cont in C, change to B at end.

Row 7: With B, ch 6, sk next 2 sts, 1 dtr in next st, *ch 1, sk next 2 sts, 1 tr in next st, ch 1, sk next st, 1 dc in next st, ch 1, sk next st, 1 Dc2Cl over next 2 sts, ch 1, sk next st, 1 dc in next st, ch 1, sk next st, 1 tr in next st, ch 1, sk next 2 sts, (work 1st dtr of DTr3Cl in next st, sk next st, work 2nd dtr of DTr3Cl in next st, sk next st, work 3rd dtr of DTr3Cl in next st); rep from * ending last rep with a DTr2Cl, working 2nd dtr in top of t-ch, turn.

Row 8: Ch 3, 1 dc in 1st st, *ch 1, 1 dc in next st; rep from * ending with 1 dc in top of t-ch, turn: 38 (44, 44, 50) dc (not counting ch-3 at beg).

For Size Small Only

Row 9: Ch 3, sk 1 st dc, 1 dc in next dc, *ch 1, 1 dc in next dc; rep from *, 1 dc in top of t-ch, change to A at end, turn.

Rows 10 and 11: With A, rep row 9 twice. Change to B at end of row 11.

For Sizes Medium and Large Only

Row 9: Ch 3, sk 1st dc, 1 dc in next dc, [ch 1, 1 dc in next dc] 8 times, ch 1, 1 Dc2Cl over next 2 dc, [ch 1, 1 dc in next dc] 10 times, ch 1, 1 Dc2Cl over next 2 dc, [ch 1, 1 dc in next dc] 9 times, ch 1, 1 Dc2Cl over next 2 dc, [ch 1, 1 dc in next dc] 9 times, 1 dc in top of t-ch, change to A at end, turn: 41 dc (not counting ch-3 at beg and counting each Dc2Cl as a dc).

Row 10: With A, ch 3, sk 1st dc, 1 dc in next dc, *ch 1, 1 dc in next dc; rep from *, 1 dc in top of t-ch, turn.

For Size Medium Only

Row 11: Ch 3, sk 1st dc, 1 dc in next dc, [ch 1, 1 dc in next dc] 12 times, ch 1, 1 Dc2Cl over next 2 dc, [ch 1, 1 dc in next dc] 12 times, ch 1, 1 Dc2Cl over next 2 dc, [ch 1, 1 dc in next dc] 11 times, 1 dc in top of t-ch, change to B at end: 39 dc (not counting ch-3 at beg and counting each Dc2Cl as a dc).

For Size Large Only

Row 11: Ch 3, sk 1st dc, 1 dc in next dc, [ch 1, 1 dc in next dc] 18 times, ch 1, 1 Dc2Cl over next 2 dc, [ch 1, 1 dc in next dc] 19 times, 1 dc in top of t-ch, change to B at end: 40 dc (not counting ch-3 at beg and counting each Dc2Cl as a dc).

For Size X-Large Only

Row 9: Ch 3, sk 1st dc, 1 dc in next dc, *[ch 1, 1 dc in next dc] 8 times, ch 1, 1 Dc2Cl over next 2 dc; rep from * 3 more times, [ch 1, 1 dc in next dc] 8 times, 1 dc in top of t-ch, change to A at end, turn: 46 dc (not counting ch-3 at beg and counting each Dc2Cl as a dc).

Row 10: Ch 3, sk 1st dc, 1 dc in next dc, *ch 1, 1 dc in next dc; rep from *, 1 dc in top of t-ch, change to A at end, turn.

Row 11: Ch 3, sk 1st dc, 1 dc in next dc, *[ch 1, 1 dc in next dc] 10 times, ch 1, 1 Dc2Cl over next 2 dc; rep from * 2 more times, [ch 1, 1 dc in next dc] 8 times, 1 dc in top of t-ch, change to B at end: 43 dc (not counting ch-3 at beg and counting each Dc2Cl as a dc).

For All Sizes

Row 12: With B, ch 3, sk 1 st dc, 1 dc in next dc, *ch 1, 1 dc in next dc; rep from *, 1 dc in top of t-ch, turn.

Change to silt pattern st as follows:
Row 13 (RS): Ch 3, sk 1st dc, 1 dc in next dc, *1 dc next ch-1 sp, 1 dc in next dc; rep from * ending with 1 dc in top of t-ch: 74 (76, 78, 84) dc (not counting ch-3 at beg), turn.

Row 14: Ch 1, sk 1 (0, 0, 0) dc, 2 dc in next dc, *sk 2 dc, (1 sc, 2 dc) in next dc; rep from * ending with sk 3 (3, 2, 2) dc, 1 sc in top of t-ch, turn.

Row 15: Work row 3 of silt pattern st.

Row 16: Work row 2 of silt pattern st, change to C at end: 24 (25, 26, 28)-(1 sc, 2 dc) groups.

Begin dec for A-line shaping as follows:
Row 17 (Dec row): With C, ch 3, sk 1st st, 1 dc in next st, 1 dc in each of next 15 (16, 17, 18) sts, 1 Dc2Cl over next 2 sts, 1 dc in each of next 17 (18, 18, 20) sts, 1 Dc2Cl over next 2 sts, 1 dc in each of next 17 (17, 18, 20) sts, 1 Dc2Cl over next 2 sts, 1 dc in each of next 15 (16, 17, 18) sts, 1 dc in top of t-ch, turn.

Row 18: Rep row 2 of silt pattern st, change to A at end: 23 (24, 25, 27)-(1 sc, 2 dc) groups.

Rows 19 and 20: With A, rep rows 3 and 2 of silt pattern st.

Row 21 (Dec row): Ch 3, sk 1st st, 1 dc in next st, 1 dc in each of next 14 (15, 16, 17) sts, 1 Dc2Cl over next 2 sts, 1 dc in each of next 16 (17, 17, 19) sts, 1 Dc2Cl over next 2 sts, 1 dc in each of next 16 (16, 17, 19) sts, 1 Dc2Cl over next 2 sts, 1 dc in each of next 15 (16, 17, 18) sts, 1 dc in top of t-ch, turn.

Row 22: Rep row 2 of silt pattern st: 22 (23, 24, 26)-(1 sc, 2 dc) groups.

Rows 23 and 24: Rep rows 3 and 2 of silt pattern st.

Row 25 (Dec row): Ch 3, sk 1st st, 1 dc in next st, 1 dc in each of next 14 (15, 16, 17) sts, 1 Dc2Cl over next 2 sts, 1 dc in each of next 15 (16, 16, 18) sts, 1 Dc2Cl over next 2 sts, 1 dc in each of next 15 (15, 16, 18) sts, 1 Dc2Cl over next 2 sts, 1 dc in each of next 14 (15, 16, 17) sts, 1 dc in top of t-ch, turn.

Row 26: Rep row 2 of silt pattern st: 21 (22, 23, 25)-(1 sc, 2 dc) groups.

Rows 27 and 28: Rep rows 3 and 2 of silt pattern st.

Row 29 (Dec row): Ch 3, sk 1st st, 1 dc in next st, 1 dc in each of next 13 (14, 15, 16) sts, 1 Dc2Cl over next 2 sts, 1 dc in each of next 14 (15, 15, 17) sts, 1 Dc2Cl over next 2 sts, 1 dc in each of next 14 (14, 15, 17) sts, 1 Dc2Cl over next 2 sts, 1 dc in each of next 14 (15, 16, 17) sts, 1 dc in top of t-ch, turn.

Row 30: Rep row 2 of silt pattern st: 20 (21, 22, 24)-(1 sc, 2 dc) groups.

Row 31 (Dec row): Ch 3, sk 1st st, 1 dc in next st, 1 dc in each of next 13 (14, 15, 16) sts, 1 Dc2Cl over next 2 sts, 1 dc in each of next 13 (14, 14, 16) sts, 1 Dc2Cl over next 2 sts, 1 dc in each of next 13 (13, 14, 16) sts, 1 Dc2Cl over next 2 sts, 1 dc in each of next 13 (14, 15, 16) sts, 1 dc in top of t-ch, turn.

Row 32: Rep row 2 of silt pattern st: 19 (20, 21, 23)-(1 sc, 2 dc) groups.

Rows 33 and 34: Rep rows 3 and 2 of silt pattern st.

Row 35 (Dec row): Ch 3, sk 1st st, 1 dc in next st, 1 dc in each of next 12 (13, 14, 15) sts, 1 Dc2Cl over next 2 sts, 1 dc in each of next 12 (13, 13, 15) sts, 1 Dc2Cl over next 2 sts, 1 dc in each of next 13 (13, 14, 16) sts, 1 Dc2Cl over next 2 sts, 1 dc in each of next 12 (13, 14, 15) sts, 1 dc in top of t-ch, turn.

Row 36: Rep row 2 of silt pattern st: 18 (19, 20, 22)-(1 sc, 2 dc) groups.

Row 37 (Dec row): Ch 3, sk 1st st, 1 dc in next st, 1 dc in each of next 11 (12, 13, 14) sts, 1 Dc2Cl over next 2 sts, 1 dc in each of next 11 (12, 12, 14) sts, 1 Dc2Cl over next 2 sts, 1 dc in each of next 12 (12, 13, 15) sts, 1 Dc2Cl over next 2 sts,

1 dc in each of next 12 (13, 14, 15) sts, 1 dc in top of t-ch, turn.

Row 38: Rep row 2 of silt pattern st: 17 (18, 19, 21)-(1 sc, 2 dc) groups.

Row 39 (Dec row): Ch 3, sk 1st st, 1 dc in next st, 1 dc in each of next 10 (11, 12, 13) sts, 1 Dc2Cl over next 2 sts, 1 dc in each of next 11 (12, 12, 14) sts, 1 Dc2Cl over next 2 sts, 1 dc in each of next 11 (11, 12, 14) sts, 1 Dc2Cl over next 2 sts, 1 dc in each of next 11 (12, 13, 14) sts, 1 dc in top of t-ch, turn.

Row 40: Rep row 2 of silt pattern st: 16 (17, 18, 20)-(1 sc, 2 dc) groups.

Row 41 (Dec row): Ch 3, sk 1st st, 1 dc in next st, 1 dc in each of next 10 (11, 12, 13) sts, 1 Dc2Cl over next 2 sts, 1 dc in each of next 10 (11, 11, 13) sts, 1 Dc2Cl over next 2 sts, 1 dc in each of next 10 (10, 11, 13) sts, 1 Dc2Cl over next 2 sts, 1 dc in each of next 10 (11, 12, 13) sts, 1 dc in top of t-ch, turn.

Fasten off.

Front

Work same as for BACK, but do not fasten off.

Continue around corner, working along side of piece for right front button lps as follows:

Row 1: Sl st in side of next sc, [ch 3, sk next dc, 2 sc before next dc] 2 times, ch 3, sk next dc, (1 sc, 1 sl st) to next dc, turn.

Row 2: 1 sc in 1st sc, [3 sc in next ch-3 sp, 1 sc in each of next 2 sc] 2 times, 2 sc in next ch-3 sp, 1 sc in sl st from beg of row 1.

Fasten off.

Finishing

Sew left side seam using A.

Waist Tie

With A, ch 65 (65, 70, 70).

Row 1: With WS facing, work along last row of front (at same corner where button lps begin): 1 sc in each dc along front, then 1 sc in each dc along back [approx. 90 (96, 102, 114) sc], ch 66 (66, 71, 71), turn.

Row 2: 1 sc in 2nd ch from hk and in each ch, 1 sc in each sc, 1 sc in rem 65 (65, 70, 70) ch, change to B at end, turn.

Row 3: With B, ch 1, 1 sc in each sc to end, change to C at end, turn.

Row 4: With C, ch 1, 1 sc in each sc to end, turn.

Row 5: Ch 1, 1 sc in each sc to end, change to B at end, turn.

Row 6: Ch 1, 1 sc in each sc to end.

Fasten off.

Sew right side seam up to button lps. Lightly steam. Weave in all loose ends. Sew buttons opposite button lps using sewing needle and thread.

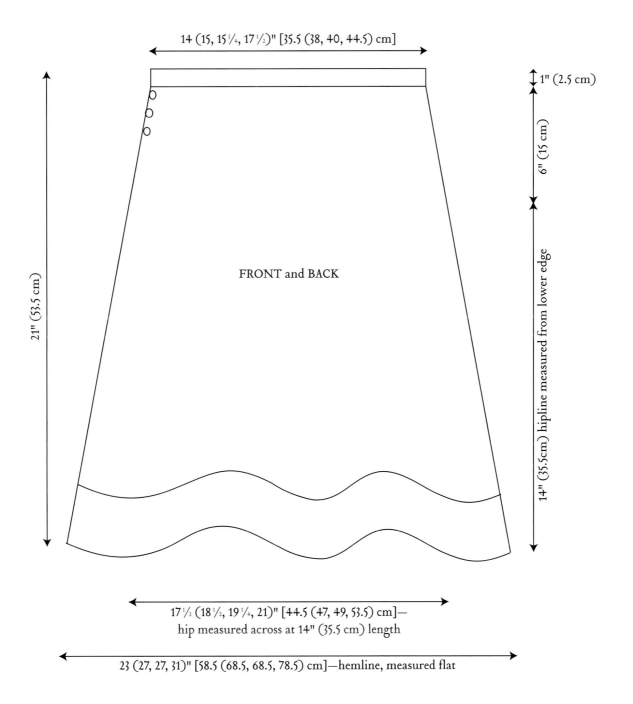

14 (15, 15¼, 17½)" [35.5 (38, 40, 44.5) cm]

1" (2.5 cm)

6" (15 cm)

14" (35.5cm) hipline measured from lower edge

21" (53.5 cm)

FRONT and BACK

17½ (18½, 19¼, 21)" [44.5 (47, 49, 53.5) cm]—
hip measured across at 14" (35.5 cm) length

23 (27, 27, 31)" [58.5 (68.5, 68.5, 78.5) cm]—hemline, measured flat

Ruffled Scarf

Finished Size
Width: 12" (30.5 cm)
Length: 60½" (153.5 cm), including ruffled ends

Materials
A bulky-weight mohair blend yarn:
total yardage required: about 492 yd
(450 m).

Shown:
Lion Brand Yarns Moonlight Mohair
(35% Mohair, 30% Acrylic, 25% Cotton,
10% Polyester Metallic; approx 82 yd
[75 m] per 1.75 oz [50 g] ball):
#203 Safari, 6 balls.

Size J/10 (6 mm) crochet hook or size
to obtain gauge.

Notions
Yarn tapestry needle

Gauge
13 sts (1 pattern repeat) = 4" [10 cm]
and 10 rows = 7" [18 cm] in pattern st
using size J/10 (6 mm) crochet hook.
Take time to check gauge.

Stitches And Techniques Used
(See pages 134-140)
Single crochet, double crochet, double
treble, multiple stitches into 1 stitch,
working into an arch.

LACE PATTERN STITCH

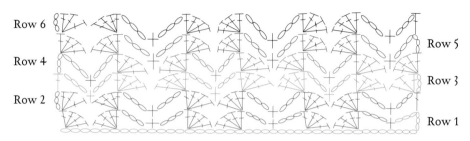

Repeat rows 3 through 6 for lace pattern stitch.

Pattern Stitches

Lace Pattern Stitch
Ch a multiple of 13 plus 6 extra.

Row 1: Sk 9 ch, 1 sc in next ch, ch 3, sk 3 ch, 4 dc in next ch, sk 4 ch, 4 dc in next ch, *ch 3, sk 3 ch, 1 sc in next ch, ch 3, sk 3 ch, 4 dc in next ch, sk 4 ch, 4 dc in next ch; rep from * to end, turn.

Row 2: Ch 3, 3 dc in 1st dc, sk next 6 dc, 4 dc in next dc, ch 3, 1 sc in next sc, ch 3, *4 dc in next dc, sk 6 dc, 4 dc in next dc, ch 3, 1 sc in next sc, ch 3; rep from * ending with 1 dc in 6th ch of t-ch, turn.

Row 3: Ch 3, 3 dc in 1st dc, sk next ch-3 sp, sk next sc, sk next ch-3 sp, 4 dc in next dc, ch 3, 1 sc bet next 3rd and 4th dc (the center space bet both 4-dc groups), ch 3, *sk 3 dc, 4 dc in next dc, sk next ch-3 sp, sk next sc, sk next ch-3 sp, 4 dc in next dc, ch 3, 1 sc bet next 3rd and 4th dc, ch 3; rep from * ending with 1 dc in top of t-ch, turn.

Row 4: Ch 6, sk 1st dc, sk next ch-3 sp, 1 sc in next sc, ch 3, 4 dc in next dc, sk next 6 dc, 4 dc in next dc, *ch 3, 1 sc in next sc, ch 3, 4 dc in next dc, sk 6 dc, 4 dc in next dc; rep from * once, ending last rep with 4 dc in top of t-ch, turn.

Row 5: Ch 6, 1 sc in sp bet next 4th and 5th dc, ch 3, sk next 3 dc, 4 dc in next dc, sk next ch-3 sp, sk next sc, sk next ch-3 sp, 4 dc in next dc, *ch 3, 1 sc in sp bet next 3rd and 4th dc, ch 3, sk next 3 dc, 4 dc in next dc, sk next ch-3 sp, sk next sc, sk next ch-3 sp, 4 dc in next dc; rep from * ending last rep with 4 dc in 3rd ch of t-ch, turn.

Row 6: Ch 3, 3 dc in 1st dc, sk next 6 dc, 4 dc in next dc, ch 3, 1 sc in next sc, ch 3, *4 dc in next dc, sk next 6 dc, 4 dc in next dc, ch 3, 1 sc in next sc, ch 3; rep from * ending with 1 dc in top of t-ch, turn.

Rep rows 3 through 6 for pattern st.

Scarf

Ch 45.

Work rows 1 to 6 of pattern st.

Rows 7 to 78: Rep rows 3 through 6 eighteen times.

Do not fasten off.

Ruffled Edging:

Note: To work a "dtr (double treble)," yo 3 times, insert hook, yo, pull through 1 lp, [yo over, pull through 2 lps] 4 times.

Row 79: Ch 4, *1 dc in 2nd ch of next ch-3 sp, ch 1, 1 dc in next sc, ch 1, 1 dc in 2nd ch of next ch-3 sp, ch 1, 1 dc in next dc, ch 1, 1 dc in sp bet next 3rd and 4th dc, ch 1, sk next 3 dc, 1 dc in next dc, ch 1, rep from * ending last rep with 1 dc in top of t-ch, turn.

Row 80: Ch 3, 1 dc in 1st ch-1 sp, *ch 1, 1 dc in next ch-1 sp; rep from * ending with 1 dc in top of t-ch, turn.

Row 81: Ch 5, 1 dtr in 1st dc, ch 1, sk 1 dc, *(1 dtr, ch 1, 1 dtr, ch 1, 1 dtr) in next dc, ch 1, (1 dtr, ch 1, 1 dtr) in next dc, ch 1; rep from * to last dc and t-ch, 1 dtr in last dc, 1 dtr in top of t-ch. Fasten off.

Attach yarn to opposite side of base ch to work ruffled edge at other end of scarf as follows:

Row 1: Ch 4, 1 dc in 1st ch-4 sp, ch 1, 1 dc in same ch as next set of 4 dc's, ch

1, 1 dc in next ch-3 sp, ch 1, 1 dc in same ch as next sc, *ch 1, 1 dc in next ch-3 sp, ch 1, 1 dc in same ch as next set of 4 dc's, ch 1, 1 dc in next ch-4 sp, ch 1, 1 dc in same ch as next set of 4 dc's, ch 1, 1 dc in next ch-3 sp, ch 1, 1 dc in same ch as next sc; rep from * ending with ch 1, sk 1 ch, 1 dc in next ch, ch 1, sk 1 ch, 1 dc in next ch, turn.

Rows 2 and 3: Rep rows 80 and 81 of first ruffled edge.

Fasten off.

Finishing

Lightly steam to flatten stitches.

Weave in all loose ends.

Stitch Glossary

These illustrations demonstrate the basic techniques and stitches used in crochet and in the patterns in this book.

Holding the Hook and Yarn
Step 1

There are two main ways to hold a crochet hook. One way is to hold it like a pencil, as shown. The other is to hold it overhand (as you hold a steak knife). Use whichever way is most comfortable for you. Many crochet hooks have a flattened area near the hook end that is intended as the place to comfortably position your thumb to hold your hook.

Step 2

As with knitting, the yarn feeding from the ball or skein must be held with slight tension as you crochet. Holding the yarn in your left hand by letting it wrap through your fingers and around your little finger as shown is a good way to maintain this tension.

Step 3

With the yarn held in your left hand as shown in the last step, use your index or forefinger, slightly raised, as a guide for the yarn to feed over as shown here. At the same time, use your middle finger and thumb to hold (simi-lar to pinching) the work that is right below your hook as you crochet. As you crochet, keep moving your left middle finger and thumb up so you are always holding the work that is just below your hook.

Slip Knot
Step 1

Almost all crochet pieces begin with a base/starting chain. To begin a base chain, make a slip knot by looping the yarn and then using the hook to pull another loop through.

Step 2

With the new loop on your hook, use your left fingers to pull on the tail of the yarn and tighten the slip knot.

Yarn Over

To yarn over, move the hook under the yarn from left to right and let the yarn catch on the hook as shown. Try to keep the yarn still (by controlling it with your left hand), using your right hand to maneuver the hook to do each yarn over. You can also move the yarn, instead of the hook, to make a yarn over, as in knitting. Bring the yarn over the hook from back to front, then back. Yarn overs are done many, many times in crochet, so you will get lots of practice doing them.

Chain Stitch
Step 1

Yarn over and draw the yarn through the loop on the hook. Be careful not to tighten the previous loop/chain; just bring the new loop through the previous loop. You have just chained 1.

Step 2

To continue the chain stitch, just yarn over and draw through a new loop on the hook again for each chain required. The slip knot does not count as a chain.

BASIC CROCHET STITCHES

All of the projects in this book use a combination of these basic crochet stitches. Here, they are illustrated as worked into a base chain. The basic stitches are worked the same way whether they are worked into a base chain or into a stitch or space of a previous row. In the illustrations, a certain number of base chains are skipped on the first row before working the taller basic stitches. This number of chains skipped is based on which basic stitch is being worked, matching the height of that stitch to form a first row of uniform height. For example, a double cro-chet row would begin with skipping three

chains because the height of three chains matches the height of a double crochet stitch. See the table under Making Crochet Fabric (page 136) for a guide to how many chains are required for the different stitch heights.

Notice that when working into each base chain, the hook should be inserted under the top two strands and above the bottom strand of each chain as you will see in the illustrations to follow. This creates a nice, firm starting row.

Slip Stitch

The slip stitch is the shortest of the crochet stitches. It is often used for joining and shaping. Insert the hook into the work, yarn over, and draw the yarn through the work and the loop on the hook in one movement.

Slip Stitch to Form a Ring

Here, the slip stitch is used to join a series of chains to form a ring, which is used when working motifs in the round. Insert hook in the first chain, yarn over, and draw the yarn through the work and the loop on the hook.

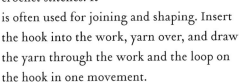

Single Crochet
Step 1
Single crochet is the next tallest stitch after the slip stitch. Insert the hook into the work, *yarn over, and draw through the work only. You now have 2 loops on the hook.

Step 2
Yarn over again and draw through both loops on the hook in one movement.

Step 3
The first single crochet is now completed. To continue, insert hook into the next stitch and repeat from * in step 1.

Half Double Crochet
Step 1
Half double crochet is the next tallest stitch after the single crochet stitch. Before inserting your hook into the work, yarn over. Now insert the hook into the work.

Step 2
*Yarn over and draw through the work only. You will have 3 loops on the hook.

Step 3
Yarn over and draw through all 3 loops on the hook in one movement.

Step 4
The first half double crochet is now completed. To continue, yarn over, insert your hook into the next stitch, and repeat from * in step 2.

Double Crochet
Step 1
Double crochet is the next tallest stitch and is very, very commonly used in crochet stitch patterns. Before inserting your hook into the work, yarn over. Now insert the hook into the work.

Step 2
*Yarn over and draw through the work only. You will have 3 loops on the hook, just as in the half double crochet stitch.

Step 3
Yarn over and draw through only the first 2 loops on the hook. You will now have 2 loops remaining on the hook.

Step 4
Yarn over and draw through the remaining 2 loops on the hook.

Step 5

The first double crochet is now completed. To continue, yarn over, insert hook into the next stitch and repeat from * in step 2.

Treble
Step 1

Treble is one of the taller basic stitches. Before inserting the hook into the work, yarn over twice. Now insert hook into the work.

Step 2

*Yarn over and draw through the work only. You will have 4 loops on the hook.

Step 3

Yarn over again and draw through only the first 2 loops. You will have 3 loops left on the hook.

Step 4

Yarn over again and draw through only the next 2 loops. You will now have 2 loops remaining on the hook.

Step 5

Yarn over again and draw through the remaining 2 loops.

Step 6

The first treble is now completed. To continue, yarn over twice, insert hook into the next stitch and repeat from * in step 2.

Taller basic stitches are made by simply doing more yarn overs on the hook before inserting the hook into the work, as in step 1 of the treble stitch. Then, they are worked like the other steps of the treble, repeating step 4 as many times as necessary until there are only 2 loops left on the hook to complete in step 5.

MAKING CROCHET FABRIC

Basic crochet fabrics start with a base/starting chain. The number of chains in the base chain determines the number of stitches, i.e. the width, of the fabric. In addition, each base chain will include a number of stitches to reach the correct height of the stitches to be used in the first row.

The flat fabric is then created by turning the work to the other side after each row is completed. The new row is then worked from right to left on top of the first row. The work is then turned to the first side again, the next row is worked from right to left on top of the second row, and so on.

Here is a guide for stitch heights:

basic stitch	chains required to reach stitch height
single crochet	1
half double crochet	2
double crochet	3
treble	4
double treble	5
triple treble	6

Each new row begins with the required number of chains (based on the guide above) to reach the height of the basic stitch used for that row. This is called a beginning or turning chain.

Generally, the turning chain is counted and treated as one of the stitches for that row for all but the slip stitch and single crochet stitch.

Turning Rows
Step 1

Here, a basic double crochet fabric is illustrated. The first row was worked into a base chain that had an extra chain 3 to match the height of the double crochet stitches. Therefore, the first double crochet was worked into the fourth chain from the hook (the first 3 skipped chains are counted as 1 double crochet stitch). Then, a double crochet was worked into each chain across to the end.

Step 2

At the end of the row, the work was turned to the opposite side. Three chains were made for the turning chain to match the height of the double crochets. The first double crochet from the previous row will be skipped since the turning chain will be treated as the first double crochet.

Step 3

Skipping the first double crochet in the previous row, 1 double crochet is then worked into each stitch across. The last double crochet of the row is worked into the top chain of the 3 chains that were from the beginning of the previous row. This is often written in instructions as working "1 double crochet in the top of the turning chain." When working into a chain from the previous row, be sure to pick up 2 strands as shown.

Changing Colors
Step 1

To change colors or join in a new ball of yarn, work the last stitch until 2 loops remain on the hook. Then, use the new yarn to make the final yarn over and draw the new yarn through the last 2 loops to complete the stitch.

Step 2

Continue just with the new yarn, letting the old yarn hang from the work. Be sure to allow at least a 6" (15 cm) tail of both the old and new yarns, which will be woven in during the finishing of the project.

STITCH VARIATIONS

Many of the crochet stitch patterns used in this book are combinations of the basic stitches reviewed above, along with some of the stitch techniques that are reviewed in this section. Specific definitions of each technique are explained in the notes for each pattern. Only the general techniques are described and illustrated here.

Multiple Stitches into One Stitch

Multiple stitches can be worked into the same exact stitch or space as part of a stitch pattern effect or to do some shaping increases. Shell stitches are common examples that use this technique, as illustrated here: 5 double crochets are worked into the same base chain just by inserting the hook into the same place each time.

Cluster Stitch
Step 1

Clusters are similar to shells, except the tops of the stitches are "gathered" instead or in addition to the bottoms. This is done by leaving the last loop of each stitch on the hook. Then, a final yarn over is made and drawn through all of the remaining loops on the hook, closing all of the stitches together to form a cluster. Here, a 3-double crochet cluster is shown. Work each double crochet into the next stitch leaving the last loop of each double crochet on the hook.

Step 2

Yarn over and draw through all 4 loops that remain on the hook to close the cluster. Sometimes, clusters are all worked into the same stitch or space, causing the bottoms of the stitches to be "gathered" as well (these may be referred to in other books as "bobbles").

Puff Stitch
Step 1

Puff stitches are simply half double crochet clusters. Because half double crochets cannot be worked until there is only 1 loop left, they are left open until the final yarn over is drawn through. Yarn over, insert the hook into the work, yarn over again and draw a loop through the work only. Three loops are on the hook.

Step 2

Repeat the last step two more times, inserting the hook into the same stitch. There are now 7 loops on the hook. Yarn over and draw through all 7 loops on the hook.

Step 3

Chain 1 to close the puff stitch firmly.

Picot
Step 1

Picots are little chain loops often used as little accents along crocheted edgings. Here, a 4-chain picot is illustrated. Chain 4.

Step 2

Insert the hook into the fourth chain from the hook and work a slip stitch to close the picot.

Step 3

Continue working more chains as indicated by the pattern.

Bullion Stitch

A bullion stitch is a unique crochet stitch that can be a bit challenging at first. It works best with a tightly cabled type of yarn. Begin by working as many yarn overs as indicated (often 7 to 10 times). Insert hook into stitch, yarn over, and draw through the work only. Yarn over again and draw though all loops on the hook, using your fingers to help as needed. Chain 1 to close the bullion stitch.

Working into an Arch

When crocheting beyond the basic crochet fabrics, many stitches are worked into spaces or arches rather than specific chains or stitches. In this example, double crochets are worked into a space created by 2 chains from the previous row. Just begin your double crochet with the usual yarn over, then insert hook into the space. Yarn over and draw through the space only. Yarn over again and draw through the first 2 loops. Yarn over and draw through the remaining 2 loops to complete the double crochet.

Working in Back Loop Only
Step 1

Unless otherwise noted, stitches are worked into stitches from the previous row by picking up both strands at the top of a stitch. Some patterns will require that the hook is only inserted into the front or back loop of the top of the stitch from the previous row because it leaves the other loop to show through as a nice looking horizontal line. In this example, the hook is only inserted into the back loop of each stitch.

Forming Ring

Step 1

Many crocheted motifs are begun with chain stitch rings. Others may require a tighter center, so they use this technique to form the center ring. Begin by wrapping the yarn into a loop and using the hook to draw another loop through.

Step 2

This new loop is the start of the beginning chain for the first round. Chain 1 to begin a first round of single crochets.

Step 3

Work the first single crochet into the ring by inserting hook into the ring. Yarn over and draw a loop through the ring only. Two loops are on the hook.

Step 4

Yarn over and draw through the remaining 2 loops on the hook.

Step 5

The first single crochet has been worked into the ring. Continue by working as many single crochets or stitches as indicated into the ring for the first round. Once the first round is complete, pulling on the tail of the yarn will tighten the ring appropriately.

Working in the Round

Step 1

Most motifs are worked in the round from the center out. Each round is worked with the right side always facing (that is, the work is never turned), unless otherwise indicated. The beginning can be a ring formed by a number of chains joined together as shown here. Begin by chaining 5. Insert hook into the first of the chains.

Step 2

Slip stitch into the first chain to join and form a ring.

Step 3

A turning chain is made to match the height of the stitches to be worked in the first round, in this case chain 3 for a double crochet round.

Step 4

Each stitch in round 1 is worked by inserting the hook into the center hole of the chain stitch ring.

Joining in the Round

Step 1

Once all of the stitches in a round are completed, the round is usually joined to close by working a slip stitch into the top of the beginning chain or first stitch.

Step 2

The following round is then worked on top of the previous round. The round starts with a beginning chain that matches the height of the stitches to be used in that round. The first stitch is then usually worked by inserting the hook into the top 2 loops of the next stitch as shown.

Fasten Off

Step 1

Crochet is fastened off with a final chain. In this example, it is done after the final round has been joined with the slip stitch. The yarn is then cut, leaving at least a 6" (15 cm) tail that will then be woven in when finishing the project, and drawn through the final loop.

Step 2

The tail can be gently pulled to tighten.

Joining Motifs
Step 1

Sometimes, motifs are joined to each other during the final round of each motif. As the final round is being worked, a motif is joined to a previously completed one with a slip stitch worked into a corresponding stitch or space of the last round of the other motif.

The last round of the new motif is then continued until the next joining point.

Step 2

Another slip stitch is worked into the other motif, creating 2 joining points. The rest of the round of the new motif is continued.

Working Around the Front of the Stem of a Stitch

Some techniques are used to create a raised effect. Here, a double crochet is worked by inserting the hook around the front of the stem of the double crochet from the previous row. This causes the new double crochet to sit at the front of the work.

Working Around the Back of the Stem of a Stitch

Here, a double crochet is worked by inserting the hook around the back of the stem of the double crochet from the previous row. This causes the new double crochet to sit at the back of the work.

Adding Fringe
Step 1

Fringe is easily added during finishing using a crochet hook. Fold the fringe yarn strand(s) in half. With the wrong side of the work facing you, insert the crochet hook into the work from front to back where the fringe should be placed. Grab the folded loop and pull it through the work only partway, forming a loop on the front of the work.

Step 2

Using the hook or your fingers, grab the ends of the fringe strand(s) and pull them all through the loop just formed. Pull gently to tighten. Trim ends of fringe if needed to even out strands.

Yarns

The yarns used in the samples for this book are shown below, at actual size, to help you find the yarn or make substitutions. Please refer to the Yarn Resources on the next page for additional information.

- Cascade Yarns Pima Tencel (50% Pima Cotton, 50% Tencel)

- Classic Elite Bazic Wool (100% Superwash Wool)

- Classic Elite La Gran Mohair
  (76.5% Mohair, 17.5% Wool, 6% Nylon)

- Classic Elite Lush (50% Angora, 50% Wool)

- Classic Elite Miracle (50% Alpaca, 50% Tencel)

- Classic Elite Montera (50% Llama, 50% Wool)

- Classic Elite Wings (55% Alpaca, 23% Silk, 22% Wool)

- Crystal Palace Yarns Mikado Ribbon (50% Cotton, 50% Viscose)

- Filatura Di Crosa Brilla (42% Cotton, 58% Viscose)

- Filatura Di Crosa Love
  (30% Merino Extrafine, 30% Acrylic, 20% Nylon)

- GGH Aspen (50% Merino Wool, 50% Acrylic)

- GGH Mystik (54% Cotton, 46% Viscose)

- GGH Soft-Kid (70% Super Kid Mohair, 25% Nylon, 5% Wool)

- Jaeger Matchmaker (100% Pure Wool)

- Karabella Gossamer (30% Kid Mohair, 52% Nylon, 18% Polyester)

- Katia Dulce Plus (50% Wool, 50% Acrylic)

- Lana Gatto Feeling (70% Merino Wool, 20% Silk, 10% Cashmere)

- Lion Brand Micro Spun (100% Microfiber Acrylic)

- Lion Brand Moonlight Mohair
  (35% Mohair, 30% Acrylic, 25% Cotton, 10% Polyester Metallic)

- Reynolds Saucy Sport (100% Mercerized Cotton)

- Rowan Kid Silk Haze (70% Super Kid Mohair, 30% Silk)

Yarn Resources

All the beautiful yarns and notions used in this book are available from the following companies. Please contact them for shops in your area or search for the item online. Many online yarn shops carry a broad selection of yarns.

CASCADE YARNS
1224 Andover Park East
Tukwila, WA 98138 USA
800.548.1048
www.cascadeyarns.com

CLASSIC ELITE YARNS
122 Western Avenue
Lowell, MA 01851-1434 USA
978.453.2837
classicelite@aol.com
www.classiceliteyarns.com

CRYSTAL PALACE YARNS
160 23rd Street
Richmond, CA 94804 USA
510.237.9988
cpyinfo@straw.com
www.straw.com/cpy

FILATURA DI CROSA YARNS
Distributed by Tahki Stacy Charles Inc.
70-30 80th Street, Building 36
Ridgewood, NY 11385 USA
800.338.YARN (9276)
info@tahkistacycharles.com
www.tahkistacycharles.com

In Canada, distributed by
Diamond Yarn
9697 St. Laurent
Montreal, QC H3L 2N1 Canada
www.diamondyarn.com

GGH YARNS
Distributed by Muench Yarns, Inc.
1323 Scott Street
Petaluma, CA 94954-1135 USA
800.733.9276
info@muenchyarns.com
www.muenchyarns.com

JAEGER YARNS
Distributed by Westminster Fibers
4 Townsend West, Unit 8
Nashua, NH 03063 USA
603.886.5041
www.westminsterfibers.com

In Canada, distributed by
Diamond Yarn
9697 St. Laurent
Montreal, QC H3L 2N1 Canada
www.diamondyarn.com

In the UK, distributed by
Green Lane Mill
Holmfirth
West Yorkshire HD9 2DX UK
44.01484.681881
mail@knitrowan.com
www.knitrowan.com

In Australia, distributed by
Australian Country Spinners
314 Albert Street
Brunswick, Victoria 3056 Australia
61.03.9380.3888
sales@auspinners.com.au

In New Zealand, please contact
Rowan Yarns for stockists.

KARABELLA YARNS
1201 Broadway
New York, NY 10001 USA
800.550.0898
www.karabellayarns.com

KATIA YARNS
Distributed by Knitting Fever, Inc.
35 Debevoise Avenue
Roosevelt, NY 11575 USA
516.546.3600
800.645.3457
knittingfever@knittingfever.com
www.knitting-fever.com

In Canada, distributed by
Diamond Yarn
9697 St. Laurent
Montreal, QC H3L 2N1 Canada
www.diamondyarn.com

LANA GATTO YARNS
Distributed by Needful Yarns Inc.
60 Industrial Parkway PMB #233
Cheektowaga, NY 14227 USA
866.800.4700
info@needfulyarnsinc.com
www.needfulyarnsinc.com

In Canada, distributed by
Needful Yarns Inc.
4476 Chesswood Drive, #10/11
Toronto, ON M3J 2B9 Canada
416.398.3700
info@needfulyarnsinc.com
www.needfulyarnsinc.com

LION BRAND YARN
135 Kero Road
Carlstadt, NJ 07072 USA
800.258.YARN (9276)
www.lionbrand.com

REYNOLDS YARNS
Distributed by JCA, Inc.
35 Scales Lane
Townsend, MA 01469 USA
978.597.8794
800.225.6340
customerservice@jcacrafts.com
www.jcacrafts.com

ROWAN YARNS
Distributed by Westminster Fibers
4 Townsend West, Unit 8
Nashua, NH 03063 USA
603.886.5041
www.westminsterfibers.com

In Canada, distributed by
Diamond Yarn
9697 St. Laurent
Montreal, QC H3L 2N1 Canada
www.diamondyarn.com

In the UK, distributed by
Green Lane Mill
Holmfirth
West Yorkshire HD9 2DX UK
44.01484.681881
mail@knitrowan.com
www.knitrowan.com

In Australia, distributed by
Australian Country Spinners
314 Albert Street
Brunswick, Victoria 3056 Australia
61.03.9380.3888
sales@auspinners.com.au

In New Zealand, please contact
Rowan Yarns for stockists.

Other Resources

SPECIALTY BUTTONS
Distributed by The Button Store
www.hushcobuttons.com

PURSE HANDLES
Distributed by M&J Trimming
800.9.MJTRIM
www.mjtrim.com

About the Author

Katherine Lee's love for crochet and knitwear design began when she learned the crafts at eight years old. As a little girl, her designs consisted of simple sweaters, little purses, dolls, toys, and many toilet roll covers. Although she pursued a corporate career path after studying industrial engineering in college and getting her MBA, her love for crochet and knitting continued. Evenings and weekends found Katherine evolving her design skills to create sweaters and accessories with intricate cabling or lace and teaching both knitting and crochet. She even took courses toward a master's degree in knitwear design while continuing her conservative daytime career.

Katherine fell in love with crochet because it allowed her to create intricate and fabulously textured fabrics from simple, classic yarns. The variety of interesting and different patterns possible with crochet has always appealed to both her engineering and creative sides. She often prefers crochet over knitting because it is faster, giving her that great sense of accomplishment from having created something from scratch. It is also more portable than knitting, requiring fewer tools.

Four years ago, Katherine decided to change her life by turning her crocheting and knitting into a full-time endeavor. She quit her corporate job and launched her own line of sophisticated hand-loomed knitwear for women, sold an exclusive line of hand-loomed baby knitwear through her online store at www.SweaterBabe.com, and began teaching crochet and knitting several times a week at a trendy local yarn shop in Los Angeles.

Today Katherine continues to teach her popular knitting and crochet classes from her home studio in the Hollywood Hills, while also selling her SweaterBabe.com line of knitting and crochet patterns online. She is also a regular contributor of both crochet and knitting designs to books, such as several books in the *Vogue Knitting on the Go!* series, *Fabulous Crochet Ponchos* (Lark Books), and *The New Crochet: 40 Wonderful Wearables* (Lark Books), as well as magazines. Her teaching talent was also showcased on an episode of the DIY network show *Uncommon Threads*. In the "Crochet Class" episode, Katherine teaches knitters how to crochet and make a great beginner shawl.

Katherine's designs are a reflection of her L.A. lifestyle, where the moderate year-round climate makes lacy cardigans and shawls easy wardrobe staples. Rather than bulky, dense crochet fabrics constructed into shapeless sweaters, all of her designs emphasize sleek, sexy shaping with feminine and flirty detailing, inspired by the latest styles worn by Los Angeles hipsters.

Throughout this book and on her website, SweaterBabe.com, you'll see many sophisticated touches—shaped hems, vibrant yet sophisticated color combinations, interesting and unexpected contrasts of open lace and textured patterns stitches, and many other design details that make her patterns beautifully unique.

This is Katherine's first book of crochet patterns, showcasing her unique ability to blend interesting detailing with sexy, yet classic shapes. All of the designs are very wearable and make Los Angeles style accessible to crocheters everywhere.

More information on Katherine Lee and her full range of crochet and knitting patterns is available online at SweaterBabe.com.

Acknowledgments

Many thanks to Mary Ann Hall for discovering me and being my wonderful editor for this book. Big thanks to Jean Lampe for her excellent and incredibly thorough technical editing. Thanks to Rosalind Wanke for her great art direction and Rochelle Bourgault for coordinating the book project. Thanks to Allan Penn for the amazing photography. And thanks to Kalpna and Kristen for helping me with crocheting the samples for this book.

This book would never have come about without the wonderful support of my husband, Scott. Thank you so much for always believing in my design talent and being my best friend and coach. Thanks, too, to my little Samantha, who is too young to know what Mommy is up to, but can look forward to many wonderful times knitting and crocheting with me (and your little sister, who is due to arrive before this book is published!). I hope you both will love to create with knitting and crochet as much as your Mommy always has and will. And of course, thanks to my parents for their eternal love and for letting me pursue my hobby all these years (much of my allowance money went to yarn!) and always being there for me! I'm thrilled to share my new career milestones with you. And to my mother-in-law—thanks for being such an enthusiastic fellow crocheter and knitter and such a great fan of my evolving new career and lifestyle. I love you all dearly and could not have accomplished this book without you.

Lastly, thank you for buying this book. Many of us have dreams of leaving our jobs to pursue more creative endeavors. Thanks to fellow knitting and crochet enthusiasts, like you, for supporting SweaterBabe.com and now my first book; because of you I have been able to successfully pursue this dream.

Please visit SweaterBabe.com to email me with your feedback on this book and with suggestions for new patterns or publications. I'd love to hear from you.

While every effort has been made to be accurate and complete with each pattern, mistakes and typos do occasionally happen. We are sorry for any convenience. Please go to SweaterBabe.com for the latest updates on any corrections.